Hearts

The Official Illustrated History of Edinburgh's Oldest League Club

Hearts

The Official Illustrated History of Edinburgh's Oldest League Club

Roddy Mackenzie

breedon **books**
PUBLISHING

First published in Great Britain in 2001 by
The Breedon Books Publishing Company Limited
Breedon House, 3 The Parker Centre, Derby, DE21 4SZ.

ISBN 1 85983 251 2

Printed and bound by Butler & Tanner, Frome, Somerset
Jacket printing by GreenShires Ltd, Leicester

Contents

Introduction

THERE is no more romantic name in world football than Hearts. The origins of the club date back to the late 19th century and, to this day, set in the cobblestones of Edinburgh's Royal Mile is a heart which marks the site of the old Tolbooth prison, where some of Edinburgh's most notorious criminals spent their last days, and which was nicknamed the "Heart of Midlothian" after Sir Walter Scott's novel.

Since their beginnings, Hearts, as founder members of the Scottish League, have been at the forefront of the Scottish game. But they have attracted interest worldwide and won a place in the heart of the nation before World War One when the entire first-team squad enlisted for active service, some paying the ultimate price.

This illustrated history attempts to pay tribute to some of the players who have, through the years, made Hearts a club that is still held by many with great affection. Some of the greatest servants to the club have also been highlighted and, in the course of writing this history, it became obvious that Hearts have been blessed with a rich bloodline of talent.

Forward players feature prominently in the club's history – from Barney Battles through to Willie Bauld through to John Robertson – and Hearts became famous for their adventurous style of play through the years.

I am indebted to several sources and, perhaps mostly, to Hearts' club historians Bill Smith, David Speed and Graham Blackwood, who work so tirelessly to add to the rich tapestry of the club's history. Their books: *A Pictorial History 1874-1984*, *The Hearts Quiz Book* and *Images of Scotland – Heart of Midlothian Football Club* have proved an invaluable source of information and they have helped with statistical information. Brian Scott's books, *Hearts Greats* and *The Terrible Trio* also provided valued reference material as did Mike Aitken's *Heart to Heart*, Norrie Price's *Gritty, Gallant, Glorious* and the excellent *The Hearts* by Albert Mackie.

In addition, I would like to thank Norman Sutherland for his personal recollections, journalist Ray Hepburn, Douglas Dalgleish at Hearts and all at Breedon Books. Every one of those mentioned has contributed to this publication in one way or another. The SNS Agency of Glasgow provided the photographs for the post-1984 era.

But, most of all, thanks must go to the players who have worn the maroon over the last century and a quarter and who have all, in different ways, contributed to the growth of Heart of Midlothian Football Club.

Roddy Mackenzie
Edinburgh
Summer 2001

The Heart of Edinburgh

THERE are conflicting theories on the birth of Hearts which only serve to illustrate that this great institution is more than merely a football club and has long been a source of discussion and debate. In his excellent history of the club, *The Hearts*, published by Stanley Paul in 1959, Albert Mackie wrote: "I do not believe any other football club in the world can claim to have aroused and retained such warmth of affection." If that sentiment has been rather overtaken by the growth of such super clubs as Manchester United and Barcelona, then Hearts are still a club that attracts affection from all over the world.

That the club seems addicted to glorious failures as much as it is to scaling the heights of the Scottish game, simply adds to the fascination. Hearts have not been short of drama both on and off the field of play through the last century and a quarter and, as Mackie observed in his history, "addicts of the happy ending need not follow such a club". As if to reinforce those words even after his history was published, Hearts famously lost the League championship in the most unlikely of scenarios in both 1965 and 1986 on the final day of those respective seasons. Hearts, as history shows, are woven into the fabric of Edinburgh life and their beginnings come out of the heart of the city. If the exact details of the club's baptism have been shrouded by the mists of time, then it does not make it any less of a compelling story.

The more favoured explanation of how Hearts came into being is that it was from a group of youngsters who, back in the latter half of the 19th century, played a basic form of football regularly on the site of the old Edinburgh Tolbooth jail in the High Street. The jail itself had been pulled down in 1817 but had been immortalised in Walter Scott's novel *The Heart of Midlothian*. A heart was set in the cobblestones to mark the site of the old prison and it remains to this day, situated outside St Giles' Cathedral.

Dating from 1386, the prison was Edinburgh's first and was the last place of residence for many of the city's most notorious criminals, including Deacon Brodie and Captain Porteous, who awaited execution at one of the seven public hanging sites in Edinburgh.

Years after the demolition of the prison in 1817, the heart was laid within an outline of the building marked in brass blocks (marked 1386, 1430 and 1610) which were the dates when extensions were added to the prison. The story goes that the authorities were unhappy at youngsters playing football on the scene of so many gruesome public hangings and sent them instead to play at the nearby Meadows, a large oasis of grass which remains to this day, and this was where Hearts started to play organised games.

Another theory is that the youngsters frequented a local dance hall in Washing Green Court (later Holyrood Square), just off the Royal Mile, which was called the Heart of Midlothian. It is said that a local policeman had joked with the youngsters that they would be better employed kicking a football than dancing and suggested they play at the Meadows. The theory goes that around 40 youths clubbed together to buy a football from Percival King's shop in Lothian Street and they formed a team and named it after their favourite dancehall. Whatever the reason for the team's name (and it was probably a combination of both theories), it was an inspired choice.

It is also said that Hearts' first captain, Tom Purdie, suggested the name. Purdie won the right to captain the team, it is said, after a one-a-side challenge with Jake Reid, secretary of the dancehall, which he won 3-2 when the latter put the ball through his own goal. These two were to play a big part in the early years of Hearts and indeed stimulated the growth of the game in Edinburgh. With football just finding its feet, it is fair to assume that the game played on the East Meadows in these formative years was a combination of rugby and football.

Association Football had started in England some ten years previously and Scotland's first club, Queen's Park, was founded in 1867. Queen's Park were permitted into the first FA Cup competition in 1872 where they were given a "bye" into the semi-finals but then lost to Wanderers. The first Scotland v England international was staged in Glasgow in November 1872 and finished 0-0 and while Association Football was taking a grip in Scotland, it was very much a west of Scotland affair. The west teams were renowned for their dribbling skills, which was very much the way football was played in the early days.

In 1873, eight clubs (Queen's Park, Third Lanark, Vale of Leven, Clydesdale, Eastern, Dumbreck, Granville and Rovers) all met to form a Scottish Football Association and also a Scottish cup competition. Decent crowds were attending matches – 4,000 for that first Scotland v England international – and it was clear the game was catching on throughout Scotland in some form or other.

Edinburgh, in the early 1870s, was regarded as a rugby city and, if you scour "football" reports in the newspapers of the time, then many will allude to rugby matches.

It was Queen's Park who were the pioneers of the game in Scotland. Queen's Park and Clydesdale had played an exhibition match at Royal High School's FP ground in Bonnington on 27 December 1873 – said to be an "invasion of a rugby stronghold" – and it was clear that there was an enthusiasm for the game in the east of Scotland.

It was in early 1874 (though no exact date has been agreed upon), that Hearts came into being as an organised club and the headquarters were at Mother Anderson's Tavern in West Crosscauseway. It was also where the players changed for matches before heading for their games on the East Meadows, where most of Edinburgh's teams had set up home (a stripping box was later set up in the Meadows for players to change). The original colours were all-white – which has been a favoured change strip for the club through the years – and these were the colours Hearts wore when they entered the Scottish Cup for the first time in season 1875-76. In the first round, Hearts drew 0-0 twice with 3rd Edinburgh Rifle Volunteers and both clubs progressed to the second round but it was as far as Hearts managed as they then went down 2-0 to Drumpellier. The 3rd Edinburgh Rifle Volunteers were credited with being the founding football team in the city and Hearts were said to be an offshoot of a team called, White Star, which would explain the early colours the team wore.

In August 1875, it is recorded that the Heart of Mid-Lothian (there was a hyphen in the name until around 1900) club had 45 members. Hearts joined the Edinburgh Football Association in 1875 but informed the association in September 1876 that they had disbanded. Several players joined St Andrew Football Club (a team of "smart, clever, young players") and persuaded the team to change its name to Heart of Mid-Lothian and so the club re-emerged in January 1877. St Andrew played in blue and, before disbanding, Hearts had adopted red, white and blue as their colours and a decision was taken to "dye" the shirts and mix the colours together and the red and blue effectively became maroon, Hearts' shirt colour to this day.

Hearts and Hibernian, a team made up of Irish immigrants and who played in green, were to emerge as the dominant teams over the next few years and the rivalry between the clubs was evident from the start. However that rivalry – bitter as it was to become on a few occasions in the years to come – helped both teams

Hearts with the Edinburgh FA Cup in 1877-78, the first trophy won by the club. Back row (left to right): George Barbour, James Whitson, Jake Reid, John Sweenie, J. Alexander. Middle row: Hugh Wyllie, Bob Winton, J. Burns, George Mitchell. Front row: Tom Purdie, Andrew Lees.

as interest in their meetings grew quickly in those early years. Hibs were officially founded in 1875 and the first reported match between the two teams took place in 1875 and finished with Hearts triumphant by 3-1. Hearts' team in that first game was recorded as: Dick; Purdie, Ovens, Barbour, Sweenie, Lees, Cochrane, Wyllie, Mitchell, Alexander and Winton.

Hearts' first trophy success came in the shape of the Edinburgh FA Cup when they beat Hibs 3-2 at Powburn in a fourth replay after the previous games had finished 0-0, 1-1, 1-1 and 1-1. John Anderson is credited with scoring the winning goal in that Final replay on 20 April 1878 but it is reported that Tom Purdie was attacked by a group of Hibs' fans as he made his way home from the Final at Powburn Toll and he escaped by taking refuge in a house at Causewayside. It is said that a local newspaper reporter was cajoled into attending the game against his better wishes and his report was given unaccustomed space in his newspaper due to the after-match attack on Purdie. While the purists may despair at the fact that off-the-field activities took precedence over the game in terms of newspaper column inches, it also sparked interest in this new game which was attracting more spectators than the traditional sports of cricket, golf and tennis.

In 1878-79, the club headquarters moved to Tom Mackenzie's "Cricket Warehouse" shop in Chapel Street and annual concerts or "soirees" were held to raise money for the club. Every Saturday, results from matches were posted in the shop window as well as those from other teams around Edinburgh as the game grew in popularity. With the Meadows getting over-populated with so many new teams springing up, Hearts were playing more of their matches at Powburn which had better spectator facilities and also at Powderhall, from 1879, where 3,000 supporters turned up in October 1880 to watch Hearts play Queen's Park. But the Edinburgh side were given a football lesson as they were humbled 8-1. However, such was the gulf in standards between teams around this time that Hearts also chalked up a 21-0 win over Anchor FC in the Edinburgh FA Cup around the same time, which remains their record win.

In January 1881, Hearts became the first Edinburgh side to play in England where they lost to Aston Villa 4-2 and Blackburn 2-0. The English game was also gaining ground but it was not until 1888 that 12 clubs formed the Football League (the brainchild of Scotsman William McGregor who was an official at Aston Villa) and it is notable that there were no clubs from south of Birmingham in that first League.

In February 1881, Hearts took over a private field in the Gorgie area of Edinburgh that became Old Tynecastle Park and was situated on Wardlaw Street, across from the present ground. Old Tynecastle was opened on 9 April 1881 with an 8-0 victory over Edinburgh side, Hanover. Queen's Park, of course, were a strictly amateur side but the bigger clubs in England had started to pay their players by the 1880s. Scotland, still a few years behind in this respect, was ripe for picking and full-back Nick Ross, said to be Hearts' first star player, was among the first to be tempted south and was signed on a lucrative deal by Preston North End.

Nick Ross, one of Hearts first great stars. Ross later joined Preston North End and played in the side which won the first English League title in 1889, and with it the FA Cup to give them the first Double.

The only way Scottish clubs could hope to hold on to their better players and so continue to attract sizable crowds was to pay wages also but this was strictly illegal at the time. In October 1884, Dunfermline protested to the SFA about Hearts using professional players after an 11-1 thrashing in the Scottish Cup and Hearts earned the dubious distinction of being the first club to be investigated by the game's governing body for illegal practices. It was alleged that two of Hearts players, James Maxwell and Chris McNee, had received 26 shillings a week (£2.30p).

Hearts were found guilty and suspended by the SFA but a month later the ban was lifted after the club appointed a new committee. But the whole debate over professionalism had been opened and clearly the SFA would have to back down at some point or else all of the best Scottish players would head south of the border to enhance the English game at the expense of Scotland. Yet it was not until 1893, nine years after Dunfermline's initial protest, that professionalism was legalised north of the border.

Hearts, meanwhile, were concerned with extending their horizons. In season 1885-86, they entered the English FA Cup but scratched when they were drawn away to Padiham and the cost of the journey proved prohibitive. The following season, Hearts took up their place and travelled to Lancashire to face Darwen in what proved to be their first and last match in the competition. Hearts were crushed 7-1 and the SFA banned all Scottish clubs from entering the competition from the following season onwards.

Off the field, Hearts were on the move again – across the road to a new ground at the present Tynecastle, which was constructed at the cost of £200. The team beat Sunderland 2-1 in their final game at Old Tynecastle on 27 February 1886 and also opened the new stadium by entertaining English opposition, beating Bolton 4-1 in front of 5,500 spectators. Tom Jenkinson, who ten months later was to become the first Hearts player to be capped when he turned out for Scotland against Ireland, had the distinction of scoring the first goal at Tynecastle and the other home scorers that day were Rab Henderson (2) and Bobby McNeill. Jenkinson, incidentally, went on to become manager of Liverpool FC.

A Silver Dawn

HIBS were the dominant team in Edinburgh around this time and in 1887 had broken the west of Scotland stranglehold on the Scottish Cup by beating Dumbarton 2-1 in the Final. From its inception in 1873-74, Queen's Park had won the trophy eight times, Vale of Leven three and Dumbarton and Renton one apiece. Hibs indeed were unofficial "champions of the world" at this stage having earlier beaten English champions Preston North End at Easter Road. Still drawing their players from Irish Catholics, there was an unforeseen setback for Hibs in late 1887 when the foundations were put in place for a new Glasgow Irish team, this time based in Glasgow. Celtic went on to lure many of the top players in the years to come.

There had been talk of forming a Scottish League and, in 1890, Peter Fairly, secretary of Renton, invited 14 clubs to attend a meeting on 20 March in Glasgow to look at the possibility of forming such a competition to complement the Scottish Cup. Hibs were not invited as it was deemed they were an Irish club at the time as their team was made up of immigrants. The team was strictly Catholic but had lost players to the emerging Celtic side. Twelve clubs (Clyde and Queen's Park were absent) attended that initial meeting – Abercorn, Cambuslang, Celtic, Cowlairs, Dumbarton, Hearts, Rangers, Renton, St Bernard's, St Mirren, Third Lanark and Vale of Leven – clearly showing the west of Scotland domination, with Hearts and St Bernard's the only east sides present.

Hearts were represented by Mr Smith and Mr Richardson and it is reported that, while they had nothing significant to put to the debate, the Edinburgh club were keen to be part of the way forward for the game. The *Scottish Sport* publication reported: "With wonted timidity, and leaning hard on the handle of a stout umbrella, Mr Smith (Heart of Midlothian)

Hearts team which regained the 'Championship of the East' by beating Leith Athletic in the 1889 Shield Final at Easter Road. Back row (left to right): Jimmy Adams, Hugh Mackay, James Cairns. Middle row: John McLeod, Willie Taylor, Johnny Hill, Isaac Begbie, Davie Baird. Front row: George Scott, John McPherson, Tom Jenkinson. Jenkinson was the first Hearts player to be selected for Scotland, scoring on his debut, against Ireland at Hampden Park in 1887.

Hearts in 1890. Back row (left to right): Jock Fairburn, Jimmy Adams, John McPherson. Middle row: Joe Newton (trainer), Davie Russell, Isaac Begbie, Johnny Hill, George Goodfellow. Front row: Willie Taylor, Willie Mason, George Scott, Davie Baird.

Cup with a win over joint League champions Dumbarton in the Final.

The cup was a protracted affair with Hearts having to come through six rounds before even reaching the semi-finals. But it meant that Hearts scored a healthy 27 goals on the way to lifting the trophy. Raith Rovers were beaten 7-2 in the first round and, while Hearts had a walkover against second round opponents Burntisland Thistle, they then beat Methlan Park 3-0 in a game played at Meggatland. Ayr (4-3), Morton (5-1) and East Stirling (3-1) were all then taken care of on the way to the semi-final where Hearts beat Third Lanark at Cathkin 4-1. The East Stirling match had great significance in a wider sense as Jimmy Adams punched out a scoring shot from an East Stirling player and it provoked an angry and sustained reaction from the home supporters. The Scottish Football Association ruled that such an offence would constitute a penalty in future matches and so Hearts literally had a hand in an historic rule change.

A crowd of 16,000 attended the Cup Final at Hampden on 7 February 1891 and Hearts scored the only goal through a shot from Willie Mason after some 15 minutes of the Final. Goalkeeper Jock Fairbairn played a big part in the Cup triumph and he was a popular figure in the Hearts' line-up. He went on to win two League championship medals and two Scottish Cup medals and was the first goalkeeper to play 100 matches for the club. He eventually left in 1899, having played 281 games for the club, a not inconsiderable total at the time. The Hearts team from that first cup success was: Fairbairn; Adams, Goodfellow, Begbie, McPherson, Hill, Taylor, Mason, Russell, Scott and Baird. Dumbarton lined up in the Final: McLeod; Watson, Miller, McMillan, Boyle, Keir, Taylor, Galbraith, Mair, McNaught and Bell.

modestly addressed himself to speech. The Hearts never did seriously discuss this matter, or consider its details, but they were just in this position – ready to go with the times."

The first Scottish League matches were played on 16 August 1890 and while Celtic attracted a crowd of 10,000 for their 4-1 defeat by Renton, rather less (between 3,000-4,000) watched Rangers defeat Hearts 5-2 at Old Ibrox. It was an inauspicious start – Isaac Begbie and William Taylor were Hearts' scorers – but worse was to follow as Celtic beat Hearts 5-0 in front of 8,000 fans the following week at Tynecastle. Hearts finished sixth in that inaugural season with Rangers and Dumbarton sharing the title after they drew 2-2 in the play-off and there were no means devised at the time to separate the teams.

Begbie, who had the honour of scoring Hearts' first League goal in that game at Ibrox, had a reputation of being an uncompromising tackler and, brought up close to Tynecastle, he had Hearts in his blood. He went on to show great leadership qualities as he captained the team in the late 19th century and helped them win two League titles and two Scottish Cups before leaving after 425 first-team appearances.

Yet, while the League form was mediocre, Hearts had the no small consolation of winning their first national trophy that season in the shape of the Scottish

The Scotland team that beat Wales 6-1 in March 1892, in the first international played at Tynecastle. Back row (left to right): J. K. McDowell (SFA), G. Sneddon (SFA), J. Orr (Kilmarnock), J. Begbie (Hearts), R. Downie (Third Lanark), J. Adams (Hearts), J. McPherson (Rangers), A. Sliman (SFA). Front row: J. Reid (referee), W. Thomson (Dumbarton), J. Taylor (Dumbarton), J. Hamilton (Queen's Park), J. Hill (Hearts, captain), D. Baird (Hearts), J. Campbell (Kilmarnock), J. M. Campbell (SFA).

the attendance was a poor one due to wintry weather in the capital.

As Hearts' fame grew, so did the club's surroundings. By 1888, the ground capacity had been taken up to 10,000 when two new stands and a pavilion were built and a roof was added to the south-east stand offering spectators the first covered accommodation by 1892. By the following year, professionalism had been made legal in Scotland and Hearts players were paid £2.00 a week for their services.

By this time, Hearts were one of the leading clubs in Scotland and, four years after the Scottish

Hearts' name was enhanced by the trophy win and the team earned the reputation for an entertaining and adventurous style of play. In a friendly match against Hibs in 1893-94, Hearts recorded a 10-2 victory at Easter Road. Tynecastle was also deemed fit enough to stage its first full international between Scotland and Wales on 26 March 1892, which the hosts won 6-1, but

Cup success, they became League champions for the first time. In 1894-95, Hearts won their first 11 games in the League to take command from the start and won 15 of their 18 games that season, scoring 50 goals in the process. The only defeats were to Clyde (twice) and the only other dropped point came in a draw with Rangers as Hearts eventually finished the season five points

Hearts in 1894-95, winners of the Scottish League championship for the first time. Back row (left to right): R. Waugh, R. Cheyne, Barney Battles (senior), J. Stirling, R. Smith, William Cox, W. Lorimer, James Mirk, J. R. Cairns, W. Amos, George Hogg, Joe Adams. Seated: Bob McLaren, Willie Michael, Isaac Begbie, Alex Hall, George Scott. On ground: Tom Chambers, John Walker.

clear of second-placed Celtic. On 27 April 1895 Hearts played an unofficial world championship game with English champions Sunderland but lost 5-3.

Hearts quickly built on that League success and regained the Scottish Cup the following season. The cup trail started with a 12-1 win at Blantyre in the first round and 5-1 wins at Ayr and 4-0 at Arbroath set up a semi-final battle with St Bernard's which Hearts won 1-0 thanks to a goal from Willie Michael. It set up an all-Edinburgh Final – the only time this has happened to date – against Hibs. The game was played at Logie Green (home of St Bernard's) – the only occasion the Cup Final has been played outside Glasgow – on 14 March 1896 in front of 16,034 spectators. The teams were: Hearts: Fairbairn; McCartney, Mirk, Begbie, Russell, Hogg, McLaren, Baird, Michael, King and Walker; Hibs: McColl; Robertson, Macfarlane, Breslin, Neill, Murphy, Murray, Kennedy, Groves, Smith and O'Neill.

Isaac Begbie, Davie Russell and Davie Baird were the only survivors from the 1891 cup win, Russell having returned from a spell at Preston. Several

hundred fans apparently stayed away from the Final for fear that the ground would not be big enough to accommodate the thousands who wanted to witness the occasion but a report at the time suggested the stadium could still have held another 8,000 spectators comfortably.

It was a Final fit for the occasion. Hibs had the upper hand in the early stages but it was Hearts who finished much the stronger. They dominated the second half to get their grip on the trophy again with a 3-1 win courtesy of goals from Davie Baird, Alex King and Willie Michael. Tom Purdie, the club's first captain, was a delighted spectator, now a member of the Hearts' committee. Baird was to be the only player to appear in three Scottish Cup winning sides for Hearts and it has proved an endurable record through the years. Begbie would have matched the record in those early years of the club but he left in 1900 to join Leith Athletic, just a year before Hearts won the Cup for a third time.

The month following the Scottish Cup triumph over Hibs – 18 April to be precise – a 17-year-old

In 1896-97, Hearts won the Scottish League championship for the second time. Back row (left to right): Davie Baird, Willie Taylor, James Sharp, Johnny Walker, J. Chapman (trainer), Jock Fairholm, James Mirk, Harry Marshall. Front row: George Hogg, Bob McCartney, Bob McLaren, Isaac Begbie.

Hearts in 1898-99, with the previous year's trophies on display. Hearts finished runners-up in the League, ten points behind Rangers who won all their matches that season. Back row (left to right): Bob. Waugh (trainer), J. Arnott, J. Fraser, R. Cheyne, R. Smith, Isaac Begbie, J. McElfrish, Albert Buick, W. Dow, D. Ireland, J. G. Robertson, G. Walker. Seated: Harry Rennie, Willie Taylor, Willie Michael, Bob McCartney, George Hogg, John Blair, Harry Allan, Bobby Walker. On ground: Joe Dodds, George Livingstone.

over the 18-game season and drew two.

It did not take Bobby Walker long to come to the fore. Although it was said at the time that he did not possess great pace, he had a deceptive style and it was said he was years ahead of his time. His play soon caught the eye of the international selectors and he was named to make his international debut on 7 April 1900 when Scotland beat England 4-1 at Celtic Park. Hearts' goalkeeper Harry Rennie, a former halfback and the first Hearts goalkeeper to be capped, also played on that occasion.

Walker went on to win 29 caps – still the most-capped Hearts player – in 13 years but that would have been worth three or four times as many in today's terms and he held the caps record for Scotland until Rangers' legendary winger Alan Morton surpassed his total in 1932. Hearts, of course, had to meet the going rate for a player of such pedigree and, while the players at the turn of the century were on £3.00 a week, Walker was also paid a £39.00 signing-on fee in 1900.

played in a trial game against Sunderland at Tynecastle, a player who was to become synonymous with Hearts' success in the years to come. His name? Bobby Walker. And he was signed on conclusion of the trial game as, even at that tender age, his skills shone through. Begbie was credited with taking the young Walker under his wing and nurturing his skills in the player's formative years and helping Walker become the complete player he was in the early part of the next century. It was a trait Walker was to follow himself as he is credited with helping a lot of younger players in their formative years at Tynecastle.

In 1897, Hearts won the League title for a second time, this time by just a two-point margin on second-placed Hibs in a tight finish which saw Rangers third, a further point adrift, and Celtic fourth, just another point less than their Old Firm rivals. This time, it was a strong finish that clinched the title as Hearts finished with wins at Third Lanark (5-1), at Clyde (5-1) and then at home to Clyde 5-0 as faltering Celtic lost their final two games. This time Hearts lost three games

Hearts' Scottish Cup winning team of 1901. Back row (left to right):Bob Waugh (trainer), Davie Baird, Albert Buick, George Hogg, George Philip, Harry Allan. Middle row: George Key, Bobby Walker, Charlie Thomson, Bob Houston. On ground: Willie Porteous, Markie Bell.

Mark Bell, an interesting character in Hearts' early history. Hearts signed Bell from St Bernards, and he later played for Southampton, Fulham and Clapton Orient before emigrating to Australia. He scored the winning goal in the 1901 Scottish Cup Final and could run the 100 yards in ten seconds.

George Kay, at 5ft 4ins tall possibly the smallest player to appear for Hearts. Right-half in the 1901 Scottish Cup winning team, he moved to Chelsea when Hearts failed to meet his wage demands and played in the Londoners' first-ever season. In 1902 he played for Scotland against Ireland.

Charlie Thomson, one of Hearts' greatest players. He joined Hearts in 1898, played 21 times for Scotland while at Tynecastle and won a further nine caps after moving to Sunderland in 1908, for a fee of £700, which also included the transfer of Tom Allan to Roker. He played at centre-forward in the 1901 Scottish Cup winning side, but was at centre-half in the club's 1906 Cup Final victory.

It was Walker who inspired Hearts to another Scottish Cup success in 1901. In the early rounds, Mossend Swifts (7-0) and Queen's Park (2-1) were dealt with at Tynecastle, before Hearts travelled west to knock out Port Glasgow 5-1 and clinch a semi-final meeting with Hibs. After a 1-1 draw, Hearts won the replay 2-1 with goals from Willie Porteous and, inevitably, Walker and it set up what was to prove one of the classic Scottish Cup finals with Celtic at Ibrox.

The teams were: Hearts: Philip; Allan, Baird, Key, Buick, Hogg, Porteous, Walker, Thomson, Houston and Bell; Celtic: McArthur; Davidson, Battles, Russell, Loney, Orr, McOustra, Divers, Campbell, McMahon and Quinn. Barney Battles and Davie Russell were both former Hearts players.

Hearts led 3-1 at one stage but Celtic pulled it back level with time running out – their three goals coming from McOustra (2) and McMahon. It was the signal for Walker, who had been causing Celtic headaches all afternoon, to turn on the style one more time. He weaved his way into the Celtic penalty area before delivering a shot which the Celtic goalkeeper could not

Albert Buick, who joined Hearts from Arbroath in 1896 and played for the club until being transferred to Portsmouth, then in the Southern League, in 1903. Known as 'Spider' because of his gangly legs, Buick, a centre-half, played in the 1901 Scottish Cup Final and then skippered Hearts when they lost to Rangers in the 1903 Final. He won four Scottish caps and after joining Portsmouth lured no less than six other Hearts players to Fratton Park over the next two seasons.

hold and Mark Bell slotted home the winning goal to give Hearts the Cup 4-3. Walker, the Hearts captain, had scored the opening goal early in the Final and Bell had scored the second goal before Charlie Thomson had put Hearts 3-1 ahead.

The Final became known as the "Walker Final" and it was afterwards that Thomson remarked that Walker must be the best player in Europe and certainly his fame was spreading outside Scotland. While comparisons are perhaps unwise given the way the game has changed over the past century, it is accepted that he was the greatest player ever to wear maroon. Hearts played matches against the FA Cup winners Tottenham Hotspur in another unofficial world championship and after securing a 0-0 draw at White Hart Lane, Hearts won the return 3-1 at Tynecastle in January 1902.

But the Cup success disguised the fact that Hearts had hardly distinguished themselves in the League and finished tenth out of 11 in 1900-01 and had to apply for re-election for the first time in their history. League success was to prove elusive after that 1897 triumph and it was to be another 61 years before Hearts could call themselves champions, yet there were to be some

Hearts in 1905. Back row (left to right: George Goodfellow (assistant trainer), Robert Mackie, George McWattie, David Philip, James Brown, George Wilson, Jas Chapman (trainer). Front: Bobby Walker, Martin Moran, George Key, Charlie Thomson, Andrew Orr, Davie Wilson.

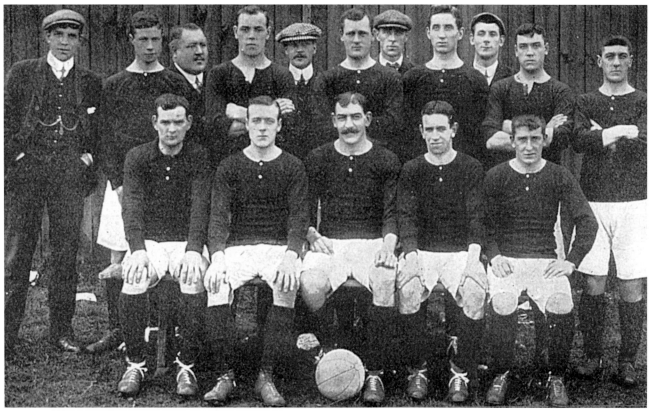

Hearts in 1907. Back row (left to right): William Waugh (secretary-manager), Isaac Tomlinson, William Cox, Frank McLaren, James Dickson, Henry Mitchell, Robert Reid, John Peddie, William Henderson, Thomas Collins, Bobby Walker. Front: Thomas Allan, William Yates, Charlie Thomson, David Phillip, Jas Dargue.

Hearts in 1908. Back row (left to right): William Scott, Bobby Walker, George Sinclair, A. Devine. Middle: Jimmy Duckworth (trainer), David Smart (assistant secretary-manager), Frank McLaren, Roddy Walker, Willie Muir, Tom Hynds, Tom Collins, James McGee (secretary-manager). Seated: George Gilmour, Peter Nellies, John Courts, Peter Cole, James Dickson.

agonisingly close calls along the way. But fortunes were rather brighter in 1901-02 and 1902-03 where Hearts climbed to third and fourth respectively.

There was still some silverware to be contested in terms of the Scottish Cup and Hearts reached another Final in 1903 but lost 2-0 to Rangers at Celtic Park after two drawn games, 1-1 and 0-0. For the first game, which attracted 28,000 to Celtic Park, Hearts lined up: McWattie; Thomson, Orr, Key, Buick, Hogg, Dalrymple, Walker, Porteous, Hunter and Baird and Rangers were: Dickie; Fraser, Drummond, Gibson, Stark, Robertson, McDonald, Speedie, Hamilton, Walker and Smith. Bobby Walker scored Hearts' goal but Stark was on target which meant a replay, also at Celtic Park, with both teams unchanged for the goalless draw.

A crowd of 32,000 watched the second replay at Celtic Park and Hearts' line-up, with Albert Buick dropping out after the first two games, was: McWattie; Thomson, Orr, Key, Anderson, Hogg, Dalrymple, Walker, Porteous, Hunter and Baird. Rangers listed: Dickie; Fraser, Drummond, Henderson, Stark, Robertson, McDonald, Mackie, Hamilton, Speed and Smith. It was

to be Rangers' trophy eventually with Mackie and Hamilton scoring the goals in the 2-0 victory.

The following season – 1903-04 – there was a first round exit in the Cup to Rangers (3-2) but Hearts hauled themselves to within sight of the League title only to finish runners-up and just four points behind champions Third Lanark.

Hearts had become a limited company in 1903 only for the venture to collapse after financial difficulties, but on 29 April 1905 the limited company was re-established with 5,863 shareholders. Football had clearly become a business and Hearts were not slow to realise the potential. Peter Fairley was the club's first manager and he also combined the role with that of club secretary.

Of course, events on the pitch have a direct relation on a club's fortunes or misfortunes and it was widely acknowledged that Hearts were one of the best teams in the country in the early years of the last century. The team won the Scottish Cup for a fourth time in 1906 in a season where they also finished runners-up in the League to Celtic.

Hearts in 1909. Back row (left to right): Thomas Collins, Willie Muir, Roddy Walker, Frank McLaren, Robert Mercer, Robert Burns, Donald Munro. Front: George Sinclair, Bobby Walker, Bail Colombo, George Gilmour, Richard Harker, Peter Nellies, Philip Cole.

Bobby Walker

BOBBY Walker is justifiably regarded as one of the greatest players ever to have played for Hearts.

He remains the club's most-capped player, having won 29 caps between 1900-13 but given that Scotland only played matches against England, Wales and Northern Ireland in the early part of last century, he would clearly have won many more caps had he been playing in the modern era.

Walker was a Scotland regular in the years leading up to World War One and his 29 caps probably equate to something between 80-90 today given that Scotland play so many more international games. He also won 14 Scottish League caps.

Indeed, he was Scotland's most-capped player until 1932 when Rangers' winger Alan Morton won the 30th of his 31 caps.

Walker was a local boy having attracted attention with his play for Dalry Primrose. He was invited to play in a trial game against Sunderland on 18 April 1896 as a 17-year-old. Walker played on the right wing and so impressed that he was signed up immediately after the game, having become an instant hero with the crowd.

He was a first-team regular the following year and won his first cap against England in front of 60,000 fans at Celtic Park on 7 April 1900 in a 4-1 win.

At that stage, Walker was commanding a £39 signing-on fee for Hearts when the regular weekly wage was just £3.

Walker indeed was Hearts' first superstar – if that term can be used – and fans used to flock from all around to see his skills. He was undoubtedly ahead of his time and he was described as the "father of altruistic football".

In the early days of football, dribbling was the art most clubs sought and teams from the west of Scotland were said to be more adept at this. Walker was a more unselfish player and was noted for his passing and for bringing team-mates into play.

He had a good football brain and much thought went into his game. He has been described as a lazy player but it was a case that when many players were charging around the field, Walker preferred to pick his moment before making the telling contribution and would not expend needless energy.

Walker did much to spread the fame of Hearts and gave the club a reputation for adventurous and entertaining football, a tradition they have attempted to hold to this day.

When Hearts won the Scottish Cup for the third time in 1901 – with a memorable

4-3 final victory over Celtic – it was known as the "Walker Final". Celtic were overwhelming favourites as they were second in the League at the time and Hearts were second-bottom and ultimately had to apply for re-election but Walker set the ball rolling for an upset by scoring the opening goal.

The Hearts' captain also set up the third for Charlie Thomson as Hearts built up a 3-1 lead only for Celtic to claw it back to level late in the game. It was the cue for Walker to swing things back in Hearts' favour and when his netbound shot was parried by the Celtic goalkeeper, Markie Bell was on hand to score the winning goal.

Walker was besieged by reporters afterwards but the modest player was unwilling to talk at any length on his heroics and it is reported that he told the journalists: "I'd rather play than speak."

Team-mate Charlie Thomson, another great Tynecastle servant, did plenty of speaking on his behalf however and labelled Walker as the finest player in Europe.

In 1902, Hearts beat Spurs over two legs to win the unofficial world championship as the club went from strength to strength with Walker pulling the strings.

Hearts lost to Rangers in the 1903 Final after three games but Walker was drawing praise from all quarters and it was said of him that he was "the greatest natural footballer who ever played" and "it is questionable if there was ever a more complete footballer in the game."

It was said that by the 1903-04 season, Walker and Thomson, Scotland's international centre-half, were carrying the rest of the Hearts' team on their shoulders such was the contribution both players made, Thomson in defence and Walker in attack.

Walker also played his part in Hearts' Scottish Cup success in 1906 when they beat Third Lanark 1-0 in the Final, setting up the only goal for George Wilson, and also helped Hearts finish runners-up in the League to Celtic.

Six years later, the club embarked on its first foreign excursion when it played matches in Scandinavia and King Haakon of Norway made a special trip to watch Walker play in a match against Kristiana Kredslag, such was the reputation of the player who was now nearing the end of his career.

Walker left an indelible mark on the club and was the first player to score 100 League goals for Hearts and he also had the distinction of scoring the club's 1,000 League goal, in a match against Airdrie at Tynecastle in November 1910.

His contribution to the growth of Hearts will never be forgotten and Walker set the standards for those who wear maroon to follow.

1896-97-1912-13
Appearances 350
Goals 123 (League)

In the Cup, Hearts beat Nithsdale Wanderers 4-1 and Beith 3-0 before putting out Celtic 2-1 in the quarter-finals in front of 50,000 fans in Glasgow. Port Glasgow were put to the sword 2-0 in the semi-final and, if the Final did not live up to the 1901 against Celtic, Hearts fans were not bemoaning the 1-0 win over Third Lanark. The teams at Ibrox that afternoon were: Hearts: G Philip; McNaught, D Philip, McLaren, Thomson, Dickson, Couper, Walker, Menzies, D Wilson and G Wilson; Third Lanark: Raeside; Barr, Hill, Cross, Neilson, Comrie, Johnstone, Graham, Reid, Wilson and Munro. Hearts wore light blue and the only goal came after Walker set up a chance for George Wilson, later transferred to Everton, and he scored the winning goal with only nine minutes remaining.

Hearts had another final appointment the following year – this time against Celtic – but they were on the end of a 3-0 reverse at Hampden after a disappointing season which also saw them finish a distant ninth in the championship.

The teams on that occasion were: Hearts: Allan; Reid, Collins, D Philip, McLaren, Henderson, Bauchop, Walker, Axford, Yeats and Wombwell; Celtic: Adams; McLeod, Orr, Young, McNair, Hay, Bennett, McMenemy, Quinn, Somers and Templeton.

No-one was to realise it at the time but it was to be another 50 years before Hearts managed to grasp the Scottish Cup again after the 1906 win. Indeed, Hearts were not to get beyond the third round again until season 1911-12 when they went on to lose 3-0 in the semi-finals to Celtic.

Lest We Forget

THE fortunes had rather sagged after 1907 and Hearts failed to finish in the top ten in four successive years and by 1911 had dropped to 14th in the table, their lowest position to date. Teams were now playing 34 matches in a League season as more and more joined the set-up.

Tynecastle had continued to move with the times. A new covered stand to replace the north-east stand had been built in 1901 and the banking around the pitch had been extended to take the capacity up to 20,000. The north and south stands were combined in 1903 and the terracing extended in 1906. In 1911, a covered enclosure "The Iron Stand" was constructed and the capacity at this stage was around 60,000. The ground staged international games with increasing regularity and there was also a Rugby League test match played at the stadium on 16 December 1911 between England and Australia which finished 11-11 as the sport sought to gain a foothold in Edinburgh.

Hearts' fame was spreading and, in 1912, the club undertook its first foreign tour when the team visited Norway. Such was the reputation of Bobby Walker, that King Haakon of Norway attended Hearts' game against Kristiana Kredslag to get a glimpse of the player.

In February 1914, Hearts sold their star striker Percy Dawson to Blackburn Rovers for a then world record fee of £2,500 in order to help fund further ground improvements – the present main stand was built at a cost of £12,178. Dawson had proved a prolific scorer in Hearts' best traditions and, having arrived in

Willie Wilson. who signed for Hearts in 1911-12 and played for the club until 1923. A forward, Wilson joined Hearts from Arniston Rangers.

Hearts in action against Celtic in the 1912 Scottish Cup semi-final at Ibrox.

Edinburgh from North Shields Athletic just three years earlier for a modest fee of £100, he scored 99 times in 117 games.

Helped by the creative skills of Walker, he was top scorer for the club in three successive seasons from 1911-12 to 1913-14 but Hearts needed the money from his transfer fee and it showed a considerable profit on their meagre investment in the Englishman. Dawson went on to spend ten years at Blackburn Rovers and won a League championship medal there, shortly after leaving Hearts.

Hearts had come out of their slump and, after finishing fourth in the League in 1912, there followed two third-place finishes in 1913 and 1914, the latter with a club record 54 points. In addition, there was a narrow 1-0 Scottish Cup semi-final defeat by Falkirk in 1913 and it was clear the recovery was almost complete. John McCartney, who had been in charge at St Mirren, had taken over as manager of the club from James McGhee on 20 January 1910 and was paid £5.00 a week and he was to forge together one of the greatest teams in the club's history.

McGhee had resigned on a point of principle the previous year when he suspended Bobby Walker for not turning up for a game but the board of directors refused to ratify it as the player was so popular. It meant Hearts were without a manager for a few months before McCartney took over.

Another reason for Hearts' upturn in fortunes under McCartney was tough-tackling full-back Paddy Crossan, who joined from Arniston Rangers in 1911 and went on to represent the club until 1925. He played 380 games for the club and also played at halfback and his fame was such that he opened a

Percy Dawson scored over 100 goals in four seasons at Tynecastle after signing from North Shields Athletic for £100. He scored within five minutes of his debut, against Partick Thistle in January 1911 and was the club's top scorer in the three seasons 1911-12-13-14. In February 1914, Hearts sold him to Blackburn Rovers for a world record fee of £2,500, of which he allegedly received £500.

Right-back Paddy Crossan played for Hearts from 1911 to 1925, before joining Leith Athletic and then opening Paddy's Bar in Rose Street. He served in World War One and was wounded on 12 July 1916, a day on which Hearts players Annand Ness, Edward McGuire and Alf Briggs were also wounded.

public house in Edinburgh's Rose Street – "Paddy's Bar" – when he retired from the game.

By the start of the 1914-15 season, there was renewed optimism on Gorgie that Hearts could recapture the League title. After beating champions Celtic in the season's opener, Hearts went on to win their first eight League matches to take a commanding lead at the top of the League. Many at the time believed this was the greatest team that had ever worn maroon but events were to overtake Hearts with Europe on the verge of war.

It was when war broke out in November 1914 that the entire Hearts squad enlisted for action along with 400 shareholders and season ticket holders. Hearts were the first British club to do so and the unselfish act may effectively have cost them the League title but there was a greater calling for Hearts to respond to. Most of the players enrolled with "C" Company of the 16th Royal Scots, Sir George McCrae's battalion.

Seven Hearts players made the ultimate sacrifice for their country and Duncan Currie, John Allan, Thomas Gracie, James Boyd, James Speedie, Ernest Ellis and Harry Wattie were all killed in action and 11 others were wounded or gassed. The redoubtable Bob Mercer, a great favourite with Hearts' fans, was gassed and suffered injuries that resulted in his premature death at the age of 37, eight years after the end of the war. Crossan, widely regarded as one of the most popular players at the time, was wounded in the Battle of the Somme and was also gassed in the war. While he played for Hearts right through to 1925, he died eight years later at the age of 37, having never regained full health.

Hearts produced a pre-season booklet for the 1917-18 season on how the players "leapt to their country's call" which included an appreciation by Lieutenant-Colonel George McCrae. He wrote: "In the closing months of 1914, much recrimination was hurled at the devotees of the world of sport, and they

Andy Wilson is a Hearts legend. He broke all the club's goalscoring records in 1918-19 and led Hearts to the Victory Cup Final for good measure. He scored 40 goals that season, 30 of them in the League. Wilson was a Middlesbrough player when he was invalided home from the war with a shattered right arm. Hearts secured his services, although he sometimes had to be smuggled out of his army barracks and played under the pseudonym of 'Nisbet'. After the war 'Boro would not release him and Wilson played non-League football with Dunfermline before returning to Teesside.

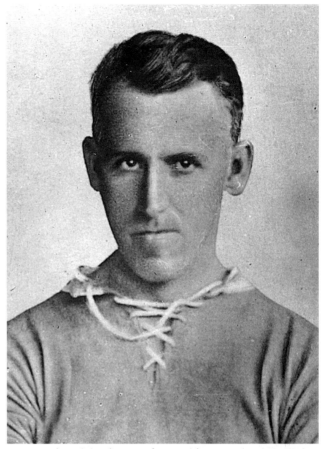

Harry Graham joined Hearts from Raith Rovers in 1913. During World War One he served in the Gloucestershire Regiment despite being exempt from military service as a dentist. A skilful inside-forward, he helped Hearts win the Shield, Wilson Cup and Charity Cup against Hibs in 1919-20. He left Hearts for Leicester City.

were freely charged with reluctance to do their bit in the great world war.

"Much of that criticism was ungenerous and unfair, made without knowledge of what had been done by the individual. The raising of a new Kitchener Battalion in Edinburgh gave opportunity of showing of what stuff Scotland's footballers were made. The Heart of Midlothian players made generous response to my appeal for recruits, and a whole company was rapidly raised, including some players from other teams in Scotland."

It concluded: "The Regiment has given a good account of itself in many a hard-fought engagement, and where danger has been greatest and the shells falling thickest, there have the "Hearts" been, all "Forwards" then. Their losses, like that of the

Regiment, have been severe. But the glory of it shall never fade, and to those of us who are left, the comradeship and good feeling which pervaded all ranks will ever be a happy recollection.

"We are proud of our fallen heroes. They have made the supreme sacrifice willingly, gladly, for a great cause."

Back home, the depleted Hearts side, who had led the League in 35 of the 37 weeks of the season eventually succumbed to Celtic when they lost their last two games to St Mirren and Morton and finished four points behind the eventual champions. The First World War meant Hearts, under John McCartney, had to rebuild again and it was not surprising that the team finished seventh in the League in 1919 and, more disappointingly, 15th at the end of season 1919-20. The team did reach the Victory Cup Final in season 1918-19 but lost 3-0 in the Final to St Mirren.

McCartney left in 1919 after nine years as manager

after a policy dispute with the board of directors and took over as manager of Portsmouth. His son William, who was just 30 when he took over and remained in control until 1935 before going on to manage the great Hibs side of the 1940s, succeeded him.

The new manager proved popular with players and fans alike and, in 1920-21, Hearts finished third in the League and also reached the Scottish Cup semi-final before eventually losing 2-0 to Partick Thistle after two 0-0 draws, the Glasgow side going on to beat Rangers in the Final.

The respected Bob Mercer, capped twice by Scotland and regarded as one of the greatest players of his generation, was released by the club on medical advice during the season. The centre-half had been given a benefit game in August 1919 against a Glasgow Select which was attended by 13,000 spectators but it was clear that he was not going to make a full recovery from his wartime experiences. He managed to play on for a couple of seasons but he collapsed during a

match at Selkirk in 1926 when he played as a guest for Hearts against the club he started out with and died on the pitch.

After the season of promise in 1920-21, Hearts failed to live up to expectations the following season and battled against relegation for most of the campaign. With three teams relegated from the First Division, Hearts finished 19th in the 22-team League to escape on the final day of the season. It took a goal from Englishman Frank Stringfellow to give Hearts a 1-0 win against Aberdeen and ensure that they would be in the top flight the following season. But nothing could disguise the fact that it was the poorest year in the club's history and there was also a third round exit in the Scottish Cup – 4-0 at the hands of Rangers, League champions from the previous season.

On 9 April 1922, the War Memorial was opened at Haymarket by Scottish Secretary of State Robert Munro to honour the players who died in World War One. Around 35,000 attended the unveiling and, every

'Big Bob' Mercer joined Hearts in 1908 and won two full Scotland caps and played five times for the Scottish League. During 1920-21 he complained of chest pains, thought to have been caused by having been gassed in World War One, and Hearts released him on medical grounds. He was replaced by Willie Porter of Raith Rovers, for whom Hearts paid their first-ever £1,000 transfer fee.

Winger George Sinclair also joined Hearts in 1908. He won three Scotland caps and played three times for the Scottish League. Sinclair saw action at Mons in World War One before his career ended in the 1920s. He later ran Sinclair's Bar at the top of Easter Road.

Remembrance Day thereafter, players and officials from the club attend a ceremony at the Memorial. It has become a landmark in the city of Edinburgh and it ensures that those who gave up their lives for their country will never be forgotten.

On the pitch, the 1922-23 season was not one that Hearts remember with any fondness. Although the League position improved to 11th, there was an embarrassing second round Scottish Cup exit 3-2 to Second Division Bo'ness. But in many ways it was a transitional year with Hearts paying out a new club record fee of £2,700 to Albion Rovers for striker Jock White. He started to pay his way immediately and scored 30 goals in his first season at Tynecastle.

Hearts were soon back on the up and their commitments were so great that they, rather remark-

Left-back Jock Wilson, along with his full-back partner Paddy Crossan, left Hearts at the end of 1924-25.

ably, turned down the offer of a challenge game from Real Madrid during the 1924-25 season as they could not fit in a suitable date. With White making his mark, the goals were flowing more freely and a total of 87 were scored in the League in 1925-26 as Hearts moved up to third place, eight points behind champions Celtic. What is more, White helped himself to four goals in three consecutive games in a 10-day period which has not been beaten since. He notched four in a 6-0 Scottish Cup win over Dundee United, scored another four in a 5-2 win over Alloa in the next round and then bagged another four in a League game against Hamilton. Not surprisingly, White finished top scorer in the League.

After beating Dundee United and Alloa thanks to the golden boot of White, holders Celtic were Hearts' third round opponents in the Cup on 20 February 1926 and such was the interest in the tie that 51,000 spectators packed Tynecastle and it was estimated that a further 15,000 were locked out. The knife-edge tie that was anticipated did not materialise as Celtic showed Hearts still had some way to go as they left

Jock Gilfillan, the Hearts goalkeeper who played in the shock Scottish Cup defeat by Bo'ness at Newtown Park in January 1923. With nine minutes remaining, the score was 2-2 when the Second Division club's Rayne hit a speculative shot and a high wind sent it sailing past Gilfillan to send Hearts crashing out of the Cup.

with a 4-0 win and went all the way to the Final again that year only to lose to St Mirren.

In 1925, Hearts had purchased Tynecastle from Edinburgh Corporation at a cost of £5,000 but there was a buy-back clause in the agreement which was not bought out by the club until 1977. In 1926, further work was conducted which led to a new entrance at Wheatfield Street and terracing was added with the help of old railway sleepers. The

Hearts team in 1925-26. Back row (left to right): George Miller, Tom Reid, Andrew Jamieson, Willie White, Alex Johnstone, Alex Wright, Tom Murphy (trainer). Front: Jimmy Smith, John McNeil, Jock Ramage, John Murphy, Willie Murray.

old "Iron Stand" was demolished and, by 1930, the capacity of the ground had increased to 55,842. The work cost the club a total of £18,000 and it was partly financed by the sale of Jock White to Leeds United for what at the time was a huge £5,700. Hearts finished the 1926-27 season in 13th but the sale of White did not appear to harm them too much as the following year, the team climbed to fourth.

The late 1920s saw another wave of optimism engulf the club and much of that was down to the fact that a goalscorer of some repute had been signed in Barney Battles and an accomplished goalkeeper Jack

Dundee United's Jimmy Brownlie grabs the ball from a Hearts attack at Tynecastle in February 1926, but Hearts went on to win this Scottish Cup second-round replay 6-0 with Jock White scoring four.

Harkness had also joined the club. Harkness, capped at full international level for Scotland by the age of 20, had signed from Queen's Park in 1928 after he had played for Scotland in the famous "Wembley Wizards" team that had beaten England 5-1. He went on to spend eight years at Tynecastle and play over 400 games for the club. He was capped a dozen times for Scotland but had to give up the game prematurely in 1934 due to a serious leg injury but went on to make his living as a sports journalist in later life.

Battles, whose father Barney senior also played for the club, had been brought up in Musselburgh but had left for America in his teenage years and signed for Boston AL as their first professional in 1926 – the country's first professional League having been established in 1921. He was actually capped for the United States in a game against Canada in June 1925 but on returning home in 1928 he signed for Hearts.

Battles scored on his debut against Queen's Park and then hit a hat-trick in his next game and went on to score 31 goals in that first season as he helped Hearts to finish fourth. He also represented the Scottish League in a game

Hearts in 1930-31, wearing maroon and white hoops and black shorts, a second strip introduced in 1927. Back row (left to right): Peter Kerr, Andy Head, Jack Harkness, Bob King, John A. Johnstone, Bob Bennie. Front: Jimmy Smith, Stewart Chalmers, Barney Battles, Lachie McMillan, Wille Murray. Battles scored a club record 44 of Hearts' 90 League goals that season.

against the Irish League where he helped himself to five goals in an 8-2 victory.

He also won a special place in the fans' affections when he achieved the unique feat of scoring 11 times in three games against Hibs within the space of a month. He notched five in an 8-2 Dunedin Cup win, another two in a 5-1 victory in the Wilson Cup and then four in a 5-1 Charity Cup win.

Hearts reached the semi-finals of the Scottish Cup in 1929-30 but crashed out 4-1 to Rangers at Hampden. The great Bobby Walker died in August 1930 at the age of 51 and crowds lined the streets of Edinburgh to pay their last respects.

On 25 October 1930, Battles won his one and only full cap for Scotland when he scored in a 1-1 draw with Wales at Tynecastle. It was to be quite a season for Battles as Hearts finished fifth in the League and scored 90 goals in the process with the centre-forward scoring a record 44 League goals which has never been surpassed. Jock White had also returned from Leeds as Hearts began to look like their old selves although the Scottish Cup interest ended somewhat prematurely when they lost 3-2 to Kilmarnock at the second round stage.

The interest in the team had never been higher and Hearts attracted a record crowd of 53,396 to Tynecastle the following season when they entertained Rangers in a third round Scottish Cup tie on 13 February 1932. It is a figure that will certainly never be surpassed at the ground. Alex Massie missed a penalty and Bob King

was sent off as Rangers escaped with a 1-0 victory. Massie, however, was a key player for Hearts in the first half of the 1930s and he was a player who commanded respect wherever he played.

He went on to win 11 full Scottish caps while at Hearts and, when he left for Aston Villa in 1935, he added another seven and he captained his country on several occasions. The inside-forward was born in Glasgow but spent a short time in America before coming back across the Atlantic and Hearts signed him in 1930 from Dublin Dolphins. In spite of his presence, Hearts struggled in the League with Battles injured for much of the 1931-32 campaign and the team slipped to eighth by the finish.

But Hearts fared considerably better the following season as they battled their way to third in the League and reached the last four of the Scottish Cup without losing a goal. After beating Solway Star 3-0 in the first round, Hearts then progressed at the expense of Airdrie (6-0) and St Johnstone (2-0) and faced Hibs in the quarter-finals at Easter Road. A 0-0 draw set up the replay at Tynecastle which Hearts won 2-0 with goals from Bob Johnstone and Willie Murray. The Hearts' defence also held firm in the semi-final against Celtic as the teams fought out a goalless draw but Hearts lost the Hampden replay 2-1.

Battles was still proving a favourite with the Hearts' fans, given his instinct for goal. He averaged more than a goal a game for the club with his total of 214 in 200 games and he was also capable of making some extraordinary individual goalscoring feats in matches.

Hearts in 1932-33. Back row (left to right): William McCartney (manager), Alex Massie, Andy Anderson, Jack Harkness, Tom O'Neill, John A. Johnstone, Bob Bennie. Front: Bob Johnstone, Jock White, Barney Battles, Jimmy Smith, Willie Murray.

Another 1932-33 line-up. Back row (left to right): Mr W. C. P. Brown, Alex Massie, Andy Anderson, Jack Harkness, Tom O'Neill, John A. Johnstone, Bob Bennie, William McCartney. Front: Bob Johnstone, Jock White, Barney Battles, Jimmy Smith, Willie Murray.

Alex Gardiner scores Hearts' first goal in their 6-1 Scottish Cup second-round match against Airdrie at Tyneside in February 1933. Gardiner was standing in for the injured Barney Battles.

None was more remarkable than a game against Cowdenbeath on 23 September 1933 when Hearts trailed 4-1 with 20 minutes remaining. Battles took matters into his own hands and scored four to give Hearts an unlikely 5-4 victory.

Not surprisingly, Hearts had the reputation of being a good team to watch but the Midas touch was still missing as Rangers dominated the Scottish game in the 1920s and 1930s. In all, Rangers won the League 15 times between 1920-39 and Celtic were the closest with four title successes in the same period. The Old

Hearts skipper John Johnstone greets Hibs' Halligan at Easter Road in March 1933. The result of this Scottish Cup fourth-round tie was a goalless draw but Hearts won the replay at Tynecastle 2-0.

Barney Battles

BARNEY Battles' goal record for Hearts has stood the test of time and it is questionable whether it will ever be beaten.

Of course, the likes of Bauld, Conn, Wardhaugh and Robertson have all scored considerably more for the club but Battles' record of 44 League goals in season 1930-31 remains a club record for the most League goals scored by a player in a season. It was almost half of Hearts' total of 90 League goals as they finished fifth in the table.

Given that Hearts only played 35 games that season, Battles' feat is all the more remarkable and indeed he was a rare commodity, having scored more goals than number of appearances he made for the club – 218 goals in 200 matches.

Battles also had the unusual distinction of playing international football for two different countries, being capped by the United States when he was residing there and also winning a full Scotland cap.

His father played with Hearts at the end of the 19th century and then went on to play for Celtic. Battles senior played – and indeed laid on the first goal – for the Glasgow side in the 1901 Scottish Cup Final against Hearts before the maroons went on to win the Cup 4-3.

Battles senior died shortly before his son was born in Fisherrow, Musselburgh, in 1905. The family emigrated to America when Battles junior was a teenager and, contrary to popular belief nowadays, there was a professional League across the Atlantic from as early as 1921.

Battles signed for Boston AL as their first professional player and his goalscoring exploits were such that he was called up for the American national team for a game against Canada in Montreal in 1925. He failed to find the net on that occasion as the Canadians won 1-0 and it was to be the only cap Battles was to win for his adopted country as international matches were few and far between in those days.

Nonetheless, two of Battles' teammates on that occasion – James Douglas and Thomas Florie – went on to play for their country in the first World Cup in Uruguay in 1930.

Rangers and Celtic were both interested in the centre-forward when he returned to Scotland in 1928 but he chose to play for Hearts where he was given a £20 signing-on fee and paid £9 a week. He was

hot property at the time and a crowd of 18,000 watched his first trial game between Hearts "A" and "B" squads in which he scored four times.

It seemed he rarely stopped scoring after that. He opened his account on his League debut against Queen's Park and scored a hat-trick a few weeks later against Hamilton Accies at Tynecastle. Battles then repeated the feat he had managed in that first trial game, when he found the net four times in a 7-3 win over Ayr United.

Not surprisingly, his scoring alerted clubs south of the border and Arsenal were reported to be set to make a big-money bid for the player who scored 31 goals during that first season at Tynecastle as Hearts finished fourth behind champions Rangers.

But Hearts managed to hold on to their prize asset who was good with either foot

and possessed an explosive shot. He also scored a large number of goals with his head and Battles was a natural finisher.

Hibs found that out to their cost during one spell of his career where he managed to score no fewer than 11 goals in three consecutive games against the Easter Road side – in the Dunedin Cup, the Wilson Cup and the Charity Cup in 1929. He scored five in a 8-2 win in the Dunedin Cup, two in a 5-1 victory in the Wilson Cup and then four in a 5-1 win in the Charity Cup.

Battles was capped once at full international level for Scotland in a 1-1 draw in 1931 against Wales (when he scored Scotland's goal) but he also won five Scottish League caps, three against the Irish League and two against the English League and indeed scored five times in an 8-2 win in one of his games against the Irish.

Battles was out for five months in the 1931-32 season due to a cartilage operation and that perhaps prevented English clubs pursuing their interest too vigorously but he was back with a vengeance the following season. In one memorable game on 23 September 1933, Cowdenbeath were beating Hearts 4-1 before Battles scored four in the final 20 minutes to give his team a 5-4 victory.

But knee trouble persisted and the player broke down on more than one occasion due to the problems. He was forced to retired prematurely at the age of 30 in 1936 due to the injury.

He was sorely missed, although Andy Black came close to emulating his League scoring record for Hearts in 1937-38 when he scored 40 League goals to finish top scorer in Scottish football.

But Battles' record now looks untouchable and the closest any post-war player has come to it at Tynecastle is 30 League goals in a season which Willie Bauld (in 1949-50) and Jimmy Wardhaugh (1955-56) both managed.

1928-29 – 1935-36
Appearances 200
Goals 218

Hearts players display the Rosebery Charity Cup which they won by beating Hibs 2-1 in May 1934.

In August 1934, Hearts played their first game at Tynecastle against a foreign side when the touring Rapid Vienna side from Austria, who also played against Rangers at Ibrox, were soundly beaten 5-1 in an exhibition match.

With Battles troubled by a knee injury for long spells, Hearts had to enlist another goalscorer in the mid-1930s and Dave McCulloch was recruited from Third Lanark in the summer of 1934. He had delivered 38 goals by the end of the season to finish as Scotland's top League scorer as Hearts finished third in the League, five points behind champions Rangers. It was a typically inconsistent year for the team – in the December, they crushed Rangers 4-1 with McCulloch scoring a brace but the following week, lost to Albion Rovers to ruin all the good work. There was also a much-celebrated 5-2 win over Hibs at Tynecastle when Hearts scored three in the final 15 minutes. McCulloch was on target twice as was the talented Tommy Walker, who was making a name for himself in the Scottish game.

Firm dominance was such that between 1905-47 only one team outside of Rangers and Celtic managed to win the League and that was Motherwell in 1932. Hearts, nevertheless, were capable of beating either half of the Old Firm on their day and finished sixth in the League in season 1933-34.

Walker had made his debut for Hearts in September 1932 at the age of 17 and was soon to be regarded as one of the hottest properties in Scotland. With Battles being forced to retire from the game prematurely in 1936 due to his constant knee problems, it was Walker who soon eased the sense of loss. The inside-forward was as much a chance-maker as a chance-taker but he was hugely popular with the Hearts support and with his fellow professionals for his sportsmanlike play and integrity. Arsenal were reportedly willing to pay a world record fee of £12,000 to prise him away from Edinburgh in 1934-35 but Hearts wanted to hold on to him.

Jack Harkness holds on to the ball against Hibs at Easter Road in September 1934.

It paid off as Hearts reached the Scottish Cup semi-final in 1935 – the furthest they had progressed in the competition for five years – and a crowd of 102,661, which is the largest to have ever watched Hearts, turned up at Hampden for the game with Rangers. It finished 1-1 but Rangers proved too strong in the replay and won 2-0 before progressing to beat Hamilton Accies 2-1 in the Final. In the same year,

Dave McCulloch was a strong centre-forward who made his name with Hearts before moving into English football. He won the first of his seven Scotland caps while at Tynecastle and Brentford paid £6,000 for him in December 1935. He helped them into the old First Division and later played for Derby County. He began his career with Hamilton Amateurs and Shotts United before joining Hearts from Third Lanark in 1934. In his first season with Hearts, McCulloch was top scorer in the country with 38 goals. He was player-manager of Alloa Athletic in 1951-52.

Hearts' distinguished chairman Elias H. Furst, who had a 30-year association with the club, retired and he is credited with steering the club through some difficult years and using his business acumen to spare the club from bankruptcy in the early part of the century.

Hearts were not finding goals hard to come by and, if at times their defensive frailties were exposed, their positive play in the years before World War Two earned them many friends. Between 1935-39, Hearts were never out of the top five and the goals were raining in. Indeed, between 1937-39, they reached at least 90 League goals in each of the three seasons. On 21 September 1935, Hearts humbled Hibs 8-3 at Tynecastle – still the highest number of goals managed by any of the teams in an Edinburgh derby and Hearts' record home League win over their rivals. Tommy Walker, Andy Black and Charlie Wipfler all scored doubles as Hearts threatened double figures and led 6-0 at one point.

In the following March, Walker endeared himself to Scottish fans everywhere when he kept his cool after the ball was blown off the spot three times to drill home a late penalty equaliser for Scotland against England at Wembley to secure a 1-1 draw and make Scotland first winners of the Home International title.

As if Hearts did not pose enough threat in front of goal, Hearts bought another centre-forward Willie Walsh from Oldham. On 13 February 1937, he gained the distinction of scoring eight goals in a Scottish Cup

Dave McCulloch is foiled by Steele of Dunfermline during the Pars' shock 1-0 League win over Hearts in January 1935.

Alex Massie, one of Hearts' finest players. He joined them from the Dolphin club of Dublin in 1930, although Hearts had to pay Bury £710 as he was registered with the English club. He won 11 Scotland caps while at Tynecastle before joining Aston Villa in December 1935. He later managed Villa.

Hearts finished runners-up to Celtic, falling just three points short in the final analysis. It was Hearts' highest finish since the 1914-15 season when the war had cruelly cut short their progress. But the feeling on Gorgie was that this was as strong a team as the one that was moulded by John McCartney and manager Frank Moss, who succeeded William McCartney in 1935, knew he had a talented team of which to boast. There were four Scotland regulars in his side (Walker, Willie Waugh, Andy Anderson and Andy Black) and 90 goals were scored in the 1937-38 season. Typically, however, Hearts could also trip up when least expected and there was an early exit in the Scottish Cup in the January when they were beaten 3-1 by Second Division Dundee United.

On the international field, Walker's reputation continued to grow and he scored the only goal of a 1-0 win over England at Wembley in 1938. While Hearts were keen to hold on to his talents, there was a queue of admirers forming to try and persuade the club to part with him. It is to Hearts' credit that they were in no hurry to sell him – partly because there was no necessity due to the healthy finances of the club.

The crowds were flocking to Tynecastle and an all-time League record attendance of 49,904 watched Hearts lose 5-1 to Celtic on 3 September 1938 in the final season before World War Two intervened and cut crowds to 8,000 due to the threat of air raids on the capital. Hearts finished fourth in the League in 1938-39 and tumbled out of the Scottish Cup at the hands of Celtic 2-1 in the third round after a 2-2 draw. Financially, Hearts announced at their AGM on 12 June 1939 that all debts had been cleared and the

tie against Stirling's Kings Park as Hearts won 15-0. However, there then followed a disappointing third round defeat at the hands of Hamilton.

With Walker proving the inspiration, Hearts had an excellent League season in 1937-38 as they threatened to break the Old Firm domination. Andy Black finished top League scorer in Scotland with 40 goals as

Hearts in 1935-36. Back row (left to right): Willie Russell, Willie Reid, Andy Anderson, Jack Harkness, Andy Herd, John Harvey, Jimmy Kerr (trainer). Front: Bob 'Fish' Murray, Tommy Walker, Alex Anderson, George Robson, Andy Black.

club was also considering building a new ground at Sighthill or Saughton Mains.

Most Hearts players enlisted for the forces for World War Two and the Scottish League was split into regional competitions. Hearts finished second to Falkirk in the East and North Division in 1939-40 and scored 104 goals in the process and, for the remainder of the war years, played in the Southern League where their best placing was fourth in 1943-44. During that season, Otto Jonsson – from Iceland – became the first

Hearts put Dunfermline under pressure in a League game at Tynecastle in August 1935.

Alex Munro, Hearts flying winger, was transferred to Blackpool in March 1937 for £3,500.

Andy Anderson was signed from Ballieston Juniors in 1929. A fine full-back, Anderson was capped 23 times for Scotland while with Hearts.

Andy Black was a fine striker. Signed from Shawfield Juniors in 1934, he scored 100 goals between 1935 and the outbreak of war in 1939. In 1937-38 he was the country's leading League goalscorer with 40. After the war he joined Manchester City.

foreign player to wear the maroon shirt.

Manager Frank Moss, a former Arsenal and England goalkeeper, had returned south early in the war to join the forces after three years in charge at Tynecastle (he was still only 31), and a new manager Dave McLean was installed in 1941. It was to be a significant appointment as McLean is credited with putting together arguably the best side in Hearts' history although the sad irony was that he died in 1951 and was not around to see the team reach its full potential.

Hearts' chairman Alex Irvine with the club's five Scotland internationals in 1935-36. Left to right are Andy Anderson, Tommy Walker, Dave McCulloch, Andy Herd and Alex Massie. All but Herd played in the same team, against Wales.

It was McLean who was responsible for signing all of the "Terrible Trio" of Alfie Conn, Willie Bauld and Jimmy Wardhaugh – for a total cost of just £200 – with Conn the first to arrive as a 17-year-old in 1944. Two years later Wardhaugh arrived and the third, and many would argue most important, piece of the jigsaw came just a month later when Bauld signed after a proposed move to Sunderland fell through.

Hearts in 1938-39. Back row (left to right): Andy Anderson, Willie Waugh, Duncan McClure, George Robson, Jimmy Dykes, Archie Miller. Front: Jimmy Briscoe, Tommy Walker, Arthur Briggs, Andy Black, Freddie Warren.

Bobby Baxter, the Middlesbrough star who guested for Hearts during World War Two. In fact, Baxter came from the Edinburgh mining community of Gilmerton.

Terrific, "Terrible" and Triumphant

AT the end of World War Two, Hearts manager Davie McLean had to rebuild the team. The Conn, Bauld and Wardhaugh era – which prompted the most successful spell in the club's history – was still to come as the Scottish League reconvened in 1945-46 with an unofficial championship where there was no relegation or promotion and no Scottish Cup competition.

Many players were still making their way back from the war and guest players were being used. Rangers finished in first place in this makeshift season with Hearts in seventh but it was not until 1946-47 that the League resumed properly. A new competition was also introduced – the League Cup – as football enjoyed a boom period after the war with optimism high in the country.

The popular Tommy Walker was back but he was not to remain at Hearts for long. After playing the first eight games of the new League campaign, Hearts could not resist the moves for the player any longer and he was transferred to Chelsea in September 1946 for £8,000 after 14 years at the club. He was to go on to become every bit as popular at Stamford Bridge as he was on Gorgie before he returned to Edinburgh to finish off his career.

The start of the 1946-47 season had been encouraging. After an early 4-1 defeat at home by Partick Thistle, Hearts lost only one of their next 12 games (to lowly Hamilton). The new League Cup competition was also finding favour with the Hearts support as the team topped their qualifying section ahead of Clyde, Kilmarnock and Partick Thistle with only one loss in their six matches. Inside-forward Alex McCrae had the distinction of scoring Hearts' first goals in the competition as he netted both of the goals in a 2-1 opening win at Clyde.

With the quarter-finals not until the following March, Hearts were free to concentrate on League matters and, with Conn and Wardhaugh starting to get amongst the goals (albeit just seven between them in this first season together), they were starting to make an impression. But successive defeats by Aberdeen (1-2) and Rangers (0-3) in late November left them struggling to keep up with the pace. Hearts picked up again but then there was a wounding festive period in which the team lost consecutive games to St Mirren (0-1), Hibs (2-3) and Third Lanark (1-4) and it was obvious that the title dream was to remain just that.

Rangers won the title ahead of Hibs by two points and Hearts had to be content with fourth place though, interestingly enough, they beat Rangers and Aberdeen, who both finished above them, in their final two games. It was not a season over-laden with goals – top scorer Archie Kelly had managed just 14 and Hearts' League total of 52 was the lowest in the top 11 finishers. It was not a failing that was to be pointed at Hearts for much longer, however.

Tommy Walker

TOMMY Walker has a special place in Hearts' history. Although he never won anything in the way of winners' medals during his spell as a player at Tynecastle, he made up for that as a manager when he inherited from Davie McLean the team that embarked on the silver streak of the 1950s and early 1960s.

A gifted footballer who went on to represent Scotland 20 times and, but for World War Two, would surely have surpassed the 29 caps won by Bobby Walker, still the most capped Hearts' player of all time.

However, Walker was more than just a footballer and, on and off the field, he commanded respect from everyone within the game.

When he left Hearts for Chelsea, he was as much admired south of the border and was seen as the perfect role model for youngsters taking up the game.

On his return north to rejoin Hearts, Chelsea produced a farewell brochure to acknowledge the contribution he had made at Stamford Bridge. Given that he only spent two-and-a-half years at Chelsea, the affection in which he was held was remarkable.

"If I were asked to define the true sportsman, I would unhesitatingly present Tommy as the complete example and that is the highest tribute I know," wrote the then Chelsea manager-secretary William Birrell.

The sentiment was echoed by Manchester City and England goalkeeper Frank Swift who wrote: "Tommy Walker is not only one of the greatest sportsmen I've ever had the pleasure of meeting but possesses a shot few other forwards can equal. As a footballer, the man is a credit to our great game."

Brought up in Livingston Station, he was capped at schoolboy level when he was at Bathgate Public School – the first player from the school to win a cap at that level. One of his first pair of boots was given to him by the parents of one of his colleagues in the Bathgate school team, when their son had been knocked down and killed in a car accident. As he later pointed out, the boots "set me off on a long and successful career".

He was taken on to the Hearts ground staff shortly before his 17th birthday and then signed professional forms not long afterwards.

It was obvious that he had the potential to go on and achieve great things in the game and he made his first-team debut for Hearts at the age of 17 in a 4-2 win over Ayr United. The inside forward with the explosive shot and unselfish play was soon to become an automatic choice both for club and country.

On his first visit to Wembley, he famously scored a penalty equaliser against

England after the ball had blown off the spot three times in the wind. The draw meant Scotland won the Home International trophy for the first time. Two years later, he was back at Wembley scoring the winning goal in the corresponding fixture.

A man of sincerity and compassion, Walker studied to become a Church of Scotland minister but World War Two interrupted his studies and he was never to conclude them.

After the war, Walker returned to Tynecastle but played only eight more matches for the club before joining Chelsea for the then considerable sum of £8,000 after scoring 190 goals in 353 appearances in a maroon shirt.

He was just as popular at Chelsea but the lure of returning to Edinburgh not much more than two years later proved too great as Davie McLean was building a team capable of challenging for honours. Walker was to play just one more match for the

club after returning in December 1948 and that was an unremarkable 1-0 defeat by Dundee a month later.

Walker was appointed assistant manager and then manager after the untimely death of McLean and indeed he was to become the most successful manager in the history of the club.

The first trophy came in the shape of the League Cup in 1954 and there followed the Scottish Cup two years later where the team bus made a detour to his home village of Livingston Station to show off the silverware that had proved elusive for fully 50 years.

There were three more League Cup successes to toast and two League championship wins as Hearts ruled the roost in Scottish football and did so by playing the imaginative, attacking football which was the hallmark of Walker's own game.

Walker also took Hearts into Europe for the first time and there were memorable games against Standard Liege, Benfica and Inter Milan as the fame of the club spread.

But success could not, of course, last forever. The watershed came for Walker and the club when Hearts lost the League title on the final day of the season to Kilmarnock in 1965 on goal average. The wound cut deep and it took the club many years to recover.

The following season, Hearts could finish only seventh in the League and went out in the qualifying stages of the League Cup and lost in the quarter-finals of the Scottish Cup.

Walker resigned as manager in September 1966 after 16 years and seven trophies at the age of 52 after there were rumblings of discontent in the dressing-room. Trainer John Harvey succeeded him.

But Walker, who won an OBE for his services to the game in 1960, returned to become a director of the club in 1974 and then vice-chairman in 1979. Hearts are unlikely to see his likes again.

1932-33-1948-49
Appearances 354
Goals 190

After beating St Johnstone (3-0) and Cowdenbeath (2-1), Hearts progressed to the quarter-finals of the Scottish Cup in that first season after the war but lost 2-1 at lower division Arbroath. It was a big disappointment but, by that stage in the season, the team had advanced to the last four of the League Cup courtesy of a 5-3 aggregate quarter-final win over East Fife. In addition, there was the prospect of an all-Edinburgh Final with Hibs drawing Rangers in one semi-final and Hearts facing Aberdeen in the other tie at Easter Road. Goals from Kelly and Johnny Urquhart gave Hearts a 2-1 lead in their game but there was an extraordinary second-half collapse and Aberdeen cashed in to the extent of 6-2 to progress to the first Final against Rangers, who had beaten Hibs in the other semi-final. The Final was to prove one-sided with Rangers crushing Aberdeen 4-0 to hoist the new trophy.

Unaware that the answer to the team's goalscoring problem lay within the club (although by this stage Bauld was serving his apprenticeship with Edinburgh City), manager McLean spent £10,000 to bring Bobby Flavell from Airdrie in the middle of the 1947-48 season with McCrae having been sold to Charlton for a then club record £9,000 during the close-season.

Flavell scored seven goals in 19 games in his first season at Tynecastle but it was another punchless season as Hearts finished ninth in the table with a meagre 37 goals in 30 games – the lowest in the top flight and less than half of what rivals Hibs scored on their way to the League title ahead of Rangers. If Hearts were having their problems, then so too were Celtic who had one of the poorest League seasons in their history and could only finish 12th.

Again, in 1947-48, the League Cup competition was to Hearts' liking and they won their opening group, ahead of Hibs, Airdrie and Clyde and managed the double over their Edinburgh neighbours with a 2-1 win at Easter Road (Urquhart and Kelly) and a 2-1 home win (Davie Laing and Kelly). There was also a 2-1 League win over Hibs to boast with Laing and Urquhart providing the goals this time in the September. Of the four games Hearts played against the eventual champions that season, they won three which was a considerable feat and the only reverse came 3-1 at Easter Road in a League game on New Year's Day.

After winning their League Cup section, Hearts faced East Fife at Tynecastle in the quarter-finals and, after a seven-goal extra-time thriller, the home side bowed out of the competition 4-3. In the Scottish Cup, Hearts knocked out Dundee 2-1 in the first round but then lost by the same score in the second round against Airdrie at Broomfield.

It was clear to everyone, that McLean's priority was to address the lack of goals as he prepared for the 1948-49 season. But things were to get worse before they were better as Hearts slumped in their opening few games and lost five of their first six League fixtures, the only victory coming in August when Flavell scored twice in a 3-2 win over Third Lanark. Even the League Cup did not rescue Hearts and just one win from their opening four games in their section and a 4-0 reversal at the hands of East Fife at Bayview, cast a cloud over Tynecastle. By the time Hearts faced East Fife again in the return game in the section at Tynecastle, Hearts were already out of contention for a quarter-final place.

It meant manager McLean had nothing to lose and his decision to give 20-year-old Willie Bauld his debut at centre-forward, flanked by Conn and Wardhaugh was to prove arguably the most inspired by any in the long line of Hearts' managers. In all, he made eight changes from the team that had lost 3-1 to Partick Thistle the previous week.

It was on 9 October 1948 that the trio played their first match together and East Fife, managed at the time by Scot Symon who went on to achieve greatness with Rangers, were the first team to feel the full force. Just 14 minutes had elapsed when young Bauld netted his first goal in maroon and he went on to contribute another two in the second half as East Fife were torn apart 6-1. Conn also helped himself to two and the other scorer that day was Laing, from the penalty spot. Over 23,000 were in Tynecastle to witness the birth of the "Terrible Trio" and few would argue that they had seen the start of something special.

For supporters who had seen their team struggle to score since football resumed properly after the war, it was a moment to savour. The following Saturday, Queen of the South visited in the final sectional game and Bauld notched another hat-trick and Conn the other as Hearts won 4-0. Two hat-tricks in two games,

Bauld was attracting his fair share of headlines. In Hearts' next 11 games, there were only two where Bauld never managed to get on the scoresheet and his eye for goal clearly rubbed off on others as the team played with a new exuberance. Hot on the heels of the wins over East Fife and Queen of the South, Hearts beat Rangers 2-0 at Tynecastle in the League with Wardhaugh and Conn scoring the goals in front of 41,000 fans. Bauld was to be an ever-present for the rest of the season and there was another hat-trick to celebrate in early April when Albion Rovers were thumped 7-1 and, inevitably, Wardhaugh and Conn were also on the scorers' list. Wardhaugh scored a hat-trick in a 5-1 win over Albion Rovers earlier in the season and Hearts had finally found their goal touch.

If there were still some fans to be convinced that Hearts were on the cusp of an exciting new era in the club's history, then a dramatic victory over champions Hibs at Tynecastle on New Year's Day 1949 surely won them over. Flavell and Bauld gave the home side a 2-0 lead but Lawrie Reilly pulled one back before Bobby Combe equalised with just three minutes left. But, in the dying seconds of a pulsating encounter, Bauld back-heeled the ball to Conn and he scored the winning goal.

However, Hearts were still dogged by inconsistency and although Bauld finished top scorer in that notable first season with 24 goals (Conn 17, Wardhaugh 13, Flavell 11), the team was only eighth in the final table. Hearts did not fare any better in the Scottish

Cup when they went out at the quarter-final stage 4-2 at home to a Dundee side who went on to finish runners-up to Rangers in the championship. Hearts had progressed with wins over Airdrie (4-1), Third Lanark (3-1) and Dumbarton (3-0) in the earlier rounds.

But there was no doubt that by the time the new season came round in August 1949, there was fresh hope over Gorgie. It was cemented by an opening 5-1 win over "A" division newcomers Stirling Albion away from home in the first match in the League Cup and the cheering news was that the summer lay-off had not blunted Bauld's boots as he marked the first game of the new season with another hat-trick. He also scored a treble a fortnight later in the return with Stirling at Tynecastle, though curiously the game resulted in a 5-4 defeat. It meant Hearts needed to beat East Fife in their final section match to qualify but, although Bauld and Wardhaugh were both on target, it was not enough to prevent a 4-3 loss.

There was also a disappointing defeat a week later by the same opposition in Hearts' first League game of the new campaign as East Fife escaped from Tynecastle with a 1-0 win but it was to be one of only five occasions in the remainder of the season that the Hearts' attack was prevented from scoring. There was an emphatic 5-2 win over Hibs in late September when Hearts led 5-0 at one point before Flavell missed a penalty to add to the tally and Hibs countered with two late goals. Flavell had scored earlier in the game and Bauld and Conn both scored twice. In all, Hearts were to score at least five in eight of their games that season with Falkirk the hardest hit in the November when they were dismissed 9-0 at Tynecastle with Flavell, Wardhaugh and Tommy Sloan all scoring twice and Conn and Bauld also amongst the goals. Wardhaugh scored four in a 6-2 demolition of Clyde in late October and, not to be outdone, Bauld scored all of Hearts' goals in a 4-2 win over

Hearts in 1949-50. Back row (left to right): Bobby Parker, Charlie Cox, Jimmy Brown, Bobby Dougan, Tam Mackenzie, Davie Laing. Front: Tommy Sloan, Alfie Conn, Willie Bauld, Jimmy Wardhaugh, Bobby Flavell.

Stirling in the December. The centre-forward scored six hat-tricks in all that season, in addition to his four against Stirling. In fact, his tally in four games against Stirling that season was 13, surely some sort of record. The "blond bombshell" finished the season with 40 goals with Wardhaugh the second-top scorer with 24 and Conn scoring 15.

Hearts gained a League double over Hibs when an astonishing crowd of 65,840 turned up for the match at Easter Road on 2 January 1950 and thousands of others were reportedly turned away from the gates. This even exceeded any of the Old Firm attendances that season and, after Gordon Smith (who was to play for Hearts later in his career) had given Hibs a half-time lead, Hearts won 2-1 through goals from Conn and Wardhaugh.

Unsurprisingly, Hearts were among the front-runners for the League title but it was Rangers who retained the title by just one point from Hibs with McLean's Hearts six points further adrift. But Hearts were looking forward to the second half of the century in the knowledge that one of the great Scottish club sides was taking shape. With Hibs also on the crest of a wave thanks to the "Famous Five", Edinburgh football had never looked brighter. There was an early Scottish Cup exit, however, that season for Hearts and after beating Dundee after a replay in the first round, Hearts were beaten 3-1 in the next round by Aberdeen at Pittodrie.

But for all Hearts undoubted progress, the League Cup had rather turned sour on them and, in season 1950-51, they once again failed to get through their qualifying section. Bobby Flavell had stunned fans by leaving the club during the close-season to sign for Bolivian side Millionairos, where he was reputedly on a huge financial incentive. It left a gap up front but Hearts nevertheless had the "Terrible Trio" to call upon and it was not as if goals were in short supply. The League Cup campaign was looking good as Hearts took seven points from their first four games but they suffered a costly 3-2 defeat at the hands of Motherwell at Fir Park and the Lanarkshire side went on to pip Hearts by just one point to win a quarter-final slot. Motherwell went on to win the trophy by beating Hibs 3-0 in the Final.

So once again, Hearts were left to concentrate on the League for the next few months and while the goals continued to flow, defensive lapses were costing the team points and twice in the season – against Partick Thistle and Falkirk – while the forwards scored four, the defence lost five and it resulted in four points dropped which would have proved valuable in the final run-in. In a season where Hibs went on to win the League with a healthy advantage on second-placed Rangers, Hearts continued to hold the upper hand in the Edinburgh derbies and won 1-0 at Easter Road in the September thanks to a Tommy Sloan goal and 2-1 back at Tynecastle with Sloan and Conn ensuring victory.

But matters were put into perspective in mid-February 1951 when manager Davie McLean died suddenly. He had moulded a truly great team and it was the supreme irony that he did not live to see it reach its full potential and finally end the trophy famine that had stretched from 1906. It was Tommy Walker, who had come back to the club as player and assistant manager from Chelsea, who took over the managerial reins. A minute's silence was observed in honour of McLean before the home match with Third Lanark on 17 February, just a few days after his death, and the team went on to honour his memory with a 4-0 win. Conn and Bauld were both on the scoresheet as was John Cumming, with his first for the club. Cumming, signed from Carluke Rovers, had made his debut for the club just a couple of months earlier but was to go on and have a 27-year link with Hearts as player and coach and win nine full Scotland caps.

Hearts, however, were knocked out of the Scottish Cup the following week at the third round stage 2-1 by Celtic (Alloa and East Stirling had been accounted for in the earlier rounds) but were to bounce back with a 8-0 win over Morton the following week with Conn helping himself to a hat-trick.

By this stage, Tommy Walker had stepped up from assistant to full-time manager and he was a most popular appointment. Conn was to finish the season as top scorer at the club with 25 goals but, in spite of winning three of their last four League games, fourth place in the table was how Hearts finished, albeit just a point behind Rangers and Dundee, who were joint-second. But Hibs finished ten points clear of those two to win the title for the second time in four years.

Hearts in 1951-52. Back row (left to right): Charlie Cox, Bobby Parker, Jimmy Brown, Bobby Dougan, Tam Mackenzie, Davie Laing. Front: Tommy Sloan, Alfie Conn, Willie Bauld, Jimmy Wardhaugh, Archie Williams.

It was clear Hearts were getting closer to honours but the defence was still giving up too many goals – 19 more than champions Hibs in the 1950-51 season. Nowhere was that more clearly illustrated than at the beginning of the 1951-52 campaign when Hearts missed out on qualifying for the later stages of the League Cup on goal average to Dundee, who eventually went on to win the trophy.

Willie Bauld had distinguished himself by scoring five times in a League Cup tie at Love Street against St Mirren but the best Hearts could manage was a 5-5 draw. Dundee were beaten 5-2 at Tynecastle in a game where the dependable Bobby Parker scored two penalties and Bauld also bagged a brace but Hearts had already lost the first game 2-1 at Dens Park and a 2-0 loss to Raith Rovers was ultimately to cost them dearly.

The goals continued to flow in the League as Hearts had won over a lot of neutral fans with their adventurous style of play. There was a noteworthy 13-game unbeaten spell between early November and late January when the team scored 45 goals – an average of over three a game. Airdrie were the worst hit with a 6-1 defeat in late December but Motherwell were also dismissed 5-0 at Fir Park in another devastating display. Conn, Bauld and Wardhaugh were all to the fore in the scoring stakes as Hearts mounted another serious title assault.

But, in typical and frustrating fashion, Hearts took only one point from their next four League games and indeed for the last three months of the season, they managed just one League win (5-2 over Stirling Albion who eventually finished bottom of the "A" Division and lost 99 goals in the process).

Hibs went on to retain the title, albeit with just a four-point cushion on second-placed Rangers and Hearts were fourth, ten points off the champions. But, if Hearts had an excuse for the faltering finish, it was that they were embroiled in a marathon Scottish Cup run which took them to the brink of their first Final appearance since 1907. With Raith Rovers (1-0) and Queen of the South (3-1) taken care of, Hearts drew 2-2 with Airdrie in the quarter-finals at Broomfield to set up an epic replay at Tynecastle which Hearts won 6-4 with Bauld hitting a hat-trick. Another Lanarkshire side awaited in the semi-finals at Hampden and two games and a period of extra-time could not separate the teams as the first game and the replay with Motherwell both finished 1-1. A total of almost 180,000 took in both games and, just two days after the replay, both teams were back at Hampden – this time in front of 59,468 fans – for the second replay. It was Motherwell who took the honours 3-1 with Conn the solitary Hearts' scorer. The Fir Park side went on to take the trophy with a somewhat more leisurely 4-0 canter against Dundee.

However, all this was serving to do was to whet the appetite of Hearts' fans who had been starved of success for too long. True, there was much to feast on in the style of football that few could match when Hearts were on their day but the craving for success was seemingly becoming greater with every passing year. But, having come so close to a Scottish Cup Final place, there was optimism that silverware would be brought back to the Tynecastle trophy cabinet in 1952-53.

There was no reason to dampen that enthusiasm at the start of the League Cup campaign as Hearts saw off Rangers, runners-up to Hibs in the League the previous season, 5-0 with goals from the "Terrible Trio" – Conn (2), Bauld (2) and Wardhaugh. Aberdeen were then beaten 4-2 at Pittodrie with Bauld getting another double and it looked as if Hearts would coast through the qualifying section. Alas, the fans were brought down to earth by successive defeats by Motherwell and Rangers and by the time Hearts completed their section with a 2-1 win over Motherwell at Fir Park, the damage had already been done and it was Rangers who qualified.

The League did not get off to the best of starts with three defeats in the opening five games and even a 1-0 home win over Celtic in late October could not dispel the gloom as it was an oasis in a four-game losing run.

Hibs managed a League double over Walker's side for the first time since the 1945-46 season but this was when the League had not fully returned from the war. It was an inconsistent season with Hearts never really recapturing the form of the opening day against Rangers in the League Cup and, curiously, the goals did not flow as freely as before, although there was a 7-0 win over Clyde late in the season when Bauld notched a hat-trick. Hearts finished fourth in the League (Rangers this time claimed the flag on goal average from Hibs).

However, the Scottish Cup was proving to be Hearts' forte and after a touch of déjà vu in the second round (Hearts beat Raith Rovers 1-0 for the second successive year with Bauld again getting the only goal), the team then knocked out Montrose 3-1 before beating Queen of the South 2-0 in the quarter-finals at Tynecastle thanks to a double from Bobby Blackwood. A crowd of 116,262 turned out at Hampden for the semi-final against Rangers on 4 April and witnessed an engrossing encounter. Wardhaugh gave Hearts the lead but Rangers won 2-1 as they fought back with goals from Derek Grierson and a late strike from John Prentice. Bauld hit the crossbar even later in the game but it was to prove another heartache. Maybe there was some sort of curse on Hearts because the closer the team seemed to get to ending their long barren spell, the more elusive the prize would become.

Hearts also started 1953-54 with a 5-0 win in the League Cup – this time at the expense of Hamilton Accies – but there was the misfortune of being grouped with Rangers again and this time the Ibrox side qualified with five points to spare on Hearts, who just pushed aside Raith Rovers for second place in the section. Early League defeats from Queen of the South and Airdrie did not augur too well but it was a campaign that gathered some momentum as the season wore on.

From mid-November to early March, Hearts only lost one game in League and Scottish Cup (a 2-0 Boxing Day defeat at home by Partick Thistle who were also flying high). After beating Hibs 4-0 in September, Hearts completed the double by winning the New Year derby 2-1 at Easter Road and, by early February, there was a fine 3-2 win over fellow title challengers Celtic at Tynecastle with Bauld (2) and

Wardhaugh – who was to go on and finish top scorer with 34 goals that season – supplying the goals. A 3-3 draw with Rangers a fortnight later (Bauld, Conn and Wardhaugh) put Hearts seven points clear at the top and the League title itself was within their grasp.

But it was to prove another mirage. In their next League game, Hearts lost 4-2 at struggling Raith Rovers and the team was to stutter badly in the final weeks. Finishing with three away games, Hearts lost two of them (1-0 to Aberdeen and 2-1 to Partick) and by then Celtic had taken full advantage and won the title for the first time since 1938, eventually by five points over Hearts. The Scottish Cup this time did not prove as drawn out as the previous season as, after early wins over Fraserburgh and Queen of the South, Hearts collapsed 3-0 in the quarter-finals to Aberdeen at Pittodrie.

Nevertheless, runners-up in the League was Hearts' highest placing since 1938, ironically in the last season Celtic had won the championship and there was still much to get excited about down Gorgie way. Conn, Wardhaugh and Bauld were still a potent force with 61 goals between them and Johnny Urquhart was also scoring with some regularity and had chipped in with 11 as four Hearts players finished in double figures.

Having now come close in the Scottish Cup and League, surely at least one of these competitions would smile kindly upon the team the following season – 1954-55 – and Hearts would finally break the hoodoo? No, it was the League Cup that was to break the spell and give the club its first trophy since 1906.

At the start of the 1954-55 season, a 19-year-old wing-half, who had played just a handful of first-team games the previous season, was maturing quickly and he soon took over the number four shirt from veteran Davie Laing. The player in question was Dave Mackay and many believe that it was more than mere coincidence that it was in his first season as a regular that Hearts ended their long separation from silverware. He played in the first three League Cup section matches and Hearts won

all three, including a 2-1 victory over champions Celtic in Glasgow when Bertie Peacock scored an own goal. Hearts comfortably qualified and also beat Celtic in the return at Tynecastle, this time 3-2, as the champions finished only third in the group behind Hearts and Dundee with just three points from their six games.

The quarter-finals paired Hearts with "B" Division St Johnstone and Hearts made no mistake by winning the first leg at Muirton Park 5-0 to make the second leg a 2-0 formality at Tynecastle. Such was the interest in the team at this juncture that over 20,000 fans turned up for the second leg even though it was academic. The draw was kind to Hearts again in the semi-finals as they faced Airdrie, also from the lower division, in the semi-final at Easter Road and there was no slipping up with Wardhaugh (2), Urquhart and Bauld scoring in a 4-1 win.

Hearts faced Motherwell, who had beaten East Fife in the other semi-final, in the Final at Hampden on 23 October 1954. The line-ups were: Hearts: Duff; Parker, McKenzie, Mackay, Glidden, Cumming, Souness, Conn, Bauld, Wardhaugh and Urquhart; Motherwell: Weir; Kilmarnock, McSeveney, Cox, Paton, Redpath, Hunter, Aitken, Bain, Humphries and Williams.

An estimated 25,000-30,000 supporters made the trip from Edinburgh to Hampden in great anticipation; after all, Hearts had won 11 of their 13 matches in League and Cup to date (their only two losses both

Hearts, winners of the League Cup in 1954, the club's first major trophy since 1906. Back row (left to right): Tommy Walker (manager), Dave Mackay, Tam Mackenzie, Freddie Glidden, Willie Duff, Willie Bauld, John Cumming, John Harvey (trainer). Front: Jim Souness, Alfie Conn, Bobby Parker, Jimmy Wardhaugh, John Urquhart.

Aberdeen goalkeeper Martin pulls down a high cross from a Hearts attack in March 1955. Aberdeen were champions of Division 'A' this season but Hearts won the match 2-0.

Alfie Conn scores against Partick Thistle in 1954-55, beating five Partick defenders.

coming against Dundee at Dens Park). On a wet afternoon, 55,640 turned up to see if Hearts could finally come good on the big occasion. There was not long to wait for the answer.

After nine minutes, Bauld headed the opening goal and, in the 15th minute, the striker scored again with a shot from the edge of the box to give Hearts a 2-0 lead. Willie Redpath pulled a goal back for Motherwell from the penalty-spot but the Edinburgh side restored their two-goal advantage when Wardhaugh headed a third goal before half-time. It looked as if the score would remain that way in a second half of few goalmouth opportunities but, in the 88th minute, Bauld completed his hat-trick with a header to make it 4-1 and an even later goal from Motherwell's Alex Bain did nothing to subdue the huge army of Hearts' fans who knew that a trophy was finally on its way to Tynecastle. Bauld, having scored a hat-trick on his debut, had now produced another treble in Hearts' most important game in many years. It is no wonder he is still held in such high esteem by supporters.

The 4-2 win had given Hearts their first trophy for 48 years and brought an immediate end to the music-hall jokes about the club and their failure to win a cup. The streets of Edinburgh were lined for the homecoming that evening and the celebrations went on long into the night. Bauld was truly the hero but captain Bobby Parker and Dave Mackay were also

toasted in many hostelries around the West End of Edinburgh. But all 11 played their part and their names at least go down in the club's history as the ones to end the long famine.

"The old grey-stone walls, the smoke-blackened walls, reverberated with the wave after wave of cheering," records Albert Mackie in "The Hearts" in 1959, "Women threw maroon rosettes to the team as if to Spanish toreadors. At McLeod Street, where part of the Saturday crowd surges into Tynecastle, there were crowds of people singing outside the public-house where the fans have their last hurried pint on their way to the match and their first to celebrate victory or drown their sorrows afterwards. This time it was undoubted and crowning victory, and the foaming pint tumblers of good strong Edinburgh ale slopped over as they were raised in salute."

Mackay had become a key figure even at so early an age and the pen picture in the League Cup Final programme in 1954 proved prophetic as it said he had "quickly developed into one of the most artistic and thoughtful middlemen in the country. Like all natural footballers, was ready to alter his original position of left-half to the other end of the line without his brilliance being dimmed. His low, measured passes to his colleagues immediately in front and the exploitation of the crossfield pass stamp him as a young man with a particularly bright future."

Alfie Conn

ALFIE Conn was the first of the celebrated "Terrible Trio" to arrive at Tynecastle and also the first to depart.

Averaging more than a goal every second game in his 408 appearances, Conn established himself as a crowd favourite in his time at the club and his son, Alfie junior, also went on to play for Hearts in addition to both Rangers, Celtic and Tottenham.

An inside forward, Conn, born in Prestonpans in East Lothian, signed as a 17-year-old from Inveresk Athletic and went on to spend 14 years at the club before joining Raith Rovers at the end of his career.

He played a big part in helping Hearts end their long trophy famine in the 1950s and left with a League championship medal in his pocket in 1958.

However, like his partners in crime up front Willie Bauld and Jimmy Wardhaugh, his talents were never really recognised at international level and he only gained one full Scotland cap – in a 1-1 draw against Austria in 1956.

Signed by Davie McLean, Conn made his debut for Hearts in October 1944 in a 4-0 win over Dumbarton at Tynecastle and, in the years immediately after World War Two, he was starting to score a few goals and was regarded as a bright prospect for the future.

His pace and thunderous shot were his main attributes but, even though he was not the tallest of players, he had good ability in the air and scored a fair number of goals with his head.

Regarded as a players' player, he slotted in well at Hearts in the 1950s and his reputation grew in the forward-line that included Bauld and Wardhaugh.

The three first played together in a 6-1 win over East Fife at Tynecastle in which debutant Bauld scored a hat-trick to take the headlines but Conn scored two that afternoon to show he would still be amongst the goals in the years to come.

Bauld finished that season as top scorer for the club with 24 goals but Conn chipped in with a respectable 17.

If Bauld and Wardhaugh were to score the bulk of the goals in the trio (although

both were to play significantly more games for the club), Conn did finish the season as top scorer in season 1950-51 with 25 goals, two ahead of Bauld and five ahead of Wardhaugh.

Conn was part of the team that won the League Cup in 1954 by beating Motherwell in the Final and ending Hearts' long barren spell without a trophy.

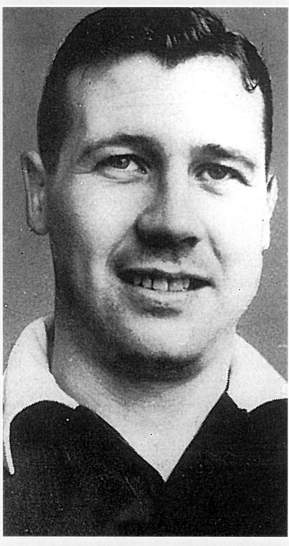

He also scored the third and clinching goal in the 3-1 Scottish Cup Final win over Celtic in 1956 to give the team the trophy for the first time in 50 years. This goal was arguably the most important of his career as it confirmed the Cup would be finally coming back to Gorgie.

Conn's initial basic wage at Tynecastle was just £2 a week but the players all received a £100 bonus when they won the Scottish Cup, so the player was, as you would expect, a popular man with his team-mates.

An ankle injury kept him out of most

of Hearts' games in the 1957-58 season when they won the championship.

He played in only five games but scored four goals and, although he did not play in enough games to warrant a medal, the club successfully obtained permission from the Scottish League to strike a replica for the popular player.

Conn had the distinction of scoring Hearts' 100th goal on that record-breaking campaign in which they finished with 132 League goals.

The century mark came when Conn struck in a 4-0 win over Motherwell at Fir Park but it was, curiously enough, a season where the "Terrible Trio" did not all play together in any League game.

The last survivor of the three with both Bauld and Wardhaugh having died prematurely, Conn still cannot explain why the chemistry worked so spectacularly with 952 goals scored between them.

"I think it was just one of those things that happen in football. We didn't talk about it in those days; we were all just happy to be in the team and getting a game. We had no idea after that first game against East Fife what we would become together," he recalled.

Conn played his final game for Hearts on 16 April 1958 in a 4-0 win over Aberdeen at Pittodrie, with the League already wrapped up.

He was transferred to Raith Rovers for a £2,250 fee in September of that year after 221 goals in 408 games for Hearts.

He rarely returned to the ground as a spectator and even watched the 1998 Scottish Cup success on television but he said he felt immense pride at watching the team end another long spell without a trophy. "When you have been a Hearts' player, the feeling never leaves you," he explained.

**1944-45-1958-59
Appearances 408
Goals 221**

The confidence of the Cup win spilled over into the League with Hearts beating Stirling Albion 5-0 and Falkirk 5-3 in their next matches with Bauld bagging a brace in each – he was to go on to score 39 goals that season – and even a 1-0 defeat by Aberdeen failed to set them back. There was a 5-1 thrashing of Hibs in the New Year's Day derby at Tynecastle when Conn, Wardhaugh and Bauld(2) all scored trademark goals and former Hibs' player Jim Souness was the other scorer as Hearts demonstrated that they had wrestled from Hibs the label of Edinburgh's top team.

Hearts were still on the fringes of the title race in April but four games without a win which included losses to Rangers and East Fife proved costly. Aberdeen held off the Old Firm challenge to win the League with Hearts only fourth, ten points off the champions. In the Scottish Cup, Hearts again received a "bye" through the first round before the "Terrible Trio" tore apart Hibs in a second-round tie at Tynecastle with Conn scoring once and Wardhaugh and Bauld twice in a 5-0 win. If Bauld had a remarkable scoring season then Wardhaugh can reflect that even his tally of 27 for the season was only enough for a distant second in the scoring charts. Hearts then went one better in the third round against Buckie Thistle as they won 6-0 with Bauld this time getting another hat-trick. But the quarter-finals brought Aberdeen and ultimately disappointment. A crowd of 47,500 turned up at Tynecastle for the tie but it finished 1-1 and Aberdeen progressed to the last four with a 2-0 win in the replay.

The Best in the Land...

ONCE you get the taste of success, you crave for it all the more and so it was with Hearts as they approached the 1955-56 season knowing that any jinx had been broken. They cruised through their League Cup qualifying round as they mounted their defence of the trophy although there was a surprise defeat by East Fife along the way. Nevertheless, Raith Rovers had been humbled 5-0 with Alfie Conn scoring a hat-trick and East Fife were beaten in the return 4-0 when a new teenage sensation announced himself with a hat-trick – Alex Young. The 18-year-old had made his debut in a 2-1 home win over Partick Thistle a week earlier and had scored the winning goal. He was to deputise for Bauld when he was injured that season but he also came into the frame for Conn as Hearts had an embarrassment of riches up front.

Indeed, Young was to outscore Bauld that season (although, admittedly, he played ten more matches) as he scored 23, with Wardhaugh scoring 34 in 45 games and Conn 27 in 38. Between the four, a staggering 102 goals were scored in all three major competitions that season as Hearts were, not surprisingly, Scotland's top scorers.

But just when it appeared Hearts could do no wrong, there was a shock quarter-final League Cup exit at the hands of Aberdeen in mid-September. In spite of a double from Young, Hearts lost the first leg 5-3 at Pittodrie and it was a similar tale in the return as

Aberdeen won 4-2 to go through on a 9-5 aggregate. There followed a 1-0 defeat by Hibs in the League and further defeats by Queen of the South and St Mirren meant that a 4-1 loss at the hands of Rangers in mid-November left Hearts trailing in the League.

But the team responded by embarking on a 23-game unbeaten run which took them into title contention and also into the Final of the Scottish Cup. Much to the joy of the Hearts fans, the goals flowed along the way – 7-1 v Motherwell, 5-0 v Partick Thistle, Stirling Albion and Dunfermline – and there was only one game that Hearts failed to score in during the run (a 0-0 Scottish Cup semi-final draw with Raith Rovers at Easter Road). Jimmy Wardhaugh helped himself to a few and scored four against both Clyde and Motherwell and also a hat-trick in a League win over St Mirren in March.

The League campaign stuttered at the end, however, and Hearts won only two of their last seven games (rather frustratingly 8-3 v Falkirk and 7-2 v Raith Rovers) and, uncharacteristically, drew a blank in two of their last three games (0-1 v Motherwell and 0-2 to Kilmarnock). So the League title went back to Ibrox with Rangers finishing six points clear of second-placed Aberdeen and seven clear of third-placed Hearts. But the Scottish Cup was a different story.

In the second round, Hearts beat Forfar 3-0 and reached the last eight with goalkeeper Willie Duff

Hearts goalkeeper Willie Duff fists the ball over the bar against Celtic in January 1955. Bobby Parker (2) guards the line.

this time – as in 1907 – and a huge crowd of 132,840 squashed into Hampden for the Final on 21 April 1956, an estimated 60,000 of which had journeyed from Edinburgh.

It was a special day for everyone at Hearts; none more so than manager Tommy Walker who had never played in such an occasion in spite of his wonderful playing career. It had been 50 years since Hearts had last won the Cup but while the debate at the time was whether Edinburgh or Glasgow was the top footballing city with Hibs having also enjoyed success in recent years, Hearts were more content to concentrate on their own affairs.

"On form, there is nothing much to separate the teams," declared the match programme, "Hearts, as they have demonstrated in recent games, are capable of rising to the heights of artistry and goalscoring and the Celtic boys are always at their best when fighting to retain or regain the trophy. It is something of a "Jubilee" occasion for the

keeping another clean sheet in a 5-0 win over Stirling Albion with Conn, Young, Bauld and Wardhaugh all finding the net (John Cumming was the other scorer). Rangers came to Tynecastle in early March and found Hearts in unstoppable form with Bauld scoring twice in a 4-0 victory. After the goalless first semi-final with Raith, Hearts won the midweek replay 3-0 thanks to two goals from Wardhaugh and a late header from Ian Crawford. So Hearts had reached their first Scottish Cup Final since 1907 and after no fewer than seven successive semi-final defeats.

What was more, they had done so in style with a total of 15 goals scored and none conceded on the road to Hampden. Celtic, who had beaten Clyde 2-1 in the other semi-final, were fittingly the Final opponents

Edinburgh club. Can they also make it a "jubilation" one by parading the Cup in triumph along Princes Street?"

Hearts lined up: Duff; Kirk, McKenzie, Mackay, Glidden, Cumming, Young, Conn, Bauld, Wardhaugh and Crawford while Celtic selected: Beattie; Meechan, Fallon, Smith, Evans, Peacock, Craig, Haughney, Mochan, Fernie and Tully. Two of Celtic's top players Bobby Collins and Jock Stein were out injured.

Hearts took the lead in the 20th minute when Crawford drilled a shot into the net from the edge of the area but just as Hearts looked to have control, there was an anxious moment when the tough-tackling Cumming had to leave the field for treatment after a painful clash of heads with Willie Fernie before half-

All the goals from Hearts' great Cup Final win over Celtic in 1956. **Top:** Ian Crawford (not in picture scores Hearts' first goal. **Middle:** In the picture this time Crawford (11) hits the second for the Edinburgh club. **Bottom:** Haughney (hidden between Tam McKenzie (3) and goalkeeper Willie Duff) scores for Celtic. **Next page, top:** Alfie Conn (8) raises his arms after scoring Hearts' third goal.

time. Yet it was a day for heroes and, with no substitutes in those days, Cumming reappeared at the start of the second half with a plaster over the wound. It was a day when all of the Hearts 11 seemed to draw upon new reserves of strength and early in the second period, Crawford scored his second after Young had set up the chance. Willie Haughney pulled a goal back for Celtic and they stormed back at Hearts. Cumming suffered another head knock but elected to soldier on as Hearts saw the Cup within their grasp. With ten minutes remaining, Bauld headed the ball down for Conn to score Hearts' third and it was clear that the 50-year wait for the Scottish Cup was over.

Hearts were given a hero's welcome on their return to Edinburgh as the team bus also passed through local villages en route to the capital. With the victory relayed over the radio, word had spread fast and the Hearts' team bus journeyed back to

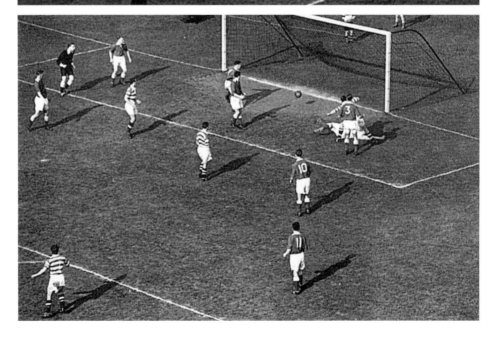

Hearts parade the Scottish Cup through the streets of Edinburgh after their 1956 triumph over Celtic.

Edinburgh via the West Lothian village of Blackburn which was Freddie Glidden's home. It also visited Livingston Station where Tommy Walker was brought up and then passed through Newbridge where Bobby Parker was from, although injury prevented the player from captaining the team on this great occasion.

The team then transferred to an open-top double decker bus on the outskirts of Edinburgh before making the final leg of journey with fans cheering them home along the route. Edinburgh Castle had been floodlit for the occasion and the bus eventually stopped at the Charlotte Rooms for the celebration dinner, with an estimated 15,000 crowding into the West End. Hostelries in the Royal Mile gave free drinks to customers and the celebrations arguably outdid the occasion when Hearts won the League Cup less than two years previously.

The League Cup, the Scottish Cup, now for the League championship. There was no reason why they could not complete the hat-trick in 1956-57. Hearts had not won the League flag since 1896-97 but few doubted that this current team was capable of delivering it back to Gorgie. In their League Cup section, Hearts fell behind to Hibs at Tynecastle with Eddie Turnbull scoring but the response was clinical – Hearts hammered home six goals without further reply through Wardhaugh (2), Conn and Crawford and two penalties from Bobby Kirk.

Falkirk were treated similarly, this time 5-0 at Tynecastle with Wardhaugh and Bauld both scoring twice but a 3-1 defeat at Partick Thistle ultimately

Despairing leaps by Milne (5) and goalkeeper Marshall cannot prevent Simpson scoring for Rangers in the 1956-57 season. But Hearts had emerged as the strongest challengers to the Ibrox club.

meant that Hearts failed to qualify from their section. The old question-marks surfaced again but Hearts made a flying start in the League, winning four and drawing one of their first five matches. Even a 5-2 home defeat by East Fife and a broken jaw for Conn which was to keep him out for almost exactly four months did not sidetrack the team and, by the end of the year, Hearts had lost just one more League game (5-3 to Rangers at Ibrox) and led the League. Even a 2-0 defeat by Hibs in the New Year derby unfazed them (it was one of only two occasions Hearts failed to score in a League game that season) and, after a run of nine League games without defeat, Hearts held a seven-point lead at the top by early March, although Rangers had games in hand.

Hearts lost 4-1 at Kilmarnock in mid-March as Rangers gained ground but again Tommy Walker's team hit back with three successive wins (over Queen's Park, Celtic and Motherwell) to set up what amounted to a League decider with Rangers at Tynecastle on 13 April 1957 – a game which drew 49,000 spectators.

It took only one goal to settle a tense contest but, unfortunately for Hearts, it came from Rangers' Billy

Simpson in the first half and it was enough to give the champions full points. Rangers were just two points behind Hearts with two games in hand and they won all four of their remaining games to snatch the title by just two points from the Edinburgh side, who took four points from their final two games. Hearts had been pipped at the post and the telling factor was that they lost both of their games to Rangers. There was also a Scottish Cup exit at the first hurdle as Rangers came to Tynecastle and left with a fine 4-0 victory to exact revenge on the Cup tie at the same ground 11 months previously when Hearts had won by an identical scoreline. At the end of it all, Hearts ended the season empty-handed.

But, if many felt it was a chance missed, the Hearts players and backroom staff were more of the opinion that it was a learning process and a stepping-stone towards that elusive title and Rangers would not have it all their own way for much longer. There was no reason for Hearts to feel like second-class citizens as they went into the 1957-58 season. Agonisingly, Heart failed yet again to get through the qualifying stages of the League Cup in spite of scoring nine in a home tie with Queen's Park and indeed only won two of their

Dave Mackay

FEW players in British football commanded the respect that Dave Mackay achieved on both sides of the border during a playing career that spanned 20 years.

Many believe it was his driving influence more than anything that led to Hearts finally grasping silverware in the 1950s and he went on to collect League championship medals in both Scotland and England.

Mackay, brought up not far from Tynecastle, won 22 caps for Scotland and also captained his country. Such was his ability that he was also "capped" for the English League in the days of League internationals when nationality did not prevent players from playing for the country where they played their football and he actually helped the English League beat the Scottish League on one occasion.

Mackay suffered two leg breaks during a career in which he was regarded as the toughest of individuals but his image rather masked the fact that he was a gifted player who could pass the ball with precision and was good with either foot.

Another inspired signing by Davie McLean, who had reputedly been keeping an eye on him from an early age after he attended a coaching clinic at Tynecastle, he was initially farmed out to Newtongrange Star as a 16-year-old where he was given a tough baptism in the junior ranks.

He was called up to the first-team squad at the start of the 1953-54 season as an 18-year-old and made his debut in early November 1953 in a 2-1 defeat by Clyde in a League game at Tynecastle, a week before his 19th birthday.

It was obvious from an early age that Mackay did not take to losing and was a fierce competitor who gave his all for the maroon shirt.

His appearances in that first season were fleeting but Hearts enjoyed their best year in the League since before the war as they finished runners-up to Celtic. It was a sign of things to come and the following season he made the number four shirt his own as Hearts won their first trophy for 50 years as they collected the League Cup with a 4-2 Final win over Motherwell.

The wing-half was not a player who figured much amongst the goals but he was a solid performer and immensely popular with his team-mates.

Mackay had to fulfil his national service in England during the 1955-56 season but he managed to travel home at weekends for games. Even when Hearts reached the 1956 Scottish Cup Final, Mackay only flew north the evening before the game and there must have been those who were concerned about his match preparations.

However, he played another commanding role as Hearts beat Celtic 3-1 in the Hampden Final in front of a crowd of 133,399 – more than double the

attendance for the 1954 League Cup Final with Motherwell.

Mackay did not have too much time to dwell on the mass celebrations in Edinburgh that weekend as he had to return to his army duties for first thing on the Monday morning.

Mackay's influence was clear and it was no surprise when manager Tommy Walker appointed him captain of the team. The player had the honour of leading the team to their first League championship of the century in 1957-58 when the team scored a record 132 League goals.

There was even a rare hat-trick for Mackay en route to the title – in a game against Falkirk which Hearts won 9-1 – but the wing-half missed the final five games of the season due to a broken foot.

His stature had grown throughout the season and it was hardly a surprise when he won his first international cap for Scotland against Spain in 1957 in a World Cup qualifying tie. He went on to play for Scotland in the 1958 finals in Sweden where he was called up for the final group match against France but, unfortunately for Mackay, it was part of a steep learning curve on the international front as Scotland tumbled out of the competition after a 2-1 defeat.

On the club front, it appeared no coincidence that Hearts' most successful spell for over half a century had occurred when Mackay was in the team and he was also prominent when Hearts won the League Cup again in October 1958 with a 5-1 Final win over Partick Thistle.

But there was widespread shock around Tynecastle a few months later when news broke that the Hearts' captain, who had also been elevated to skipper of the national side at the time, was to leave the club in a £30,000 transfer to Tottenham Hotspur.

The London club were mid-table in the old English First Division at the time but, not much more than a couple of years after Mackay's arrival, they had won the League and Cup double – the first team to achieve the feat in the 20th century.

He also helped Spurs' tremendous run which saw them become the first British side to win a European trophy – the Cup-Winners' Cup – but Mackay missed the 5-1 Final win over Spanish Cup holders Atletico Madrid in Rotterdam due to a stomach injury.

In 1968, Mackay signed for Brian Clough's unfashionable Derby County, then in the Second Division. Apparently there was a chance that he could have returned to Hearts but the Derby manager proved very persuasive and did not want to miss out on the Scot.

Mackay helped Derby win promotion to the First Division and, later in his career, was voted joint English Player of the Year with Manchester City's Tony Book.

In his playing career, Mackay won ten winners' medals – a testament to his approach to the game – before he went on to become a successful manager with Swindon, Nottingham Forest and Derby.

He spent some years in the Middle East in Kuwait and Dubai before returning to settle in England.

1953-54-1958-59
Appearances 208
Goals 32

John Cummings scores against Newcastle United under the new Tynecastle floodlights in October 1957.

six games in the section with Kilmarnock claiming the quarter-final berth.

But the League campaign started with a bang – 6-0 v Dundee and then 7-2 v Airdrie – and the goals did not dry up. Queen's Park were hit for another eight in November and, in the same month, Falkirk were thumped 9-1 with Dave Mackay scoring a rare hat-trick and Alex Young notching four.

After a 2-1 defeat by Clyde in late November, Hearts won 15 successive League games before their return game with Clyde in the middle of March which finished 2-2 and this time there was little Rangers could do about it. Hearts won at Ibrox 3-2 in the October and this time they set a pace that no-one could match. The final run-in had to be completed without the influential Mackay who had broken a bone in his foot and was to miss the last five games. But a 4-1 win over Raith Rovers gave Hearts a new Scottish League scoring record and surpassed the 119

Motherwell amassed while winning the title in 1931-32. Kilmarnock forced a 1-1 draw at Rugby Park as the champagne was kept on ice but in their third-last game of the season, Hearts knew they could wrap up the title against St Mirren at Love Street.

The sun shone brightly as Hearts (Marshall; Kirk, Thomson, Cumming, Milne, Bowman, Blackwood, Murray, Young, Wardhaugh and Crawford) took the field and Alex Young scored after just seven minutes to make it 1-0 at half-time. Ryan equalised for St Mirren in the 59th minute but Wardhaugh headed Hearts back in front shortly afterwards. Hearts were not moving as fluently as in previous matches and it was no surprise when Wilson equalised for St Mirren. It looked as if Hearts may have to wait until another day for the title but, 17 minutes from time, Young was on the spot again to touch the ball home from close range after Crawford had lobbed it into the penalty area and, in spite of home claims for offside, the goal stood. Hearts held on for the two points and there was a pitch invasion from their jubilant supporters when the final whistle came.

The *Edinburgh Evening Dispatch* printed a special issue that night declaring in banner headlines: "Hearts are Home!". It captured the mood of Hearts fans everywhere: "If at first you don't succeed, try, try, try again. That's what Hearts have been doing for 61 years and today, 12 April 1958, the long years of League flag frustration are over. Hearts, high scoring, record breaking Hearts, are champions again!"

In a record-breaking season, only Third Lanark prevented Hearts from scoring (in a 0-0 draw in October) in a remarkable season which saw Hearts score a total of 132 goals for only 29 against in their 34 matches with Wardhaugh finishing top scorer with 37 goals. Jimmy Murray, who had come in for the injured Conn, scored 29 and Young, named ahead of Bauld for much of the season, scored 26. For all that is spoken about the "Terrible Trio", it is worth noting that although Wardhaugh played in 30 League

Jimmy Wardhaugh nets against Raith Rovers at Tynecastle in March 1958 and Motherwell's record of 119 goals in a League season is broken.

Jimmy Wardhaugh

No player has scored more goals in the maroon of Hearts than Jimmy Wardhaugh and, given the way the game has changed in recent years under players' freedom of contract, it is safe to assume that no player ever will.

Although John Robertson beat Wardhaugh's record of League goals in the not-too-distant past, his tally of overall goals – 376 in 519 games – puts Robertson's 310 in 720 matches in the shade, although it has to be acknowledged that defences have tightened up considerably in the modern game.

Another inspired signing by Davie McLean, who brought all three of the "Terrible Trio" to the club, Wardhaugh was born at Marshall Meadows, Berwick, and signed, at the age of 17, for Hearts from Shaftesbury Park a month before the arrival of Willie Bauld.

He was an accomplished sporting all-rounder, having played rugby and cricket to a high level at school.

He made his first-team debut in a 3-2 win over Celtic on 21 August 1946, when he scored the first of his remarkable total for Hearts and was a player of promise in that first season, although he spent much of his time in the reserve team with Alfie Conn.

Wardhaugh played 11 games in that first season and scored just one more goal, against Clyde, but he was still very much serving his football apprenticeship.

What was obvious in those early days was that Wardhaugh was supremely fit – something he maintained throughout his career – and he had an infectious enthusiasm for the game.

Standing just 5ft 8ins, he was not the tallest of strikers but was physically very strong and also had great heading ability.

Wardhaugh did not command a regular first-team place until the 1948-49 season although, ironically, he was the only member of the "Terrible Trio" who did not score in the game against East Fife in October 1948, when the three played together for the first time.

That season, he scored 13 goals in 26 appearances – a goal in every other game – which was a respectable return. By the following season (1949-50) he had upped the ratio to 24 in 39 games, including a four-goal blitz against Clyde in a 6-2 win at the end of the October.

But it was Bauld who was regularly finishing top of the Tynecastle scoring charts every season (although Conn outscored the two other members of the trio in 1950-51). But from 1953-54 to 1957-58, Wardhaugh was top club scorer in four out of the five seasons.

In April 1953, he scored Hearts' goal in a 2-1 Scottish Cup semi-final defeat by Rangers at Hampden in a tie that drew 116,262 fans to the stadium and Hearts finished fourth in the League that year for the third successive season.

But the goals of the trio had Hearts challenging for honours before too much longer and when they finished runners-up to Celtic in the First Division in 1953-54 and scored 70 goals in the process, Wardhaugh scored 27 goals in his 28 League games and scored 34 in 37 appearances overall.

The trophy finally arrived in the shape of the League Cup in 1954 when Bauld scored a hat-trick and Wardhaugh scored the other goal in a 4-2 Final win over Motherwell. He scored four goals in the qualifying group and then also netted in the quarter-final against St Johnstone and notched two in the semi-final win over Airdrie at Easter Road.

In one productive spell late in the year, he scored eight goals in as many games and the competition between the three bore fruit as Hearts were scoring as never before. Not that any of the three was selfish

– there just seemed to be enough goals for them all to share.

In 1955-56, Wardhaugh set the standard when he scored four goals twice in matches within the space of a month, in a 5-1 win over Clyde in the November and a 7-1 victory over Motherwell in mid-December. He also hit a hat-trick of hat-tricks that season as Hearts climbed up to third in the final League table but significantly were the highest scorers in the division with 99 goals.

He also scored two of the three goals that killed off Raith Rovers in the Scottish Cup semi-final replay in 1956 and picked up another winner's medal as part of the team that went on to defeat Celtic in the Final.

The following season the goals continued to come as this time Hearts came within two points of champions Rangers and it became clear that a championship medal would shortly be added to Wardhaugh's growing collection.

Sure enough, he played in 30 of the 34 League games in 1957-58 when Hearts finally won the title and almost averaged a goal-a-game as he finished with 28 League strikes and was well clear in the overall scoring stakes with 37 in 39 games. Three hat-tricks in the first couple of months of the season signalled his intent.

Wardhaugh played in the team that won the League Cup in 1958 but that season was to play only 14 League games and, when Hearts regained the title in 1960, he played no part in it and had been sold to Dunfermline for £2,000 in the November after just four League Cup appearances. His last goal for the club came in a 2-2 draw with Aberdeen at Tynecastle.

He was capped only twice for Scotland – in 1955 against Hungary and in 1957 against Northern Ireland – but he also represented the Scottish League on nine occasions.

Wardhaugh went on to command respect as a sports journalist after hanging up his boots but he died prematurely at the age of 48 in January 1978.

1946-47-1959-60
Appearances 519
Goals 376

Hearts, champions 1958. Back row (left to right): Bobby Kirk, Tam Mackenzie, Gordon Marshall, Dave Mackay, Freddie Glidden, John Cumming. Front: Johnny Hamilton, Alfie Conn, Willie Bauld, Jimmy Wardhaugh, Ian Crawford. Inset: Jimmy Milne, Bobby Parker, George Thomson, Alex Young, Jimmy Murray, Andy Bowman, Bobby Blackwood.

John Cumming joined Hearts in 1950 and made 613 senior appearances, scoring 58 goals. he became trainer in 1967, retiring in 1976.

games that season, Bauld only managed nine and Conn five. Bauld and Conn indeed had not played enough games to obtain League medals but, after gaining League permission, additional medals were struck.

As Hearts entered the 1958-59 season, their forward-line was the most feared in Scotland. Ironically, in their opening game – a League Cup tie at Ibrox – it was a rare occasion where that forward-line failed to function and Rangers won the tie 3-0.

But Hearts came back and won the return at Tynecastle 2-1 with goals from Bauld and Jimmy Milne and beat both Raith Rovers and Third Lanark twice in their other section matches to top the group ahead of Rangers. In the League, Hearts had opened with a 6-2 win over Dunfermline and followed up by crushing Hibs 4-0 in a game where Ian Crawford scored twice.

On 3 September 1958, Hearts defended Scotland's honour as they played their first-ever European tie when they faced Belgian champions Standard Liege in the first round of the European Cup. Hearts made a bright start with Crawford scoring Hearts' first European goal to put the Scottish champions ahead but the Belgians produced a strong

Royal Standard Liege are put under pressure at Tynecastle in Hearts' first venture into European football, in 1958.

Smith of Partick Thistle heads a goal in the 1958 Scottish League Cup Final. But it was Hearts who won, 5-1.

second half performance to go on to win 5-1. The second leg was something of a formality but Hearts restored some pride when Bauld scored twice to give them a 2-1 win on the night but the team went out 6-3 on aggregate.

Remarkably, Hearts had to play their League Cup quarter-final with Ayr United at Somerset Park the following night when they made only three changes (Danny Paton, Young and Wardhaugh coming in for Bobby Blackwood, Bauld and Crawford) but there were no signs of any tiredness after the European encounter as Hearts won 5-1 against the Second Division side and booked their place in the last four with a 3-1 return win at Tynecastle.

A crowd of 41,000 turned up for the semi-final with Kilmarnock at Easter Road and Hearts finished comfortable 3-0 winners with goals from George Thomson, Crawford and Bauld. It set up another tilt at silverware and Hearts fans had never had it so good.

This time, Partick Thistle were the Final opposition at Hampden Park on 25 October 1958 and Hearts were overwhelming favourites to lift the trophy. Manager Tommy Walker surprisingly omitted Young from his side as the teams lined up: Hearts: Marshall; Kirk,

Thomson, Mackay, Glidden, Cumming, Hamilton, Murray, Bauld, Wardhaugh and Crawford; Partick Thistle: Ledgerwood; Hogan, Donlevy, Mathers, Davidson, Wright, McKenzie, Thomson, Smith, McParland and Ewing.

Any hopes Partick had of an upset were effectively over inside ten minutes as Hearts led 2-0 after Bauld and Murray both netted. By half-time it was 4-0 with Bauld and Murray on target again and Hearts had another piece of silverware in the bag. Understandably, the second half was something of an anticlimax –

Dave Mackay shows off the League Cup in 1958, watched by Johnny Hamilton, Bobby Kirk, Gordon Marshall, George Thomson, Ian Crawford and Freddie Glidden.

Willie Bauld

THERE have been many candidates but only one player can claim the title of "King of Hearts" - Willie Bauld.

Jimmy Wardhaugh may have scored more goals in total for the club but it was Bauld who captured the Hearts of fans on Gorgie.

That he won only three full international caps for Scotland remains something of a mystery but he had cruel luck with injuries and he had the misfortune to be vying for a place with legendary Hibernian forward Lawrie Reilly, who went on to play for Scotland on 38 occasions.

It is difficult to imagine a player of Bauld's talents not gaining an automatic place for Scotland these days. Described in his time as the most "natural" of centre-forwards in the Scottish game, he was as dangerous off the ball as he was on it as his positional sense and timing were a lesson in the art of leading the front line.

Bauld was not the tallest striker but he had exceptional ability in the air and often troubled more imposing defenders with his timing to get his head to crosses.

Brought up in the mining village of Newcraighall on the outskirts of Edinburgh, Bauld attracted attention from an early age from clubs both north and south of the border.

The young Bauld was a fervent Hearts supporter but he could easily have missed out on a Tynecastle career as, when a teenager, he signed provisional forms to play for Sunderland. Fortunately for Hearts, the deal was never formalised and the then Tynecastle secretary Jimmy Kean stepped in to sign the player.

Dave McLean was the Hearts manager at the time (he signed all three of the "Terrible Trio" for a cost of just £200) but, for all of his reputation locally, Bauld had to be patient and wait for his first-team chance.

McLean farmed the forward out to Newtongrange Star and Edinburgh City and the player later admitted that it was a good apprenticeship for him as it prepared him both mentally and physically for the rigours of the Scottish First Division.

Yet, when he did eventually get his chance just three months short of his 21st birthday, it was clear that he could not wait to show his manager that he was ready for the step up.

A hat-trick on his debut against East Fife on 9 October 1948, at Tynecastle signalled his arrival in a 6-1 win, the first of his 355 goals for the club coming after just 14 minutes of the game. It was the first time that McLean had used what later became known as the "Terrible Trio" and it paid off spectacularly with Conn also scoring twice.

Not unsurprisingly, all three were in the attack for the following week's game against Queen of the South when this time Hearts won 4-0 with Bauld helping himself to another Tynecastle hat-trick.

Understandably, he was an instant hit with the supporters who had never seen such a dramatic entrance from a young player. Virtually from the first moment they set eyes on him, Bauld was to occupy a favoured place in their hearts.

It was not long before the centre-forward gained international recognition and he won all three of his caps for Scotland in 1950 (against England, Switzerland and Portugal) but, after that, Bauld had to content himself with club honours, and fortunately, there were plenty of those.

Under Tommy Walker, Hearts enjoyed the most successful spell in the club's history and, typically, Bauld was to the fore when the club ended 48 years without a major trophy by capturing the Scottish Cup in 1954. Hearts beat Motherwell in the Final 4-2 with Bauld scoring a hat-trick and he played a significant part in Hearts' progress to the Final with nine goals on the way to Hampden.

When Hearts won the League title in 1958 with a record 132 goals, Bauld played less of a part and indeed made only nine appearances. Similarly, when Hearts recaptured the title two years later, he played in just 17 of the 34 games.

The one criticism that Bauld received during his playing days was that he used to drift in and out of matches but his work-rate was never questioned by playing colleagues and he had the knack of being in the right place at the right time when it came to scoring goals.

In all, he scored 355 goals in 510 appearances and his final goal came in February 1962, by which time his appearances were more fleeting, in a 2-1 win over Third Lanark. He was given a testimonial by the club against Sheffield United nine months later but his association with Hearts was to end in some bitterness as his final cheque for his testimonial game came with expenses deducted. Bauld was so aggrieved that he did not set foot in Tynecastle again for another 12 years.

Bauld died at the age of just 49 after he collapsed after attending a supporters' club function and his passing was greatly mourned by Hearts fans everywhere.

1948-49-1962-63
Appearances 510
Goals 355

Dave Mackay holds aloft the Scottish League Cup after Hearts' 1958 triumph over Partick Thistle.

George Smith headed a goal for Partick only for man-of-the-match Murray to lay the ball on for Johnny Hamilton to score a brilliant fifth as Hearts ran out 5-1 winners. Hearts had reason to believe this could be the first leg of an historic treble as their League form was exhilarating.

Bauld had scored five goals in an 8-3 destruction of Third Lanark in late September and Raith Rovers, Queen of the South, Falkirk and Aberdeen had all lost five goals in matches against Hearts in late 1958. Hearts led the League by two points when they faced Rangers in the top-of-the-table clash at Ibrox in mid-December and Walker's side were significantly without Dave Mackay through injury. It proved a turning point in the championship as Rangers romped to a 5-0 victory. Hearts were visibly shaken at the result and won only one of their next five games, scraping a 3-2 win over Airdrie at Broomfield. By early March, Hearts trailed Rangers badly and a decision was taken to sell Mackay to Tottenham Hotspur in a £32,000 deal.

It looked a premature decision by the club with Mackay such a key player for the club but Hearts made light of his absence and won four of their next five matches to move four points behind leaders Rangers with the Ibrox side due to visit Tynecastle on the penultimate day of the season. Goals from John Cumming and Bobby Rankin gave Hearts a 2-0 win and it set up a final day decider with Hearts facing Celtic and Rangers meeting Aberdeen. Hearts needed to beat Celtic and hope that Aberdeen, not enjoying the best of seasons in the League but through to the Cup Final, could upset Rangers, if they were to take the title on goal average. Aberdeen kept their half of the deal by beating Rangers 2-1 at Ibrox and, at half-time at Celtic Park, Hearts led through a Rankin goal. But, not for the last time, Hearts were to miss out on the final day as Bertie Auld pulled Celtic level early in the second half and Eric Smith scored midway through the second half and it was sufficient to give Celtic a 2-1 win and give Rangers the title by two points.

Rangers had also knocked Hearts out of the Scottish Cup that season – 3-2 at Ibrox in the second round after Hearts had beaten Queen of the South 3-1 in their opening tie – and the campaign finished in some disappointment. It was St Mirren who went on to lift the Scottish Cup that year with a 3-1 Final win over Aberdeen.

Tommy Walker made a surprise signing at the start of the 1959-60 campaign when he brought in former Hibs' favourite Gordon Smith who, at 34, many felt would play only a handful of matches in maroon. There was, nevertheless, no shortage of interest and a crowd of 12,000 turned up to watch him play in his first reserve game for the club. He made his first-team debut in a 2-0 League Cup win over Kilmarnock at Tynecastle in late August and he went on to play an important part in a successful season for the club, playing in all but five of the League games and also winning a League Cup medal.

His eagerly anticipated first goals came when he scored a double in a 2-2 draw at Stirling Albion in late September and he also played his part against former club Hibs in a 2-2 draw at Tynecastle when Jimmy Murray scored both goals. But Smith's first game back at Easter Road was not against Hibs but in a League Cup semi-final against Second Division Cowdenbeath in early October. Hearts had emerged unbeaten from a qualifying section that had contained Aberdeen, Kilmarnock and Stirling Albion and beaten Motherwell 7-3 on aggregate in the quarter-finals after

Alex Young in action against Third Lanark in the 1959 League Cup Final at Hampden.

a fine 6-2 second leg win at Tynecastle. Everyone expected a one-sided semi-final and so it proved with Hearts coming through 9-3 winners with Ian Crawford helping himself to four of the total.

Hearts faced Third Lanark in the Final at Hampden on 24 October. Hearts: Marshall; Kirk, Thomson, Bowman, Cumming, Higgins, Smith, Crawford, Young, Blackwood and Hamilton; Third Lanark: Robertson; Lewis, Brown, Reilly, McCallum, Cunningham, McInnes, Craig, D Hilley, Gray and I Hilley.

Hearts wore their change strip of white and maroon candy-stripes and were unrecognisable in the early stages as Third Lanark took a shock lead when Gordon Marshall fumbled the ball and Matt Gray scored. Hearts came back strongly but passed up numerous chances and a surprise looked a distinct possibility. But Hearts scored twice in two minutes to turn the tide – firstly, Johnny Hamilton equalising when his long-

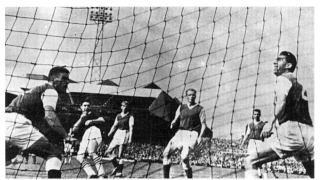
Jimmy Murray scores against Hibs at Tynecastle in September 1959. Joe McLelland and John Grant are on the line.

range shot was deflected into the net in the 57th minute and then Alex Young scoring what proved to be the winning goal with a typical piece of opportunism. It was Hearts' third League Cup triumph in six seasons and, with the club also topping the League at this stage, there was optimism that more silverware could be added before the season was through.

Hearts did not disappoint as they won their next five League games after the Final to show they had not over-indulged in the celebrations, including a 6-2 win over Third Lanark days after the Final when Bauld, left out of the Final team, made his point by scoring a hat-trick. Hearts had also won a crucial game at Ibrox 2-0 but there was a setback to the title hopes in early December when Hearts lost back-to-back games against St Mirren and Motherwell and failed to score in either.

It was to prove a temporary reversal in fortunes. Hearts were only to lose one more League game that season (against Kilmarnock in March) as the goals started to flood in again. Alex Young – who went on to finish top scorer that season with 28 goals – fired a hat-trick at Easter Road in a thrilling 5-1 win on New Year's Day. Kilmarnock, who put Hearts out of the Scottish Cup in a first round replay at Rugby Park 2-1, emerged as the closest title challengers with Rangers faltering and Dundee and Motherwell also failing to sustain a challenge.

Rangers' Telfer, Niven and Caldow look crestfallen now as Wardhaugh (left of picture) races away to celebrate a goal.

Willie Bauld is just beaten to the ball by Rangers' Telfer with goalkeeper Niven waiting in vain and Caldow looking on.

Hearts players and officials with the League Cup in October 1959. Back row (left to right): Donald Macleod (assistant trainer), Andy Bowman, Alex Young, Gordon Smith, Gordon Marshall, Tommy Walker (manager), Billy Higgins, Bobby Kirk, George Thomson, John Harvey (trainer). Front: Mr R. Tait (director), Ian Crawford, Mr Wilson Strachan (vice-chairman), John Cumming, Mr Nicol Kilgour (chairman), Bobby Blackwood, Mr Alex Irvine (director), John Hamilton, Mrs Austin Eadie (director).

Hearts, First Division champions 1959-60. Back row (left to right): George Robertson, Gordon Marshall, John Brown, Bobby Blackwood, John Cumming, Tom Lough, Jim McFadzean, Andy Kelly, Willie Bauld, Alan Finlay. Middle row: Donald Mcleod (assistant trainer), Gordon Smith, Alex Young, Jimmy Milne, Jimmy Murray, George Thomson, Andy Bowman, Johnny Harvey (trainer). Front row: Bobby Kirk, Ian Crawford, Johnny Hamilton, Billy Higgins.

Willie Bauld heads towards the Celtic goal at Parkhead.

Higgins, Smith, Young, Bauld, McFadzean and Crawford.

It was to prove another high-scoring affair in which Hearts had to battle all the way for the necessary point after falling behind early in the game to a Tommy Bryceland goal. Tommy Gemmell also scored for St Mirren but Young and Crawford had scored for Hearts as the game was tied 2-2. Gerry Baker put St Mirren back in front only for Young to equalise in a goalmouth scramble. But Gemmell made it 4-3 from the penalty spot only for Bauld to have the final say for Hearts with the late goal which made it 4-4 and gave Hearts the necessary point for the title. It was fitting that Bauld should get the clinching goal – he had played more often than in Hearts' previous title success and chipped in with 10 goals in his 17 League appearances.

But Hearts came back strongly from the League defeat by Kilmarnock in March to beat Aberdeen 3-0 at Tynecastle and then Clyde 5-2 in early April with Ian Crawford this time getting a hat-trick. Gordon Smith had also enjoyed a marvellous season for Hearts, removing any doubts that he could still play at this level and, two years and four days on from when they captured the title at Love Street for the first time in 61 years, Hearts were back in Paisley requiring just a point for the title on 16 April 1960. This time Hearts lined up: Marshall; Kirk, Thomson, Cumming, Milne,

Hearts wound up their campaign with a 2-2 draw at Raith Rovers as they finished the season four points ahead of Kilmarnock and 12 ahead of third-placed Rangers, scoring 102 League goals in the process (compared with Kilmarnock's 67 although, curiously, seventh-placed Hibs were top League scorers that season with 106). Incredibly, no fewer than seven Hearts players finished with goal tallies into double figures. Hearts had won two major trophies in the same season, the first time, and to date the only time, the club had managed such a feat.

All Good Things Must End

IF 1959-60 was to be one of the most memorable in Hearts' history – a League Cup and, more importantly, another League Championship to celebrate – few could have predicted that it would take Hearts almost another 40 years to collect another two trophies.

Interestingly enough, the 1959-60 season was the first since World War Two that neither of the Old Firm had occupied one of the top two places (Rangers were third and Celtic a distant ninth), with Kilmarnock runners-up. It was only to happen on one more occasion in the 20th century – in 1964-65 – when the roles were reversed and Kilmarnock edged Hearts for the title in a cruel finish for the Tynecastle side.

Of the team that clinched the League title in 1960 with that 4-4 draw at St Mirren in the penultimate match of that season, only two players were missing from the next season's opening League game against St Johnstone the following August (Hearts won 3-1) with Willie Bauld and Jim McFadzean replaced by Bobby Blackwood and Johnny Hamilton.

But from the early months of the 1960-61 season, it was clear that teams saw Hearts as a major scalp. They lost 2-1 in a League Cup play-off with Clyde at neutral Celtic Park which cost them a quarter-final place, coming less than a fortnight after having beaten the same opposition 6-2 in the qualifying section.

In the League, Hearts won their opening two games but then went ten games without a victory before

Johnny Hamilton scored 157 goals, including 20 penalties, for Hearts between 1955 and 1967.

scraping a 1-0 win over Raith Rovers at Tynecastle in late November thanks to a goal from Blackwood. It was a day when the Hearts supporters made their feelings known in no uncertain terms to the club's directors,

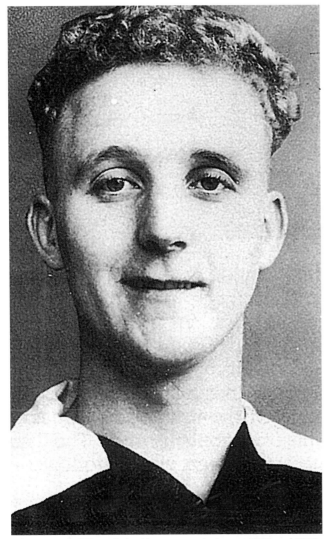

Alex Young's 150 goals for Hearts came between 1954 and 1960.

Benfica went on to beat Barcelona 3-2 in the Final in Berne that season and, the following season with a certain Eusabio scoring twice, retained the trophy with a 5-3 Final win over the great Real Madrid side who included Di Stefano, Puskas and Gento in their number. There was another Final appearance in 1963, this time at Wembley, when Benfica went down to AC Milan, so Hearts were far from disgraced in their performances.

But the mediocre League form was a cause for disgruntlement and Tommy Walker decided changes had to be made. Willie Bauld and Gordon Smith both found their names missing from the team-sheets by the tail end of the year as the manager sought the correct blend.

Walker was intent on rebuilding what was clearly a team that was past its peak. Conn, Mackay, Young and Wardhaugh had already departed and Bauld's appearances were not as frequent. The manager brought in goalkeeper Jim Cruickshank, an amateur from Queen's Park but who had played for Scotland at Under-23 level, and defender Davie Holt, another amateur who had played for Great Britain at the 1960 Olympic Games in Rome and who was to become a permanent fixture at left-back for most of the decade.

In a season of transition, Hearts were to finish a disappointing eighth in the League, pipped on goal average by arch-rivals Hibs for seventh place. The Scottish Cup campaign started brightly enough with Danny Ferguson scoring a hat-trick (his only goals of the season) in a 9-0 rout of Tarff Rovers at Tynecastle. Narrow wins at Kilmarnock and Partick Thistle followed as Hearts reached the last eight but a defeat by St Mirren at home when Don Kerrigan scored the only goal in the quarter-finals ended hope of silverware for another year.

It was the first time since season 1956-57 that Hearts had failed to win one of the three major domestic trophies and Hearts fans had come to expect a glimpse of silverware. Season 1961-62 was another barren year but was not without its flirtations with glory. For the first time, there was progress in Europe and there was another League Cup Final appearance.

In Europe, Hearts were invited to compete in the Inter-Cities Fairs Cup (later to be the UEFA Cup), and beat Luxembourg's Union St Gilloise on a 5-1

who had a few days earlier sold the popular Alex Young and George Thomson to Everton in a combined £58,000 deal. Many thought even that early in the season that the club was slipping towards the wrong end of the table and selling Young in particular – who had scored 26 goals the previous season – was a foolhardy move.

Preoccupying the team in the early days of that season were the small matter of two European Cup ties against Portuguese champions Benfica. The first leg at Tynecastle drew a crowd of close on 35,000 and expectation was high that Hearts could upset a team who was shortly to reach their peak. But a late goal from Alex Young in the home tie was not enough to prevent a 2-1 home defeat and an early goal from Aguas in the return leg in Lisbon effectively killed the tie and Hearts eventually lost 3-0 to go out 5-1 on aggregate.

Blackwood in action against St Mirren's goalkeeper Forsyth and defender Riddel in 1960.

In the League Cup, Hearts had reached another Final but were taken to extra-time in the semi-final by Stirling Albion at Easter Road before coming through with goals from Willie Bauld and Willie Wallace for a 2-1 win. Rangers, who had also been taken to extra-time by St Johnstone in their semi-final tie, stood between Hearts and another trophy. The Final took place at Hampden on 28 October 1961, and there was a surprise for Rangers with Tommy Walker selecting 17-year-old Alan Gordon at inside-left ahead of Bauld or Blackwood, the youngster having made his debut just a week earlier in a 2-1 win over Celtic at Tynecastle.

Teams: Hearts: Marshall; Kirk, Cumming, Polland, Holt, Higgins, Ferguson, Elliott, Wallace, Gordon and Hamilton; Rangers: Ritchie; Shearer, Caldow, Davis, Paterson, Baxter, Scott, McMillan, Millar, Brand and Wilson.

Gordon was to play an important part for Hearts in the Final. Rangers took the lead in the first half when a shot from Jimmy Millar deceived Gordon Marshall and crept in at his post. The equaliser did not arrive until the 77th minute when referee Bobby Davidson ruled that Gordon had been pushed in the penalty area by Harry Davis and the ever-dependable John Cumming shot the penalty past Billy Ritchie. Extra-time brought no further goals.

Due to a postponement because of frost and Hearts' European commitments, the replay did not take place until 18 December – a Monday night and just two days after Hearts had fought out a 3-3 draw with Kilmarnock in the League. This time Hearts lined up: Cruickshank; Kirk, Cumming, Polland, Holt, Higgins, Ferguson, Davidson, Bauld, Blackwood and

aggregate, winning 3-1 away with goals from Norrie Davidson (2) and Bobby Blackwood and winning the home leg 2-0 with Willie Wallace and Robin Stenhouse on the scoresheet. It was the first time Hearts had won a European tie and the reward was a clash with Italian giants, Inter Milan. Standard Liege, Benfica and now Inter Milan on successive European campaigns – there was no shortage of glamour ties for the Tynecastle support.

Inter defended in depth in the first leg in Edinburgh and escaped with a 1-0 victory through a first half goal from Humerto. It was a different side of Inter that Hearts saw in the San Siro Stadium in the return, as the Italians cantered to a 4-0 victory to go through 5-0 on aggregate.

Hearts line-up in 1961. Back row (left to right): Ferguson, Holt, Marshall, Barry, Polland, Higgins. Front row: Henderson, Blackwood, Wallace, Docherty, Hamilton.

Hamilton. Rangers were: Ritchie; Shearer, Caldow, Davis, Baillie, Baxter, Scott, McMillan, Brand and Wilson. Millar gave Rangers a seventh-minute lead but Hearts hit back immediately with Davidson heading the equaliser from a Cumming free-kick a minute later. However, Rangers turned on the style after this and scored again through a Ralph Brand header and an Ian McMillan shot and only some inspired goalkeeping from Jim Cruickshank prevented Rangers from winning by a greater margin than the 3-1 that clinched the trophy.

Hearts were to finish sixth in the League by the end of the season with Dundee winning the title ahead of Rangers and Celtic. In the Scottish Cup, Hearts went out at the third round stage in a seven-goal thriller to Celtic at Tynecastle 4-3, the winning goal coming from a controversially retaken penalty kick from Pat Crerand with just four minutes left.

At the end of the season, Bauld announced his retirement at the age of 34 after 355 goals in 510 appearances. His last game was in a 1-1 draw with Aberdeen at Tynecastle on 10 February, 1962, and his last goal for Hearts came just three days earlier in a

2-1 win over Third Lanark, also at Tynecastle. He was given a testimonial game against Sheffield United in November of that year when a crowd of 15,000 turned up to pay tribute to the "King of Hearts" but there was a bitter ending as the board deducted the cost of the match ball and other expenses from his final cheque. It was to be 12 years before he set foot in Tynecastle again.

On the field of play, Hearts were doing quite nicely without Bauld at the start of the 1962-63 season and there was another trophy for their supporters to toast before the autumn was through. Hearts came through a League Cup qualifying section that included Celtic, to beat Morton 6-1 on aggregate in the two-leg quarter-final and thump St Johnstone 4-0 in the semi-final, again at Easter Road, with a hat-trick from Willie Wallace and one from Willie Hamilton. Wallace was emerging as a genuine goalscoring talent and finished the season with 25 goals, the highest by a Hearts player since Alex Young in 1959-60.

Kilmarnock awaited in the League Cup Final at Hampden on 27 October 1962, and the teams lined up thus: Hearts: Marshall; Polland, Cumming, Barry,

Gordon Marshall goes to block a shot from Celtic's Divers in 1962.

Hearts' goalkeeper Gordon Marshall saves from Brian McIlroy of Kilmarnock watched by Andy Kerr (Kilmarnock) and Willie Polland (Hearts) in 1962.

By the early 1960s, Billy Higgins was one of only four Hearts players to survive at Tynecastle from the League Cup-winning side of 1959.

Goalkeeper Gordon Marshall, another of the few from the 1950s who was still at Tynecastle in the early 1960s.

Holt, Higgins, W Hamilton, Wallace, Paton, Davidson and J Hamilton; Kilmarnock: McLaughlan; Richmond, Watson, O'Connor, McGrory, Beattie, Brown, Black, Kerr, McInally and McIlroy. The referee was Tom Wharton.

The only goal of the game came after 26 minutes of play when Willie Hamilton provided the cutback for Davidson to score from close range. But the drama was far from over as Hearts were pinned back in defence in the final minutes as Kilmarnock pressed for the equalising goal. They thought they had found it in the final minute when Frank Beattie headed past Marshall from a free-kick from Jim Richmond. Kilmarnock's celebrations were cut short as referee Wharton ruled that an offence had occurred before the "goal" and Beattie was penalised.

Television pictures proved inconclusive and Kilmarnock felt a strong sense of injustice as Cumming climbed the Hampden steps to receive the League Cup trophy for Hearts. The wound was obviously deep but the Ayrshire side would take full revenge a few years later when they plundered the League title from Tynecastle on the final day of the 1964-65 season. For Hearts, the winning of that League Cup was not without cost and the curse that came with it meant it was the last piece of significant silverware that Hearts won for almost 36 years.

Hearts showed some improvement in the League that season and finished fifth with Rangers taking the title but Celtic again brought their Scottish Cup ambitions to an abrupt end – this time in the second round – with a 3-1 win at Parkhead with Wallace inevitably scoring the Hearts' goal. It was an

Hearts in 1961-62, wearing their 'lucky' candy-striped shirts. Back row (left to right): Danny Ferguson, Davie Holt, Gordon Marshall, Roy Barry, Willie Polland, Billy Higgins. Front: Tommy Henderson, Bobby Blackwood, Willie Wallace, John Docherty, John Hamilton.

Willie Wallace scored 21 goals when Hearts narrowly missed the title in 1964-65.

inconsistent campaign overall – whereas Hearts scored six goals in matches against both Airdrie and Clyde, they also lost 5-0 at home to Rangers and 7-3 the following week at St Mirren when Wallace took over in goal after only 15 minutes due to an injury to Marshall (Hearts had beaten the Paisley side 5-0 at Tynecastle earlier in the season).

Tommy Walker had been carefully rebuilding his side. Marshall went to Newcastle United with Hearts having a more than capable replacement in Cruickshank and John Cumming was nearing the end of a career in which he gave the club tremendous service. Hearts had climbed to fourth in the League by the end of the 1963-64 season (sixth, fifth, fourth in successive seasons showed Hearts were moving in the right direction) and just eight points off champions Rangers. But there was a disappointing defence of the League Cup with Hearts failing to get through a qualifying group which included Motherwell, Falkirk and Partick Thistle. The Scottish Cup was just as unremarkable with Hearts falling at the third round stage when they were beaten at home 2-1 by Motherwell in a replay (Tommy White scored the Hearts' goal) after getting a 3-3 draw in the first game at Fir Park. In Europe, Hearts were involved in the Fairs Cup again. There was a creditable 2-2 draw with Lausanne Sports in the first round first leg in Switzerland with Tommy Traynor and Danny Ferguson giving Hearts a 2-0 lead but they could not complete the job at Tynecastle and were held 2-2, with this time John Cumming and Johnny Hamilton finding the net.

Hearts lost the toss of the coin to host the play-off game and found themselves travelling to Switzerland again where Wallace and Ferguson were both on target but it was not enough to keep Hearts from going down 3-2 and out of Europe for another year. Wallace was still catching the eye and this time contributed 30 goals – the most by a Hearts player since Jimmy

Hearts in 1963-64. Back row (left to right): Chris Shevlane, David Holt, Jim Cruickshank, Willie Polland, Alan Anderson, Billy Higgins. Front: Johnny Hamilton, Willie Wallace, Tommy White, Frank Sandeman, Tommy Traynor.

Wardhaugh's 37 in the remarkable championship year of 1958.

Season 1964-65 was one that was to go down in Tynecastle folklore, but for the wrong reason. Once again the League Cup campaign was inglorious – only one victory in the qualifying group, and that coming – against Partick Thistle – too late to prevent an early exit and there was also a 6-1 defeat by Celtic at Parkhead to digest. An 8-1 victory over Airdrie in the first League game of the season suggested that this was going to be another season where Hearts were frustratingly inconsistent.

Motherwell again thwarted Hearts' Scottish Cup

hopes with a 1-0 third round win at Fir Park in January after Hearts had put out Falkirk and then Morton (after a replay). But by that stage, Hearts were looking capable of recapturing the League title with Rangers and, in particular, Celtic finding the pace too hot to handle. Hearts were unbeaten in their first 16 games and had won 12 of them. Ironically, as it would turn out, that first defeat – deep into December – was at Kilmarnock where Gordon scored in a 3-1 reversal. It resulted in Hearts questioning themselves as there were back-to-back losses to Hibs, now managed by Jock Stein, and Dunfermline at the turn of the year.

A narrow win over Partick Thistle in late January

Willie Wallace scores against Partick Thistle in the early stages of 1964-65.

put Hearts three points clear at the top but there was a huge setback a month later when Hearts were torn apart 7-1 by Dundee at Tynecastle in a result that was to have great significance on the outcome of the championship. To their credit, Hearts did not let the nature of the loss knock them out of their stride and won six of their next seven games (the other being a 1-1 draw with Dundee United) to stand within touching distance of the title when they entertained closest challengers Kilmarnock in their final League game at Tynecastle on 24 April 1965.

A crowd of 37,275 packed into the stadium that day in the knowledge that a draw, or even a single-goal defeat, would give Hearts their first League flag for five years (when they had finished four points clear of Kilmarnock). Hearts lined up: Cruickshank; Ferguson, Polland, Anderson, Holt, Barry, Higgins, Jensen, Wallace, Gordon and Hamilton, with Kilmarnock naming: Ferguson; King, McGrory, Beattie, Watson, McLean, Murray, McInally, Black, Sneddon and McIlroy.

Hearts hit the post early on through Raold Jensen but Kilmarnock scored twice in a three-minute spell through Dave Sneddon and Brian McIlroy and the home side found themselves 2-0 down after just half an hour. Still, there was plenty of time to rectify the situation and Hearts dominated the second half as they went in search for the one goal that would secure the title on goal average. Kilmarnock stood firm, however, and the closest Hearts came was a Gordon shot in the 84th minute which brought out the best in Bobby Ferguson.

The Ayrshire side held on to their two-goal margin of victory to win the League with a goal average that was just 0.042 better than Hearts. Ironically, had goal difference been used in 1965, Hearts would have won the title but by the time goal difference was used in preference, Hearts were also to suffer as they lost the League on an equally dramatic day in 1986 at Dens Park. Ironically, had goal average counted on that day, then Hearts would have won the League on that occasion.

It took time for events of the 1964-65 season to sink in and Hearts finished seventh the following season and a distant 11th the season after that – 1966-67 when Celtic were sweeping all before them, including the European Cup, with a certain Willie Wallace in their ranks. Indeed, Hearts were not to finish in the top three in the League again until they again lost the title on the final day of the season in 1986.

Between times, there was major change at the club and Hearts had to suffer one of the blackest spells in their history before fate would allow them to once again clamber up to the top table. After League reconstruction in the mid-1970s, Hearts were relegated from the new Premier Division not long afterwards and, at one stage, there was a huge question mark against their future as the club faced mounting debts.

Many believe the rot set in back in the mid-1960s after the painful way the League was lost in 1965 and Tommy Walker's days in charge neared an end.

After Hearts had again tumbled out of the League Cup in the preliminary section, it was clear at the start of the 1966-67 season that all was not well in the dressing-room and many of the top players, including

Stout hearts in Hearts' defence – goalkeeper Jim Cruikshank with Chris Shevlane, left, and Davie Holt.

Hearts boss Tommy Walker pictured at his desk.

Three minutes from time and Donald Ford (second left) scores the only goal of the Scottish Cup quarter-final replay against Rangers at Tynecastle in March 1968 before a crowd of over 44,000.

While Harvey was moulding his own team, the question remained of who could provide the goals to fill the considerable void left by the departure of Wallace. Hearts did not have to look too far. Donald Ford, who had been an amateur at the club as he was studying for accountancy qualifications, signed professional forms and was making an impact in front of goal. Modest and unassuming, he scored 16 goals in the 1967-68 and was to go on and find the net 188 times in 436 appearances as well as going on to win three international caps for Scotland.

If Hearts had made little impact in the League that season, there was the consolation of a Scottish Cup Final appearance against Dunfermline at the end of April. It was a thrilling cup run, with Dundee United beaten 6-5 in the second round at Tannadice in a memorable encounter with Jim Irvine scoring the winning goal five minutes from the end. Ford then endeared himself to the Hearts fans by scoring the only goal of a quarter-final replay against Rangers in front of a crowd of 44,094 at Tynecastle (after Hearts had drawn 1-1 at Ibrox) and Morton were taken care of in a marathon semi-final tie. The first game ended 1-1 with Jensen scoring the goal and Jensen scored the penalty winner in extra-time in the replay at Hampden in a 2-1 win with George Miller also on the mark for Hearts.

Cruickshank, Wallace and Roy Barry, had tabled transfer requests. Barry was granted his wish and moved to Coventry and while Wallace did not remain at Tynecastle for much longer with Celtic's Jock Stein coming in for him, Cruickshank was to stay for a few more years yet.

But all the unrest inevitably brought a casualty and it was the manager Walker, who shouldered the blame. He was told by the Board that they were considering terminating his contract and, in the circumstances, Walker chose to resign. In his 16 years in charge, he had brought seven trophies but it was clear that Hearts were struggling to live up to the burden of success that previous teams had brought.

Hearts promoted from within and trainer John Harvey took over as manager and started with a 3-1 win over Dundee on 1 October 1966. There was to be no lasting success however, and the departure of Wallace in mid-season for what many believed was a knock-down price of £30,000 meant the goals did not flow as freely. That was blindingly obvious in the spring of 1967 when Hearts did not score in six successive League games, their worst drought since World War Two. Within months of leaving, incidentally, Wallace had won Scottish League, Scottish Cup and European Cup winners' medals to more than make up for events of 1965.

So it was a confident Hearts team that lined up in the Final on 27 April 1968: Cruickshank; Sneddon, Anderson, A Thomson, Mann, Jensen, Townsend, Miller, Ford, Irvine and Traynor; Sub: Moller; and Dunfermline fielded: Martin; W Callaghan, McGarty, Barry, Lunn, Edwards, T Callaghan, Robertson, Lister, Paton and Gardner; Sub: Thomson.

After a goalless first half in front of a 56,365 crowd, Dunfermline took the lead in the 56th minute after a misunderstanding between Cruickshank and Arthur Thomson presented Pat Gardner with a chance which he gratefully accepted. Bert Paton was then fouled by Cruickshank in the area and John Lister scored from

Jim Cruickshank

NO player was more synonymous with Hearts in the seventies than Jim Cruickshank. The ever-dependable goalkeeper, who started out as an amateur with Queen's Park, played for 17 years at Tynecastle and went on to win six full caps for Scotland.

Cruickshank played in two Scottish Cup finals for the club – in 1968 and 1976 – and was a member of the team that just missed out on the League championship in 1965 but for all his consistent service, there was no winner's medal to mark his long career at Hearts.

He played a total of 610 games for the club and kept 102 clean sheets in 394 League matches which was a noteworthy return given that the club had mixed fortunes during his years there. Only Henry Smith played more matches between the posts for the club but Cruickshank is regarded by many as Hearts' greatest-ever goalkeeper.

A gifted athlete, the Glasgow-born goalkeeper was a former Scottish schools' long jump champion yet stood only 5'10". But his agility and commanding presence in the penalty area made up for any lack of inches and, having made his debut for Hearts at the age of 17, he was soon to establish himself as a favourite with the Tynecastle supporters.

He signed for the club in May 1960 as a 17-year-old and was capped at schoolboy, youth, amateur, Under-23 and Scottish League level before winning his first full cap for Scotland against West Germany in 1964 in a 2-2 draw in Hanover. Although he reportedly played well in the game – and it was a fair result given that the Germans were to reach the World Cup Final two years later – it was to be another six years before he won his second cap (against Wales). Given that he only played six times for his country, Cruickshank can boast that his international career spanned 11 years as his final cap, against Romania, did not arrive until 1975 in a 1-1 draw at Hampden.

Cruickshank made his Hearts debut in October 1960 in a narrow 1-0 defeat by Ayr

United at Somerset Park and he went on to play four more games that season, although it was not until the 1963-64 season that he became a regular first-choice with Gordon Marshall having departed to Newcastle United. He did, however, deputise for the injured Marshall in the 1961 League Cup Final replay against Rangers when he was promoted at the eleventh hour and did not know he was playing until less than an hour before kick-off. It was not to be a fairytale ending as Rangers claimed the trophy.

When Cruickshank did establish himself in the team, he was seemingly an immovable object and did not miss a League game for four years. But he then had competition for the jersey with Kenny Garland challenging him for the berth and between 1972-75, the two goalkeepers were sharing the first-team duties. Ultimately, Cruickshank was to finish on top and make the jersey his own again from 1975-77 and by the time he left the club in 1977, Garland had already hung up his gloves, frustrated at his lack of first-team opportunities as the perennial understudy.

The goalkeeper played a big part in Hearts' run to the Final of the Texaco Cup in 1971 and it was indeed a pity that he could not mark his long years of service with a major trophy to boast of. There were, however, a number of highlights in his long career.

He claimed the headlines in 1967 during an Edinburgh derby when he made a triple penalty save, a rare event in the game. He managed to get his hand to Joe Davis's initial kick and then stopped the Hibs' striker's follow-up effort. The ball broke to Allan McGraw but Cruickshank somehow recovered to block his effort too.

The Hearts goalkeeper gained a reputation as something of an expert at saving spot kicks and he was a popular figure with Hearts fans, particularly for his bravery in the penalty area and his willingness to give his all for the cause.

Unfortunately, his Tynecastle career ended bitterly in 1977 after the club refused to recognise his 17 years of service with a testimonial match for his then record number of appearances for the club.

It was a sad way for his association with the club to end and, even when he signed for Dumbarton at the end of his career, Hearts refused him permission to train with them in Edinburgh. Cruickshank did not linger long at Dumbarton and retired from the game a few months later.

For all the acrimony in his final days at Tynecastle, it did nothing to soil what had gone before and Cruickshank holds the distinction of being one of the Hearts' greats.

After his departure, Hearts found it hard to replace him with Brian Wilson, Ray Dunlop, John Brough, Thomson Allan and Ian Westwater all getting chances in the years ahead but it was not until the arrival of Henry Smith that Cruickshank's gloves were finally filled.

1960-61-1976-77
Appearances 610

the resultant penalty to make it 2-0. Hearts pulled a goal back when John Lunn turned a Rene Moller cross into his own net with 20 minutes still remaining. However, Gardner settled it with a third goal for Dunfermline to cap a disappointing afternoon for Hearts.

There were no sour grapes in the Hearts' camp. "Dunfermline deserved to win," Donald Ford recalled, "Man for man, they were the better team

Hearts in 1969-70. Back row (left to right): Johnny Cumming (trainer), Alan MacDonald, Dave Clunie, Rene Moller, Jim Cruickshank, Alan Anderson, Eddie Thomson, Ernie Winchester. Front: Roald Jensen, Tommy Traynor, Peter Oliver, Donald Ford, Jim Brown, Andy Lynch, Neil Murray, George Fleming.

and they had a terrific blend of enthusiasm, strength and skill. Alex Edwards was a big factor and I think they were also better prepared for the Final."

It had been Hearts' first Scottish Cup Final since they won the trophy in 1956 and it was to be another eight years before they made it to another. The Final appearance failed to disguise what had been a mediocre season for Hearts given what had happened in the previous ten years and, while there was promise in the new-look side with the likes of Cruickshank, Ford, Alan Anderson and Jim Townsend, they failed to progress through the group stages of the League Cup for the next six seasons and, in the League and Scottish Cup, there were only occasional shafts of light.

In the 1969-70 season, there was some encouragement – a 2-0 win over Celtic in Glasgow in November and a 5-0 win over Airdrie shortly before Christmas in which Ford scored twice, and a defence and goalkeeper who did not give up many goals. Cruickshank kept 17 clean sheets in 38 appearances as Hearts went on to finish fourth in the League with only champions Celtic boasting a better goal difference.

It was enough to gain qualification to a new cross-border competition, the Texaco Cup, the following season – a competition which was to provide consolation for teams that missed out on European places and, initially and in Scotland at least, it was to

prove popular. Nowhere more so than amongst Hearts supporters who turned out in decent numbers to support the tournament. Indeed, outside of matches against the Old Firm and Hibernian, Hearts' best three attendances of the 1970-71 season were for Texaco Cup matches.

Yet Hearts did not make the most auspicious of starts in the competition. Drawn against a strong Burnley side, who included England international Ralph Coates in their ranks, they lost the first leg 3-1 at Turf Moor. But there was a stirring performance in the return where over 15,000 fans turned up to see if Hearts could come back. Goals from Jim Brown and Kevin Hegarty had tied the aggregate scores by half-time and an own goal from Gene Waldron and a further strike from Andy Lynch gave Hearts a 4-1 win on the night to qualify for the second round on a 5-4 aggregate. Airdrie provided the next hurdle but Hearts cleared it comfortably with Donald Ford scoring four times in a 5-0 win at Broomfield and a 3-2 home defeat in the return was not surprising as Hearts coasted through. Given the Anglo-Scottish nature of the tournament, it seemed strange that it was another Lanarkshire side, Motherwell, who awaited Hearts in the semi-finals.

By that stage, Hearts had made a change of manager. John Harvey, who it transpired had been a reluctant manager after the resignation of Tommy Walker, stepped down to remain as trainer with special responsibility of bringing on the young players. His health had suffered with all of his management duties and he was happy to step down. Bobby Seith, who had been manager at Preston North End for over two years before being sacked the previous season, was invited to take over at Hearts in December 1970, at the age of just 38. While Hearts still struggled to make an impression in the League, it was the Texaco Cup that gave the fans some welcome respite.

The semi-final with Motherwell drew some 21,301 fans to Tynecastle but it was the visiting team who finished happier with a 1-1 draw giving them the chance to settle the tie on their own turf. The reliable Ford had given Hearts the lead but Jim Muir had equalised in the second half.

The return game was televised live and drew 25,259 to Fir Park as Motherwell sensed it could be their year after putting out Stoke City, with Gordon Banks, and Tottenham Hotspur, including Martin Chivers and Alan Gilzean, on a more glamorous route to the semi-finals. It was a tense tie and, after a goalless first half, Brian Heron opened the scoring for Motherwell early in the second period. The goal looked to be sufficient to put Motherwell through but, deep into injury-time, a Ford shot was parried by home goalkeeper Billy Ritchie and George Fleming netted to take the tie to extra-time. Motherwell did not recover from the body-blow and Ford scored a typical opportunist effort in the second half of extra-time to take Hearts into a Final confrontation with Wolverhampton Wanderers.

The English side were not treating the game lightly and named a strong team for the first leg at Tynecastle which drew an impressive 25,027 crowd; Hearts: Cruickshank; Sneddon, Thomson, Anderson, Kay, Brown, Townsend, Wood, Carruthers, Ford and Fleming: Subs: Young, Garland; Wolves: Parkes; Taylor, McCalle, Munro, Parkin, Wagstaffe, Bailey, O'Grady, McCalliog, Curran and Gould; Subs: Dougan, Smith. Wolves were lying third in the English First Division at the time but Ford headed Hearts in front early on to put the Edinburgh side ahead. But it brought false hope and the English side took control after this and finished worthy winners with Mike Bailey and Hugh Curran scoring before half-time and Curran making it

3-1 with his second goal late in the game. It left Hearts with a seemingly impossible task in the return leg at Molineux but Hearts took a strong travelling support.

The teams lined up: Wolves: Parkes; Taylor, McCalle, Munro, Parkin, Wagstaffe, Bailey, O'grady, McCalliog, Curran and Gould; Subs: Dougan, Smith; Hearts: Cruickshank; Sneddon, Thomson, Anderson, Kay, Veitch, Townsend, Wood, Laing, Ford and Fleming; Subs: Carruthers, Young. Hearts caught their opponents off guard and when Fleming put them ahead midway through the first half to leave them just a goal adrift on aggregate, there was belief that the task was not insurmountable. But Wolves were well organised in defence and shut Hearts out for the remainder of the tie to become the inaugural winners of the gold trophy on a 3-2 aggregate.

But, if the Texaco Cup was a thrilling ride while it lasted for Hearts, the League programme finished in anti-climax as Hearts could only finish 11th in the table after losing four of their last five games. The Scottish Cup ended at the second round stage with a 2-1 home defeat by city rivals Hibs. But Ford had a productive season up front and finished top scorer with 23 goals and the promise of much more to come in a maroon shirt.

Hearts could not repeat their run to the Final in the next season's Texaco Cup and indeed they failed to get beyond the first round but they were extremely unfortunate not to beat a Newcastle United side which had won the Fairs Cup in 1969, having put Rangers out in the semi-finals. An Andy Lynch goal was enough to give Hearts a 1-0 victory in the home leg and Hearts looked to be holding on for a goalless draw in the return at St James' Park until the powerful Malcolm Macdonald equalised with five minutes left.

Macdonald was again on target in extra-time but Alan Anderson headed an even later goal to take it to 2-2 on aggregate and send the tie into a penalty kick decider, the first time Hearts had been involved in such a scenario to decide a cup tie. Jim Townsend and Ford both failed to score with their attempts and, although Cruickshank saved Terry Hibbett's effort, Newcastle went through 4-3 on penalties.

But, if the result was unkind on Hearts, it was clearly not going to unsettle them and they returned from Tyneside to beat Rangers at home and string

Hearts in August 1971. Back row (left to right): David Clunie, Eric Carruthers, Peter Oliver, Ian Sneddon, Jim Cruickshank, Alan Anderson, Kevin Hegarty, Andy Lynch, Tommy Veitch, Roy Kay. Front: Jimmy Brown, Brian Laing, Donald Ford, Eddie Thomson, Jim Townsend, Wilson Wood, George Fleming, Ernie Winchester.

together an impressive run of results which saw them lose just once in their next ten games. Hearts were looking in better shape to challenge for a European place than they did the previous season but then followed a slump where they did not win in eight matches. There was a chastening 6-0 defeat by Rangers in the January of 1972, the week after Hearts had leaked five goals at home to Dundee which had cost Cruickshank his place in goal, and Kenny Garland took over for the rest of the campaign. Hearts finished sixth in the table, but 21 points behind champions Celtic, who also ended Hearts' Scottish Cup interest, winning a replayed quarter-final tie at Tynecastle with a Lou Macari goal separating the teams.

There was another mixed bag of results for Hearts in the 1972-73 season. League Cup interest again did not extend beyond the qualifying section but Hearts recovered from this and managed to climb to third in the League by mid-December after a run of just one defeat in nine games (that being at Celtic Park) and including a win at Ibrox when Ford scored the only goal of the game. Hearts had come through the first

round of the Texaco Cup at the expense of Crystal Palace but went out to Motherwell in the next round and squandered a two-goal lead at Fir Park in the process. But the festive season was calamitous. Not only did successive defeats by Dundee and St Johnstone put serious question marks against any title credentials they may have been holding but the meeting with Hibs at Tynecastle on New Year's Day in 1973 will go down as one of the blackest days in the club's history.

There was no warning of what was to follow when Hearts made a promising start. But it was a day when little went right for the home side and poor defending cost them dearly as Hibs ran out 7-0 winners. It is a result that has been regurgitated before many a derby since and, although Hearts won their following game against Dumbarton, it was a false recovery as, the following month, Hearts tumbled out of the Scottish Cup at the first hurdle after a replay with Airdrie.

Indeed, there was only to be one more victory that season – a narrow 1-0 home win over Falkirk at Tynecastle courtesy of a Jim Brown goal. If 36,000 had

Hearts in 1973-74. Back row (left to right): Peter Oliver, Ian Sneddon, Alan Anderson, David Graham, Kenny Garland, Jim Cruickshank, John Gallacher, Jimmy Cant, Eric Carruthers. Middle: Bobby Seith (manager), Jim Brown, David Clunie, David Dick, Roy Kay, John Mckay, Harry Kinnear, Jim Jeffries, Drew Busby, Willie Gibson, John Cumming (trainer), John Hagart (coach). Front: Donald Ford, Bobby Conn, Tommy Murray, John Stevenson, Kenny Aird, Billy Wilson, Gordon Welsh, Donald Park, Ralph Callachan. Sitting on the ground are the club's 'S' form signings.

been drawn to Tynecastle for that fateful New Year's Day game, then, apart from games against the Old Firm, crowds had dwindled at Tynecastle with 6,000 or 7,000 more commonplace.

The hangover from that defeat by Hibs was a lasting one and Hearts slumped to tenth in the final table, having scored just four goals in their final ten games and at one stage finding the net just once in seven matches. But, such is the unpredictability of city derbies, there was some measure of revenge the following September when there was a comfortable 4-1 victory to savour with goals from Kenny Aird, Donald Ford and Drew Busby along with an own goal from Eric Schaedler. Recovery indeed.

It came in the middle of a 13-match unbeaten run for Hearts, including a remarkable 3-0 win over Rangers at Ibrox (Busby 2, and Rab Prentice were the scorers) and a 1-0 win over Everton at Goodison Park

(with Busby again on the mark) in the Texaco Cup (Hearts drew 0-0 in the return at Tynecastle to go through to the second round). Bobby Seith's team were top of the League in the early days of that 1973-74 season but the challenge could not be sustained. They tumbled out of the Texaco Cup on an 8-0 aggregate to Burnley and Celtic brought their unbeaten League run to an end with a 3-1 win at Tynecastle in late October.

Yet again it was around Christmas that Hearts' challenge faltered and home defeats by Ayr United, Morton, Rangers and St Johnstone within the space of little more than a month meant the title was once again out of reach with Celtic claiming their ninth successive championship under Jock Stein and this time it was the resurgent Hibs who came closest to them, caught just four points adrift in the final analysis. Hearts were a distant sixth but had shown considerable improvement on the previous season and there was finally a Scottish Cup run to speak of.

The campaign started with a 3-1 win over Clyde and, while Hearts took two games to get past Partick Thistle in the next round (Ford scoring a hat-trick in the 4-1 replay at Firhill), a home quarter-final tie with Ayr United would give them the chance to reach the last four for the first time since 1968. Hearts were held to a draw by an Ayr side managed by future Scotland manager Ally McLeod at Tynecastle but two goals in extra-time by Ford gave Hearts a 2-1 win in the replay at Somerset Park to put them into the semi-finals.

Dundee United – managed by Jim McLean – awaited in the semi-final at Hampden and, for the third successive round, the tie went to a replay after a 1-1 draw in the first game. This time, luck deserted Hearts and it was United who went through to secure a Final place against Celtic with a 4-2 victory. After the start of the season had promised so much, it was a flat ending with no European place as consolation. However, Ford's goals – 29 in all that term – earned him a place in Scotland's squad for the World Cup finals in Munich in 1974, the first Scottish squad to attend such an event since 1958.

But 1974 was a turbulent year for Hearts. There was early optimism at the start of the new campaign when Hearts came through their League Cup section for the first time since they won the trophy in 1962 but it gave their supporters false hope and that turned to dismay when Hearts went out of the competition in the two-leg quarter-final to Second Division Falkirk, 1-0 on aggregate. Hearts were to go out of the Texaco Cup at the first round stage a few days later (to Oldham) and a 4-1 defeat at home to Aberdeen in early October was to be Bobby Seith's last game in charge. He tendered his resignation on the eve of a trip to Tannadice and it was not surprising that Dundee United took full advantage and sent five goals past Kenny Garland without reply the following day.

For the first time, but not for the last, Hearts attempted to lure Jim McLean away from Tannadice to become their new manager but the approach was unsuccessful. In any case, John Haggart, who had been appointed caretaker manager in the interim, had been achieving some decent results – not least of which was a 1-1 draw against eventual champions Rangers – and he was given the job on a permanent basis. Haggart admitted he had never anticipated becoming manager but, during that first season, he at least made Hearts more resilient. There was just one defeat in 20 matches between mid-October and the end of the following February. However, typically, that defeat came at perhaps the least expected place – a 3-1 loss at Arbroath, who were to finish the season bottom of the League.

Marooned

SUCH had been the fall in attendances throughout Scotland in the early 1970s, that a decision on League reconstruction was taken to go with a 10-14-14 three-division set-up which would see teams in the new Premier Division meeting four times a season in a bid to create a more competitive environment and entice the crowds back to the game.

Hearts crucially took eighth place in the old First Division in 1974-75 to qualify for the top flight of the new set-up, albeit with just four points to spare on 11th club Airdrie. The price of failure was great and it was not until 1980 that Airdrie won a place at the top table again. In the Scottish Cup, Hearts reached the last eight but lost a tense quarter-final replay 3-2 against Dundee at Dens Park.

At the start of 1975-76, the Texaco Cup had been replaced by the Anglo-Scottish Cup, a competition which failed to capture the imagination of its predecessor. Hearts advanced through the first round against Queen of the South but then went out at the next stage to Fulham, 5-4 on aggregate. Hearts again failed to negotiate their League Cup section that contained Celtic. There was a deflating 2-1 defeat at lower League Dumbarton, although Hearts took some revenge by winning the home tie 6-0.

It set them up for their opening game in the new Premier Division and a crowd of 23,646 turned up to watch them face city rivals Hibs at Easter Road. Hibs started as favourites and justified the tag by taking the two points with a solitary strike from Scotland international Joe Harper. Defeat by Rangers followed swiftly but Hearts took to the new surroundings and

Willie Gibson scores Hearts' first goal in their 2-1 win over Rangers at Ibrox in November 1975.

there was a victory at Ibrox to enjoy in the November – Willie Gibson scoring both goals in a 2-1 win.

But successive defeats at the hands of Hibs, Rangers and Dundee in early January proved a serious setback. The cut-throat nature of the new division was to become clearer as the months progressed and, though Hearts were in mid-table for most of that first season, only a handful of points separated them from the relegation zone. St Johnstone had been cut adrift early and it was obvious they were going to become early casualties but the second relegation place was between Dundee, Dundee United, Aberdeen, Ayr United and Hearts.

It was a tension-packed final few weeks of the season for Hearts but narrow single-goal wins over Ayr United and St Johnstone were to prove invaluable and Hearts took fifth place in the table ahead of Ayr on goal difference. But there was just a three-point cushion on the three teams immediately below them, Aberdeen, Dundee United and Dundee who all finished on the same points. It was goal difference that proved crucial with Dundee the unlucky team to drop into the First Division with St Johnstone. That Dundee United survived by the skin of their teeth was to prove significant as Jim McLean was to turn them into Premier Division champions within a few short years and to the brink of a European Cup Final place. Dundee, on the other hand, did not return to the top flight until 1979 and it demonstrated the thin line between success and failure.

But if the League was to prove a nail-biter for Hearts' fans, then the Scottish Cup run was no less dramatic. At least, however, there was the reward of a Cup Final place at the end of it and the Final loss to Rangers, who won the inaugural Premier Division, at the start of May was tempered by the fact that Hearts qualified for the European Cup-Winners' Cup through the back door. Although Hearts were not drawn to face Premier opposition in any of the rounds up to the Final, it took them eight games to set up the clash with Rangers (curiously, when Hearts finally won the trophy again in 1998, they reached the Final against Rangers without facing top-League opposition).

In 1976, it took Hearts two games to get past Clyde in the third round, and three games and extra-time to get past Montrose in the quarter-finals (Ralph Callachan finally settling it at neutral Muirton Park in Perth). Hearts also made heavy weather of the semi-final against Dumbarton and drew the first game at Hampden 0-0. It all finally came good in the replay with Hearts winning 3-0 with an own goal from Walter Smith setting them on their way and Prentice and Busby completing the job but there were just 11,273 to witness the semi-final replay.

Hearts were without the dependable defender Dave Clunie for the Final due to injury and lined up: Cruickshank; Brown, Gallacher, Kay, Burrell, Callachan, Shaw, Jefferies, Busby, Gibson and Prentice; Subs: Aird, Park. Rangers were: McCloy; Greig, Forsyth, Jackson, Miller, McLean, Hamilton, MacDonald, Johnstone, Henderson and McKean; Subs: Jardine, Parlane.

If the Cup semi-final attendances were poor, Hearts fans turned up in their thousands to see if their heroes could reproduce the Final of 20 years previously when they had beaten Celtic in front of a near 133,000 crowd at the stadium. The crowd was not as large but Hearts had a fair representation in the 85,250 attendance and there was some optimism that the Cup would come back to Gorgie.

Yet in one of the most dramatic starts in Cup Final history, Hearts found themselves a goal down after less than a minute. It is recorded that referee Bobby Davidson started the game a minute early and so Hearts were technically behind even before 3 pm that day. It was Jim Jefferies, who was finally to bring the trophy back to Tynecastle as manager of the club 22 years later, who conceded the first free-kick of the game on Rangers' young striker Derek Johnstone. Tommy McLean floated over the free-kick and Johnstone met it perfectly to glide a header past a bemused Jim Cruickshank, whose first task of the Final was to pick the ball out of his net.

It was not the kind of start Hearts had anticipated and it left them with an uphill struggle. When Alex MacDonald volleyed in a second goal before half-time when Cruickshank was unsighted, it was clear that Hearts would have to wait a while longer to re-acquaint themselves with the old trophy. The second half was a more even-balanced affair with both teams hitting woodwork and John Greig clearing off the line for Rangers but any lingering hopes Hearts held of pulling it back died nine minutes from time when Johnstone nabbed his second goal with an opportunist effort. There was some consolation for Hearts with an even later goal from Graham Shaw but, by then, the red, blue and white ribbons had been tied to the Cup and it was not long before Greig made his way up the steps to collect it as Rangers celebrated the domestic treble. It was difficult to disagree with Hearts manager John Haggart's assessment that his team had lost "killer goals at killer times".

If Hearts had not performed to expectations in the Final, then at least there was the consolation of a Cup-Winners' Cup place with Rangers having qualified for the European Cup by virtue of winning the League. It was to prove a memorable campaign, if only because it gave Tynecastle one of its greatest nights the following season.

Hearts had made a bright start to the new season, had qualified from their League Cup section and had suffered just one defeat in their first eight domestic matches. There was a tough European tie to face up to

Hearts, July 1976. Back row (left to right): John Gallacher, John Hay, Jim Cruickshank, Roy Kay, Cammy Fraser. Middle: Jim Brown, Ralph Callachan, Sandy Burrell, Don Murray, Jim Jefferies, David Clunie. Front: Willie Gibson, Kenny Aird, Graham Shaw, John Hagart (manager), Drew Busby, Donald Park, Bobby Prentice.

against the East German side Lokomotiv Leipzig and a trip behind the Iron Curtain. Hearts were put through their paces in the first leg and lucky to escape with a 2-0 defeat given that the East Germans missed a late penalty. It did not deter an 18,000 crowd turning up at Tynecastle for what proved to be a thrilling return. It looked a familiar Scottish hard-luck story at half-time with Hearts having levelled the scores on aggregate through goals from Roy Kay and Willie Gibson but then Fritche scored an invaluable away goal shortly before the interval which left Hearts having to score twice to go through.

The second half was on a knife-edge with Hearts mindful that Leipzig were well organised at the back and venomous on the break and, for long enough, it looked as if the East Germans would hold on. But spurred on by some fine wing play from Prentice,

Hearts made it 3-1 in the 74th minute with a goal from Jim Brown. The home side still needed another to avoid going out on the away goals rule and it arrived shortly afterwards when Drew Busby scored with a header. Even at 4-1, Hearts had to tread warily as another Leipzig goal would still put the East Germans through. But, with just five minutes left, Willie Gibson settled it beyond doubt with a fifth goal which sparked a pitch invasion at the final whistle. Although Hearts were later fined by UEFA for this intrusion, it was a minor footnote to a memorable tie.

When the second round paired Hearts with SV Hamburg, no-one saw a reason why Hearts could not claim another major scalp. The feeling was not doused after the first leg in which, though Hearts lost 4-2, they had scored away goals through Busby and Donald Park and had held their own for most of the game and did

Donald Ford

LIKE many of his predecessors at Tynecastle, Donald Ford was not bestowed with too many international caps but his goals were testament to a fine Hearts' career where he continued the tradition of gifted centre-forwards at the club.

An accomplished cricketer (his talents took him to the verge of the Scotland international team although he never won a full cap at the sport unlike his brother Malcolm), Ford first signed for Hearts as an amateur player as he was completing his studies as a chartered accountant.

Slightly-built, there were fears that he was not sturdy enough for the demands of the Scottish First Division but his lightning pace and his natural awareness of where the goal was stood him in good stead.

He was also an industrious player who always gave full commitment to the cause and it was a pity that his years at Hearts coincided with a time when the club failed to win silverware.

In many ways, he was a late recruit to the big time as he played in the West Lothian Juvenile League before being signed by Bo'ness United where he played on the right wing. Within a few months, Hearts came in to offer him signing terms in 1964 after he played in a couple of trial games at Tynecastle.

Signed by the great Tommy Walker, he made his debut in the ill-fated 1964-65 season when he first appeared as a 19-year-old in a 4-2 win over Celtic and went on to play nine games in that first season.

However, he did not play in the final game of the season at home to Kilmarnock when Hearts famously let the League flag slip from their grasp.

Not long afterwards, Ford showed his flair for goal when he scored five times in an experimental "no offside" game against Kilmarnock which Hearts won 8-3.

Hearts' fans bemoaned the loss of Willie Wallace to Celtic in 1966-67, but Ford proved a more than capable successor and, even when the team was not enjoying the best of spells, the centre-forward was always worth a goal.

He was top scorer for the club in eight successive seasons between 1968-75. In 1967-68, he notched 16 goals including a famous winner in a Scottish Cup replay against Rangers at Tynecastle.

Hearts went on to reach the Final that season but lost out 3-1 to a strong Dunfermline team inspired by Alex Edwards.

There were many landmarks in a career awash with goals but, in 1971, he scored two hat-tricks in three games – against Morton and then Aberdeen – and, two years later, he had the rare feat of scoring a hat-trick of penalties against Morton.

Ford also fondly recalls a hat-trick he scored against Partick Thistle in the 1973-74 season when the then Scotland manager Willie Ormond was an interested spectator in the stand.

Ormond selected Ford for the World Cup finals in Germany at the end of the season but there was stiff competition for places with Denis Law and Joe Jordan in the squad and the Hearts' player did not get a game.

However, he was capped three times for Scotland – against Czechoslovakia and West Germany from the substitutes' bench and he started the Home International Championship game against Wales.

He also played his part in guiding Hearts to the Final of the short-lived Texaco Cup – a competition contested between teams from England and Scotland who had missed out on Europe – in 1971 when they lost to Wolverhampton Wanderers.

It was a competition that Hearts seemed to enjoy as they had a memorable aggregate win over Tottenham, after they lost the first leg 3-1 at White Hart Lane and won the return 4-1.

Hearts had a useful side in 1973-74 and led the League for the first couple of months with Ford forming a decent partnership with Drew Busby. During that season, Ford scored 29 goals but Hearts could not sustain the title challenge as injuries and suspensions caught up with them.

Ford played under a number of managers at Tynecastle and obviously had the utmost respect for Tommy Walker, although it was always going to be difficult for him to maintain the level of success that the team enjoyed in the 1950s and early 1960s.

John Harvey, the respected trainer at the club, inherited the managerial reins and Ford also played under Bobby Seith and John Hagart. There had not been much investment in the playing side of the club in the seventies and Ford could see it was a club in decline when he left.

Ford spent 12 years at Tynecastle and scored a total of 188 goals in 436 matches but left in May 1976 to play for a short spell at Falkirk. He missed out on playing in the 1976 Final against Rangers, which Hearts also lost, as he was absent for a large part of that season because of a serious knee injury.

He was instrumental in helping Wallace Mercer take control of the club when it looked as if it could go out of business and his influence ensured that Mercer had the support to put the club back on an even keel.

Ford spent time as a radio sports analyst with former Hearts' team-mate Alan Gordon and, a professional photographer, he now runs the Donald Ford Gallery in South Queensferry.

1964-65-1975-76
Appearances 436
Goals 188

not lose a fourth until the dying embers of the game. It did not escape the notice of Hearts' fans that, although there was a two-goal deficit to claw back again, it was a better result than Hearts had obtained in Leipzig. But any over-enthusiasm was misplaced as Hearts found themselves outclassed in the return leg in Edinburgh in front of 25,000 fans. Hearts were 2-0 down at half-time and Hamburg went on to win 4-1 to go through comfortably on aggregate with Gibson providing the only moment of joy with his consolation goal.

The exit came just a week after Celtic had ended Hearts' League Cup interest with a 2-1 semi-final win at Hampden when Kenny Dalglish scored twice in response to an early opener from Brown but it was a bad-tempered tie with Prentice later sent off.

However, if Hearts had been keeping good company in the Cup competitions at home and abroad, their League form was requiring some attention. The nature of the Premier Division meant that if you were not challenging for the title, you were effectively involved in the relegation dogfight. By the turn of the year it was obvious Hearts were not going to dispute the title with Celtic and Rangers or the emerging Aberdeen and Dundee United. Three successive defeats in the February – to Celtic, Kilmarnock and Motherwell – left Hearts in no doubt that they were in a predicament. A Scottish Cup run where they reached the semi-final against Rangers rather put a false gloss on things but there was to be no Final appearance this time with Colin Jackson and Sandy Jardine scoring in a 2-0 win at Hampden to book a place in the Final.

By this stage, Hearts were in the middle of a six-game losing streak and facing up to the harsh reality that they could be relegated for the first time in their history. A costly 2-1 home defeat in early April by fellow relegation candidates Ayr United was painful to endure and when Hearts lost at home to Rangers, it was significant that many fans stayed away. The proud traditions of the club offered no protection and, although Hearts managed to avoid defeat in their final five matches and won two of their last three, there was to be no escapology act.

Hearts needed wins and not draws and a 2-2 draw at Kilmarnock proved the final nail in the coffin. Haggart resigned as manager a few days later and there

was to be a major clear-out at the end of the season with players such as Cruickshank, Clunie, Aird and Kay all released. There was to be no easy route back to the top for Hearts.

Indeed, there followed a period where Hearts flitted between the First and the Premier Divisions – seemingly too good for the lower League but not good enough for the top ten. It was not until season 1983-84 when the club was under new ownership and Alex MacDonald had brought some stability as manager that the club could start to contemplate regularly competing for major honours again.

Relegation had hit everyone hard but there was some degree of optimism that Hearts' time in Division One would not be prolonged. A new, and experienced, manager had been appointed shortly after relegation was confirmed with Willie Ormond, one of the Famous Five across at Hearts' arch-rivals Hibs, taking over the reins. Ormond had not long previously taken Scotland to the World Cup finals for the first time in 16 years and was unlucky not to get the national team past the group stages as they missed out on goal difference after an undefeated campaign against Zaire, Brazil and Yugoslavia.

In spite of his association with the green half of Edinburgh, his appointment was warmly welcomed and it was thought an imaginative appointment. Ormond had enjoyed a successful stint previously at St Johnstone. There was no doubting Hearts were favourites to win the First Division but there were early warning signs: a 2-2 draw with Dumbarton in the season's opener and defeats by Hamilton, Morton and Montrose in a dismal October. But there was a second round League Cup win over Morton in spite of the fact that they were beaten 2-0 at Cappielow (a 3-0 home win in which Eamonn Bannon scored twice enough to carry Hearts through).

But a run of nine wins in 11 League games through November to January put Hearts back on course for promotion. There was an early Christmas present for the fans with a 7-0 demolition of Arbroath at Gayfield with Willie Gibson and Drew Busby both helping themselves to hat-tricks. The belief was growing that Hearts were still a Premier Division side in First Division clothing and that belief was aided by a run to the semi-finals of the League Cup.

In a dramatic quarter-final with Dundee United, Hearts came back from a 3-1 first-leg defeat to square the tie at 3-3 with a 2-0 win at Tynecastle (future captain Walter Kidd getting his first goal for the club) and, after extra-time did not prove decisive, it was left to the lottery of penalty kicks but Hearts clinched a place in the last four by squeezing through 4-3 in the shoot-out.

Celtic awaited in the Hampden semi-final on the first day of March and, although Hearts gave a good account of themselves, goals from Joe Craig and George McCluskey before half-time put Celtic through. The loss came hard on the heels of a shock Scottish Cup exit at the hands of Dumbarton. Hearts had drawn at Boghead but lost the replay 1-0 at home on another frustrating night for the home supporters.

But Hearts at least seemed to have tightened up in defence and strengthened their promotion bid and it was to be their last defeat that season. A run of 23 unbeaten League games – stretching back to a 2-0 loss to East Fife in mid-November – meant Hearts were always in the promotion picture. It was a three-horse race alongside Morton and Dundee and there was a significant 1-0 win at Morton in March. But, typically for Hearts, the issue was not decided until the final game of the season after they had dropped points to Montrose and Queen of the South in the final run-in. Morton were already assured of the title but Hearts had to beat Arbroath at Gayfield to avoid the possibility of being overtaken for the second promotion place by Dundee.

If Hearts had enjoyed a seven-goal win on the same patch earlier in the season, there was no sign of a swagger to them that day. A certain Albert Kidd, who was to prove a more painful thorn in the flesh for Dundee a few years later, threatened to ruin the afternoon with a couple of efforts that came close for Arbroath. But Hearts came through an anxious afternoon when Bannon headed what proved to be the only goal in the first half. The fears amongst their supporters that they would come to grief on the final day of a season again came to nothing.

So Hearts were back in the Premier Division but it was to be a difficult step up. Successive defeats by Aberdeen and Celtic in their opening two games where Hearts leaked a total of eight goals and scored only once was a clear warning to them that the environment was much tougher than in Division One. The first win did not arrive until near the end of September when a Malcolm Robertson goal was enough to beat Motherwell at Fir Park. There were some glimmers of hope – Hearts beat both Aberdeen and Celtic in October and followed up with a 2-1 win at Easter Road – but a calamitous collapse at the end of the season meant the stay in the top flight was a short one.

Hearts had sold Bannon to Chelsea in January, a move that was foolhardy with the benefit of hindsight. In early April, it still looked as if Hearts could survive as they put together wins over Dundee United and Motherwell but there followed three consecutive home defeats (to Partick Thistle, Dundee United and Celtic) and there was to be no recovery. Hearts lost their last ten League games and scored just two goals in the process and, by the end of the campaign, apathy had set in with just 2,700 turning up for the final home game against Morton. Hearts finished 11 points short of safety with just eight wins in total in the 36-game campaign. In the League Cup, Hearts were knocked out 7-2 on aggregate by Morton and, in the Scottish Cup, there was a painful 2-1 quarter-final loss to endure against Hibs at Easter Road.

Hearts were going nowhere fast and, although Ormond remained in charge, there was another haemorrhage of players at the end of the season with long servants such as Jim Brown and Drew Busby among the casualties.

Although the club was clearly in some financial difficulties and there was little money for Ormond to spend on new players, they made a bright start to life back in the First Division and won their opening five League games. But then Hearts hit another run of inconsistency and there were defeats at the hands of Raith Rovers, Motherwell and Hamilton. Even in the games Hearts won, the performances were far from convincing and, although they shared the leadership of the League with Airdrie at the time, Ormond was sacked in early January a few days after a 3-3 draw with Clydebank.

Alex Rennie, Ormond's assistant, took over as caretaker but Hearts needed a fresh approach and, by early March, former Newcastle United and Scotland defender Bobby Moncur was appointed as the man to guide the club into a bright, new era.

Frank Liddell, scorer of some vital goals for Hearts. In April 1980 he scored the goal which have Hearts promotion, against Berwick Rangers, and followed up that with the goal which clinched the championship title, against Airdrieonians.

His first task was to take the First Division leaders to Ibrox to face Rangers in a Scottish Cup quarter-final and, although Hearts were dismissed 6-1, they had played encouragingly in the first half and had led through an own goal from Tom Forsyth. It left Moncur and Hearts to concentrate fully on the League and their attempt to get straight back to the Premier Division. A dozen games remained and there was no adverse reaction from the Rangers' defeat with Hearts keeping a clean sheet in four of their next five games. There was a home loss to promotion rivals Ayr United but Hearts secured their place back in the Premier Division with a 1-1 draw against Berwick Rangers. It left them playing Airdrie in the title decider at Tynecastle and a late goal from Frank Liddell gave Moncur's side the necessary 1-0 victory to go up as champions. Although Hearts spent four seasons in Division One in the late 1970s and early 1980s, this was to be the only occasion they went up as champions.

Moncur went for experience in his bid to establish Hearts in the top League and midfield player Alex MacDonald, 32, was signed for £30,000 from Rangers,

Hearts, First Division champions in 1980. Back row (left to right): Walter Kidd, Cammy Fraser, John Brough, Thomson Allan, Ronnie McLafferty, Grant Tierney, David Scott. Middle: Bobby Masterton, Robert Stewart, Graham Shaw, Pat McShane, Colin More, Frank Liddell, Des O'Sullivan, Derek O'Connor. Front: Peter Johnstone, Gordon Marr, Ian Black, Kenny McLeod, Jim Jefferies, Willie Gibson, Malcolm Robertson, Francis Farmer, Lawrie Tierney.

Hearts staff for the new Premier League season of 1980-81. Back row (left to right): Alfie Conn, Robert Stewart, Colin More, Craig Robertson, Ian Westwater, John Brough, Ronnie McLafferty, Gary Mackay, Frank Liddell, Jim Docherty, Jim Denny. Middle: Tony Ford (assistant manager), Bobby Moncur (manager), Walter Kidd, David Bowman, Chris Robertson, Stuart Gauld, Pat McShane, Stewart Porter, Bobby Masterton, Scott Maxwell, Steve Hamilton, Andy Stevenson (physiotherapist), Ian Brown (reserve-team coach). Front: Archie White, Malcolm Robertson, Gordon Marr, Derek O'Connor, Jim Jefferies, Cammy Fraser, David Scott, Willie Gibson, Paul O'Brien.

It was clear that more change was needed. Willie Gibson, Derek O'Connor, Jim Jefferies and Malcolm Robertson – who were all great servants to the club – were nearing the end of their careers. Hearts finished bottom of the Premier Division at the end of the season, had been bundled out of the Scottish Cup after a replay with Morton and had lost a lamentable 71 goals.

Clearly, there was a gulf between the First Division and top League and Hearts – relegated three times in five years – needed to do more than paper over the cracks. What Moncur had shown a willingness to do in his first season (and it was to prove a shrewd investment for the future) was to introduce two 16-year-olds, Dave Bowman and Gary Mackay. He was also to sign another promising young player who had been attracting an increasing amount of interest for the number of goals he was scoring at schoolboy level – John Robertson.

which was to prove a significant buy, and former Rangers and Celtic forward Alfie Conn and Motherwell defender Willie McVie were both signed on free transfers.

In spite of the new blood, it was another difficult season for Hearts – there was an early League Cup exit at the hands of First Division Ayr United and the League was a constant struggle. Early wins over St Mirren and Kilmarnock gave false hope and Hearts did not win a League game for over two months and when that record was finally broken – a 2-0 win over Kilmarnock at Tynecastle in early December – there followed a miserable run of another 12 games without a win bonus for the players. Remarkably it ended with a 2-1 home victory over Rangers but by then it was too late to turn the tide. There followed four defeats on the trot for the loss of a total of 15 goals with Celtic scoring six without reply on All Fool's Day.

Hearts had slipped badly since the heady days of the late 1950s and early 1960s, but few realised how badly. The financial situation was dire and, for a club that prided itself in its history, Hearts were well short of the required standards. There was no money to invest in the transfer market and, while there was some promise in the young reserve players breaking through, that promise could come to nothing if results dented their confidence. It was clear that Hearts were in deep crisis and there was still a slow, painful road to recovery. Indeed, matters were to get worse before they were better.

A Change In Fortunes

THE summer of 1981 was to prove a pivotal one for the club. For the club to survive, it was obvious that major change was needed from top to bottom. The then chairman of the club, Archie Martin, was honest enough to accept this and in order to attract fresh money into the club, he persuaded the shareholders to open up the club and create 350,000 new £1 shares. Kenny Waugh, an Edinburgh bookmaker who was later to gain control of Hibernian, and Wallace Mercer, a local property developer put together rival consortia. Waugh made an initial bid of £255,000 for controlling interest in the club but Mercer, who admitted that he had given little initial thought to getting involved, was prompted to make a counter bid by former Hearts centre-forward Donald Ford.

Mercer tabled a first bid of £265,000 but then raised another £85,000 through the consortium to cover all of the £350,000 shares. At this, Waugh raised his offer to £350,000. It was left to the board to decide on who was the better prospect for the future of the club.

On 3 June 1981, the board voted on which bid to go with and, of the board, directors Alex Naylor and Iain Watt went for Mercer and Martin and Bert McKim for Waugh which meant that former player Bobby Parker had the casting vote. He went with Mercer and the 34-year-old property developer won control on a 3-2 majority. In some ways, he was the reluctant owner and had it not been for Ford's influence, he would not have contemplated getting involved, he was to state later.

As Mercer outlined in Mike Aitken's book *Heart to Heart* some years later, "I'd been watching Hearts for a few years and was very saddened by what I saw. My wife Anne and I had bought some shares just as a gesture. We knew that Hearts were hitting the skids and that the club's bank had made this statement to the effect that unless they had a flotation to raise a substantial amount through £1 shares, then the club could be closed…The last thing on my mind was to get involved in the ego trip of buying, running or managing a football club. Apart from anything else, I didn't have any experience in football whatsoever."

Yet if Mercer was shy at coming forward initially, he was to prove no shrinking violet. It was apparent from the start that he had a talent for courting the press and no-one could ever accuse him of being dull during the tenure at Hearts.

There were difficult decisions to be taken and Mercer applied business principles to running a football club, without doubt because it was the only way he knew how. It was clear from the outset there was no magic wand to be waved but Mercer was not slow to make changes. Out went Martin and Naylor became the new chairman with Mercer filling the vice-chairman role in spite of the fact that he had control of the reins.

Also, Mercer and team manager Moncur did not hit it off and the manager's chair was vacant again

Hearts first-team squad pictured in 1981-82. Back row (left to right): Walter Borthwick (coach), Stewart MacLaren, Derek Addison, Walter Kidd, Roddy MacDonald, Henry Smith, Derek O'Connor, Willie Pettigrew, Chris Robertson, Brian McNeill, Andy Stevenson (physiotherapist). Front: Peter Marinello, Peter Shields, Pat Byrne, Tony Ford (manager), Alex MacDonald, Alex Hamill, Derek Strickland.

when Moncur resigned within a matter of weeks ("I didn't like the cut of his jib and I was delighted when he resigned," Mercer famously once said). Dundee United's Jim McLean and Leicester City's Jock Wallace were the two favoured options but both rejected Mercer's overtures and it was a 36-year-old Englishman Tony Ford who took over. But the new owner was to later confide that he saw this as only a stop-gap arrangement.

There was a budget for new players before the start of the season and centre-half Roddy MacDonald became Hearts' record signing at the time when he arrived from Celtic for £55,000. For much less money (just £2,000 in fact), goalkeeper Henry Smith arrived from Leeds United where he had been in a strong goalkeeping contingent at Elland Road which included David Harvey, David Stewart, John Lukic and David Seaman, who were all to play international football at some stage (Smith also went on to represent his country). A sum of £30,000 was paid to Dundee for rugged midfield player Stewart McLaren and a new side was starting to take shape.

The new season started well with Hearts beating Aberdeen, who had finished second in the previous season's Premier Division, and another top ten club Airdrie, in their League Cup section with Chris Robertson scoring the only goal in both matches. There was also a 1-1 draw with fellow relegated side Kilmarnock but all the early good work came to naught as Hearts lost to all three sides in the return games and finished third in the qualifying group to miss out on the later stages of the competition. So at least the way was clear to concentrate on the League and their attempt to climb out of division one.

It was to be another season of highs and lows. The club spent £110,000 – another record – to bring striker Willie Pettigrew from Dundee United and at least Hearts were starting to think big again. There was an early home defeat by old rivals Kilmarnock which was ultimately to prove costly but there were encouraging signs with wins over St Johnstone, Queen of the South and Raith Rovers in successive matches. Pettigrew was paying his way with some valuable goals and there was an imaginative signing of former Hibs and Arsenal favourite Peter Marinello, who had been playing in America.

But, by Christmas time, inconsistency had dogged Hearts to such an extent that they were looking for another manager. Ford had been given little chance to turn it around and a 3-1 defeat at Dumbarton followed by a stumbling 1-1 draw with Queen's Park meant he was dismissed early in December. Hearts were rudderless yet came through a tricky first round Scottish Cup tie 4-1 at East Stirling only to crash 3-0 at home to promotion rivals and League leaders Motherwell a couple of days later. At this juncture, it looked as if Hearts would toil to win promotion but it was to be in the Scottish Cup that one of their darkest days occurred in mid-February.

With the club needing the money a cup run would generate, Hearts fell at home to Forfar when Steve Hancock scored the only goal of a second-round tie at Tynecastle. The result brought home the harsh reality of Hearts' plight and, perhaps the only saving grace, was that there were not much more than 5,000 Hearts fans there to witness it. The scars would take a long time to heal.

Less than half that number turned up for the next home game against Queen of the South at Tynecastle such was the apathy directed towards the team. Alex MacDonald had been appointed player-coach in the wake of the Forfar disgrace and, though no-one could know it at the time, the appointment was to prove an inspired one. There was also a debut in that Queen of the South game for John Robertson, who was to go on and become such a favourite with the crowd.

Hearts won the game 4-1 with Robertson coming on as a substitute and getting the chance to play alongside his older brother Chris up front and realise one of his ambitions. There were plenty more to realise for the young striker in the years ahead but, such were the many changes around Tynecastle in the weeks and months ahead, that this was the only occasion that the brothers played together for Hearts. Chris Robertson did manage to get on the scoresheet that day but his young brother would have to wait a few months for his first goal in maroon.

Under Macdonald, there were some encouraging early results – 3-0 and 4-0 respectively against Ayr United and Raith Rovers and then a 5-1 win over

Queen of the South. Of course, being the kind of season it was, there were also mishaps and a 2-1 defeat at Clydebank in late March put another question-mark against promotion. But there followed seven successive wins where Hearts scored 19 goals for the loss of only three but, not for the first time, it all went wrong for Hearts as they reached out for promotion. With Motherwell having taken the title, there was a 5-2 home defeat by Dumbarton and then a fraught 0-0 draw at Kilmarnock in the penultimate game of the season when victory would have assured a Premier Division return.

Chris Robertson gets airborne to score against St Johnstone at Tynecastle in April 1982.

The final home game against champions Motherwell was another sorry affair. A crowd of almost 15,000 packed Tynecastle knowing that a draw would probably be enough to clinch second place ahead of Kilmarnock. As it transpired, Motherwell greedily helped themselves to both points with a headed goal from Willie Irvine. There was trouble amongst the Hearts supporters in the second half and Mercer went down from the directors' box in an appeal for calm. Hearts missed out by a point and Kilmarnock, with a 6-0 win over Queen of the South, plundered the promotion place. Scarves were thrown on to the Tynecastle pitch at the end by disgruntled fans as Hearts were consigned to the First Division for another year.

Even in the gloom, there was some light, however. Mercer was later to recount that the depth of feeling he witnessed first-hand that afternoon convinced him that there was a passion amongst the fans that, if

Hearts squad which won promotion in 1982. Back row (left to right): Walter Borthwick (coach), Willie Pettigrew, Roddy MacDonald, Henry Smith, John Brough, Walter Kidd, Stewart MacLaren, Alan Rae (physiotherapist). Front: Alex MacDonald (manager), Peter Marinello, Peter Shields, Gerry McCoy, David Bowman, Gary Mackay, Pat Byrne, Sandy Jardine (assistant manager). The trophy is the East of Scotland Shield.

It was time to take stock on and off the park. Mercer sold some of his shareholding in the club to Lanarkshire businessman Douglas Park and bookmaker Pilmar Smith also joined the board. Mercer, who now held a 43 per cent shareholding, became chairman and there was a major fillip to the club on the park with former Scotland defender Sandy Jardine joining as assistant player-manager to MacDonald on a free transfer from Rangers. But the financial problems would not go away and when Derek Addison was sold to St Johnstone for £55,000, the money went straight to the bank to pay off creditors. Hearts, who were in debt to Dundee United to the tune of £165,000 after signing Addison and Pettigrew, were subsequently banned from buying players by the SFA for failing to settle their debt to United.

In many ways, season 1982-83 was another crunch year for the club. Had promotion not been attained, then Hearts would surely have resorted to part-time football and the debt situation meant that there were grave concerns for the future of the club. There was early promise – Hearts rattled seven goals past Clyde in a League Cup tie with Pettigrew scoring four (it was Hearts' highest tally in a game for almost five years) and Hearts won their League Cup section ahead of Premier Division Motherwell.

MacDonald and Jardine were building a side that had a good blend of youth and experience. Dave Bowman and Gary Mackay were featuring regularly and, in addition to the management pairing, Hearts also signed former Rangers and Scotland winger Willie Johnston, who had been playing with Vancouver Whitecaps. There was a more robust nature about the team and, while they lost their opening League Cup game at Motherwell, Hearts then went 13 matches without defeat before losing narrowly to Raith Rovers in early October. There was also a good run in the League Cup for the fans to cheer with Premier Division

By season 1983-84, when the club was under new ownership, Alex MacDonald (above) brought some stability as manager.

channelled in the right direction, would provide the cornerstone for recovery. MacDonald, too, had shown himself to be an astute manager and it was just the frustrating habit Hearts had of contriving to mess things up in the Final few days of a season that had proved costly. But this had not been the first occasion, nor would it be the last.

Hearts in the 1983 close season. Back row (left to right): Walter Borthwick (coach), David Bowman, Derek O'Connor, Roddy MacDonald, Henry Smith, Stewart Gauld, Stuart MacLaren, Jimmy Bone, John Binnie (reserve-team coach). Front: Alex MacDonald (manager), Donald Park, John Robertson, Walter Kidd, George Cowie, Willie Johnston, Gary Mackay, Sandy Jardine (assistant manager).

St Mirren beaten in a two-leg quarter-final to set up a semi-final measuring stick against Rangers.

Hearts gave a good account of themselves in both legs and, after losing 2-0 at Ibrox, Hearts did well in the second leg at Tynecastle but went down 2-1 with a late strike by Derek Johnstone settling the issue in Rangers' favour.

But there was a new optimism around Tynecastle. Almost 19,000 had turned up at the second leg at Tynecastle – the biggest crowd the stadium had held for over four years – and Wallace Mercer's ability to sell the club off the field had led to a shirt sponsor for the first time.

The defeat by Rangers did not distract Hearts from the League. Another ten games went past without a loss and there was a memorable New Year's Day win over title rivals St Johnstone when a healthy crowd of 14,554 turned up to witness Pettigrew scoring the only goal. Hearts were on course for promotion but there were still some stutters to come – successive League defeats by Partick Thistle and Dunfermline caused

some concern – but there was a more settled look to the team (MacDonald was only to use 17 players in the entire campaign).

Hearts also reached the quarter-finals of the Scottish Cup but the run came to an abrupt end at Parkhead with a 4-1 defeat by Celtic in a game where Willie Johnston was sent off for the 19th time in an eventful career. It left Hearts to concentrate on their priority – getting promotion.

John Robertson, by this stage, was enjoying his first extended run in the first-team and, alongside Willie Pettigrew and Derek O'Connor, was helping himself to a share of the goals. There were hat-tricks for the 19-year-old to celebrate against Queen's Park, Partick Thistle and Dunfermline and, although he also managed to score trebles in cup competitions, it was a curious footnote to his career that he never managed a Premier Division hat-trick.

Hearts faltered again with the finishing-line in sight and, with Clydebank and Partick Thistle also in the promotion picture with Hearts and St Johnstone, there was a worry for the Edinburgh side when they went for four matches in April without a League win. But, with two games remaining, Hearts needed just two points to guarantee a Premier return. This time, there was no slipping up and a 4-0 win at Dumbarton with John Robertson scoring twice and Gary Mackay also on the scoresheet confirmed Hearts would be rejoining the top League. The club celebrated by offering tickets at just £1 for the final League game against Hamilton at Tynecastle which, although Hearts won 2-0, was not enough to prevent St Johnstone, who had won their final game against Dunfermline, winning the First Division by a single point.

But the contrast with events 12 months previous were marked. MacDonald and Jardine had moulded together a team that was playing with a new assurance and the home attendances were such that only four other teams in Scotland boasted better. The Tynecastle side were also scoring goals again – 79 in the League – and it was only the Old Firm that ended their cup campaigns. What is more, there was a feeling – later to prove accurate – that Bowman, Mackay and Robertson were all future Scotland international players. This time the step up did not seem quite as steep.

MacDonald had no room for manoeuvre on the transfer market but he brought back 30-year-old Donald Park, who had been with Partick Thistle, and also secured former Scotland forward Jimmy Bone, who had first made his name at Firhill. Bone was to prove a perfect foil for John Robertson up front and Robertson was later to admit that he was one of the guiding influences on his career. Yet, at 34, Bone's days of playing up front at the top level were clearly numbered.

With Sandy Jardine, Willie Johnston, Park and MacDonald himself listed for the opening Premier game away to St Johnstone, Hearts were soon to attract the tag of "Dad's Army".

Yet the joke was on the other teams in the division as Hearts beat St Johnstone in their first game courtesy of a solitary goal from Bone and went on to lead the League by winning their first five games. Hibs were beaten 3-2 in a memorable encounter at Tynecastle when Robertson scored two and laid on the other for Bone. Rangers were also beaten in Edinburgh (Robertson, Bone and Alex MacDonald

getting the goals) and it was not until the first day of October that Hearts tasted defeat in the League for the first time (0-2 at home to Aberdeen).

Yet, while enjoying such a good run in the League, Hearts were taken to a replay and penalties by Cowdenbeath in the League Cup qualifying round before progressing. However, there was a latent bonus in that manager MacDonald had a couple of chances to look at a promising young player in the opposing ranks, one Craig Levein who went on to play in defence for both Hearts and Scotland and was later to fill the manager's chair at Tynecastle.

It was evident there was a new togetherness about Hearts that seemed to stretch from the boardroom to the dressing-room. MacDonald was repaying the faith shown in him by Wallace Mercer and, in turn, the "old guard" that the manager had brought to the club were all putting in the extra mile to make it work on the park. On a shoestring budget and with a group of players who many felt were over the hill, MacDonald had established Hearts in the top League and had ensured that there would not be another season battling against the drop.

Hearts failed to get through their League Cup section with Rangers topping the group but, in the League, they were holding their own. There was the satisfaction of going through the season undefeated by their city neighbours Hibs (the three remaining games were drawn) and Hearts were proving difficult to beat. Although they only won two of their final 11 League games, they only lost one (to Aberdeen) and they

Donald Park, in his second spell with Hearts after four years with Partick Thistle, heads his side's second goal in the 2-2 draw against St Johnstone at Tynecastle in April 1984.

Tynecastle pictured in May 1984, from the Gorgie Road terraces.

plus points in the season. Robertson, in his first Premier campaign, had contributed a splendid tally of 20 goals and Bone had also weighed in with nine. Levein had been brought from Cowdenbeath for just £35,000 and, after an initial spell in midfield, he was to slot into the defence alongside the experienced Jardine to hasten his progress. There was also, of course, a European draw to look forward to that summer. Hearts had only won ten League games that season (the same number as relegated St Johnstone) but had also only lost ten.

finished a respectable fifth, a couple of places above Hibs and 13 points clear of relegation. A 1-1 draw in their third-last game against Celtic at Tynecastle clinched a UEFA Cup berth with Willie Johnston coming off the substitutes' bench to score. It was eight years since Hearts had played in Europe and this was a moment for the fans to cherish after such a long period of instability.

There was a fourth round exit in the Scottish Cup to Dundee United at Tannadice but there were many

The European draw had paired Hearts with Paris St Germain and it proved a timely lesson for Alex MacDonald's side as they were outclassed 4-0 in the first round first leg UEFA Cup match in France. Robertson scored twice in the return at Tynecastle as Hearts restored some pride with a 2-2 draw but it was

Hearts squad on the eve of the 1984-85 season. Back row (left to right): Walter Borthwick (coach), Stewart MacLaren, Derek O'Connor, Craig Levein, Roddy MacDonald, Henry Smith, Brian Whittaker, Jimmy Bone, David Bowman, John Binnie (reserve-team coach). Front: Alex MacDonald (manager), Donald Park, Kenny Black, John Robertson, Walter Kidd, Gary Mackay, George Cowie, Willie Johnston, Sandy Jardine (assistant manager).

clear that Europe was to be a steep learning curve for Hearts. On the domestic front, Hearts had enjoyed another early derby win over Hibs and progressed to the semi-finals of the League Cup when Roddy MacDonald scored the only goal of a quarter-final tie with Dundee.

Jim McLean's Dundee United were the opposition in the two-leg semi-final and Hearts went out 5-2 on aggregate after losing a bad-tempered first leg at Tynecastle 2-1 when Dave Bowman and United's Dave Narey were sent off for exchanging punches. Robertson had netted in a 1-0 win over Rangers in early October and, a couple of weeks later, the young striker had another partner-in-crime up front when Sandy Clark became the latest former Rangers player to find his way to Tynecastle. Clark made a scoring debut in a 3-2 win at Morton (Robertson was also on target, along with another ex-Ranger Kenny Black).

The Clark-Robertson combination clicked from the start, with the former's heading ability laying on scraps for the voracious Robertson to thrive on. Hearts eventually finished seventh in the League and missed out on European qualification but again it was a season absent from relegation worries.

There were some highlights along the way: another unbeaten season against Hibs, a 6-0 Scottish Cup win over Inverness Caledonian when Gary Mackay scored four times and another victory over Rangers late in the season at Tynecastle. But there was a narrow Scottish Cup quarter-final defeat by Aberdeen after a replay. Hearts had led for most of the first game at Tynecastle only for Eric Black to score a late equaliser and Billy Stark decided the tie at Pittodrie after Hearts' defender Roddy MacDonald was sent off. The season ended rather flatly with five successive defeats and it was time for Alex MacDonald to take stock of his squad.

MacDonald himself had been restricting himself to the substitutes' bench towards the end of the campaign and Jimmy Bone, Willie Johnston and Derek O'Connor had departed. John Colquhoun was the most significant signing of the close season – at a bargain £75,000 from Celtic – as Hearts embarked on what was to be a landmark season. There was no warning of what was to follow in the months ahead as Hearts opened with a creditable 1-1 draw at home to Celtic (Colquhoun repaying some of his transfer fee with the

goal) and then there followed a crushing 6-2 defeat at St Mirren.

August was a month of mixed fortunes as Hearts scraped through a third round League Cup match against Stirling Albion 2-1 after extra-time and there had been a 3-1 defeat by Rangers at Ibrox. At least Hearts kept up their supremacy over Hibs with a 2-1 win at Tynecastle when, for once, Robertson was not on the scoresheet and it was left to Colquhoun and Sandy Clark to get the goals. September was even less noteworthy as they tumbled out of the League Cup 1-0 to Aberdeen and suffered League defeats at Aberdeen, Motherwell and Clydebank; the last two clubs were ultimately to suffer relegation that season.

Yet after that 1-0 defeat at Clydebank at the end of September, Hearts put together a terrific run and were unbeaten for the next seven months, League and Cup. The Robertson-Clark pairing was at its most potent in the 1985-86 season but opposing defences also had the pace of Colquhoun to worry about and the probing runs of Gary Mackay, who had a fine season. Hearts also had unsung players like Neil Berry and Kenny Black who played above themselves when the chips were down. Defensively, Sandy Jardine and Craig Levein were a solid partnership and Henry Smith proved the most dependable of goalkeepers.

A win over Celtic in October thanks to a Robertson goal signalled a turn around in fortunes. Rangers were humbled 3-0 at Tynecastle in mid-November (Clark 2, Robertson) as Hearts grew in self-belief. To show this was not a freak result, Hearts went to Ibrox shortly after Christmas and returned with a 2-0 win courtesy of a brace from Colquhoun.

MacDonald's side took seven out of a possible eight points off Hibs that season and, as Hearts gathered pace in the League, so too did the Scottish Cup campaign. Rangers were beaten in a thrilling third-round tie at Tynecastle 3-2 in a game which saw Colin McAdam get his one and only goal for Hearts (Mackay and Robertson were the other marksmen that day). By the end of February, it was clear that Hearts intended to stick around for a while longer.

Eight successive victories then took Hearts to the brink of the League title and also into the Final of the Scottish Cup for the first time in ten years. Hamilton Accies (2-1) and St Mirren (4-1) had been taken care of in the Cup and it led to a semi-final against Dundee United at Hampden. Hearts had warmed up for the tie with another 3-1 (Robertson 2, Clark) win over a Rangers side who had slipped to mid-table. Hearts took a huge travelling support to Hampden in anticipation of a final place and they were not to be disappointed with Colquhoun scoring the only goal early in the game.

The clubs met again in League business at Tannadice a week later and this time Hearts produced one of their best displays of the season with a 3-0 victory in which Robertson scored two wonderful goals and Clark netted the other. Now, most people were convinced this would be Hearts' year and a League and Cup double was on the cards.

Hearts were, after all, five points clear of both Celtic, who admittedly had games in hand, and Dundee United now and required just four points from their last three games – against Aberdeen, Clyde-bank and Dundee. To all intents and purposes, the title race appeared to be over. Celtic were making a decent fist of it under manager Davie Hay but Hearts, who had surely learned a painful lesson from 1965, had their fate in their own hands. What is more, everyone appeared to believe it and the media were all but engraving the name "Heart of Midlothian" on the League trophy.

Yet Alex MacDonald, stubbornly refused to publicly acclaim his team as champions. When it was put to him after the Dundee United win, he flatly refused to accept that the title had been secured on Tayside. It proved to be a wise approach.

Television were convinced that Hearts' home game against Alex Ferguson's Aberdeen was effectively the title decider and so the game was switched to a Sunday for a live screening. But, under the spotlight, Hearts froze and trailed to a disputed penalty from Peter Weir for most of the game. Neither side created too many chances but Colquhoun came to Hearts' rescue with an equalising goal just three minutes from time and many felt that was the necessary point to take the title from Celtic's grasp. There would surely be no slip-ups in the final games against Clydebank and Dundee. After all, just three points (and more realistically, two, given their goal difference advantage over Celtic) would be enough now.

But Clydebank, who had won just two games away from home all season, proved stubborn opponents in that penultimate game. Over 20,000 fans packed into Tynecastle and there was a collective sigh of relief when Gary Mackay scored a superb individual goal late in the first half that proved sufficient for a 1-0 victory. Hearts were now undefeated in 31 matches, 27 of which were in the League and the silverware was all but nestling in the trophy room at Tynecastle. Celtic had moved to within two points by winning their games in hand but Hearts still held a four-goal advantage on goal difference.

This was the scenario on that final day of the Premier Division season: Hearts needed a point or a narrow defeat against Dundee at Dens Park to win the title for the first time since 1960 while hoping that Celtic did not stack up the goals in their final game against St Mirren at Love Street.

More than 10,000 Hearts supporters made the journey to Tayside and the title celebrations had begun even before the kick-off. Yet there had been concerns in the Hearts' dressing-room in the week leading up to the match. Brian Whittaker, John Colquhoun and Craig Levein had all been suffering from viruses and, while Whittaker and Colquhoun were both able to play; Levein was left at home, listening to the game on the radio. It was to prove as agonising an afternoon for him as it was for the legions who filled the terraces of Dens Park.

Levein's place went to the experienced Roddy MacDonald but, for only the fourth occasion that season, the rock-steady defensive partnership of Levein and Sandy Jardine had been torn asunder. The Hearts' team that afternoon was: Smith; Kidd, MacDonald, S Jardine, Whittaker, I. Jardine, Berry, G. Mackay, Colquhoun, Clark and Robertson with Kenny Black and Billy Mackay listed as substitutes.

Hearts had a strong early penalty claim turned down when Sandy Clark appeared to be fouled by Colin Hendry in the area but nothing was given. Still, Hearts looked assured and, with Dundee not giving them too many problems, a goalless draw was not the worst of outcomes for Alex MacDonald's side and indeed one he would have readily accepted.

Yet the news from Love Street was discouraging. Many fans had travelled with pocket radios to track events elsewhere and, by half-time in Paisley, Celtic had swept to a 4-0 lead. The fifth goal came not long into the second half and the restlessness on the Dens Park terraces now seemed to translate itself on to the field of play. Dundee, who still had an outside chance of winning a UEFA Cup place ahead of Rangers, looked the more relaxed team as the second half wore on and it became a case of Hearts digging in and hoping to hold out for the scoreless draw that would still leave them champions.

Yet it was the Dundee substitute Albert Kidd who was to decide the destination of the title. With barely seven minutes left, he took advantage of some slack marking at a corner to slam the ball past Henry Smith. There was no way back for Hearts and Kidd was later to add a solo second goal which was the final nail in the coffin.

The Hearts' bench were stunned by the events. Celtic had won the title on goal difference in the most unlikely of circumstances and tears flowed freely amongst the Hearts fans. Many stood on the terraces staring into space at the final whistle and this was a defeat that hurt deeply and none of the players, management or directors could believe it. This was to complete the rehabilitation of Hearts after MacDonald and Mercer had dragged them out of the First Division a few years previously. Instead, it was another sorry tale of glorious failure. Only Hearts could have surrendered the title in such a manner and there were inevitable comparisons with 1965.

The Scottish Cup Final against Aberdeen arrived just a week later and clearly Hearts, for all their talk in the build-up to the big match, were finding it hard to lift spirits after such an experience. Levein was back and there was a starting place for Black with Ian Jardine injured as Hearts lined up: Smith; Kidd, S. Jardine, Levein, Whittaker, G. Mackay, Berry, Black, Colquhoun, Clark and Robertson with Billy Mackay and George Cowie on the bench. Alex Ferguson's Aberdeen were: Leighton; McKimmie, McLeish, W. Miller, McQueen, Bett, Cooper, McMaster, Weir, McDougall and Hewitt; Subs: Stark, J. Miller.

John Hewitt opened the scoring for Aberdeen after just five minutes and it was an uphill battle for Hearts after that. Hewitt scored his second shortly after half-time and, although Neil Berry hit the crossbar for

Hearts midway through the second period, substitute Billy Stark finally killed the game off as a contest with Aberdeen's third goal. Walter Kidd was sent off late in the game when, already booked, he threw the ball at Frank McDougall as Hearts' frustrations at how the season had ended finally boiled over.

Yet, after the 3-0 defeat, Hearts fans remained to acknowledge what had been a memorable season when the club had gone to the brink and been within touching distance of the two biggest prizes in Scottish football. There was a rousing reception waiting for the team when they returned to a reception in an Edinburgh hotel as Hearts, even given the lack of silver polish, had become a big-time club again. They had finished the season 15 points better off than Rangers, who could only finish fifth, and even Ferguson's much-acclaimed Aberdeen were left trailing in the League.

Yet that season was to prove a watershed in the Scottish game. Rangers took immediate steps to ensure they would not be left trailing to such an extent again and brought in former Liverpool and Scotland midfielder Graeme Souness as their new player-manager and gave him a licence to spend money on the top British talent. It was to up the stakes in the Scottish game and, those that could not keep up, were to be left engulfed in the tidal wave. Yet Hearts had plenty to look forward to. MacDonald had forged a settled side who were capable of holding their own against the Old Firm and there was a UEFA Cup return in 1986-87 where Hearts were drawn to face Dukla Prague in the first round. Considering where the club was a few short years before, the transformation was remarkable.

The following season, there was an early setback when Hearts were knocked out of the League Cup unexpectedly at the hands of Montrose (2-0 at Tynecastle) but Hearts won the home leg of their European tie against Dukla Prague 3-2 with goals from Clark, Robertson and former English youth cap Wayne Foster, who had arrived in the summer from Preston North End on a free transfer.

It was one of MacDonald's traits as a manager that he was able to get the best out of bargain-basement players and the likes of Foster, Berry, Ian Jardine, Kenny Black and later Mike Galloway were all great servants to the club but obtained for next to nothing. Hearts went out of Europe on the away goals rule, however, when they lost 1-0 in the return in Prague in front of a meagre crowd of just 3,500, one of the lowest to watch Hearts in European competition.

The League campaign was a long one with the Premier Division stretched to 12 teams and involving 44 games which many felt was too taxing on the top players, especially if their team had extended runs in cup competitions and there was also international duty to consider.

There was a notable 1-0 victory over Celtic in December where Berry found the net and, the same month, Hearts scored 11 goals without reply against Hamilton (7-0) and Falkirk (4-0) but still no Premier Division hat-trick for John Robertson, who scored a double in each game. The win over Hamilton was Hearts' biggest win for nine years.

Hearts were to finish fifth in the League that season, just missing out on a European place, but there was a fine, if ultimately disappointing, run in the Scottish Cup again. It took Hearts three games to get past Kilmarnock in the third round but then there was a terrific 1-0 fourth round victory over Celtic with Robertson getting the all-important goal at Tynecastle.

Hearts made the semi-final after beating Motherwell 1-0 in a replay at Fir Park courtesy of John Colquhoun. St Mirren were the semi-final opponents and Hearts started the game as strong favourites. With both Old Firm teams out of the competition and Aberdeen also out, it looked as if it could finally be Hearts' year.

But they fell behind in the semi-final to a goal from Ian Ferguson in the first half and although Gary Mackay equalised, Hearts lost a late goal when former Celtic striker Frank McGarvey beat Henry Smith. It was a result that had been unexpected and St Mirren went on to lift the trophy for the first time since 1959 when Ferguson, now a sought-after commodity in the Scottish game and to end up at Ibrox before too long, scored the only goal of the Final against Dundee United.

The 1987-88 League campaign started well for Hearts with only one defeat in the opening dozen games (0-1 to Celtic in Glasgow), although there was a quarter-final loss to Rangers (1-4) in the League Cup at Ibrox. The good run was ended by Hibs of all teams, 2-1 at Easter Road which was MacDonald's first loss in an Edinburgh derby as Hearts' manager.

With John Robertson finding the net with regularity (he scored 31 times that season), Hearts were stringing together some impressive results – 3-0 v Dundee United, 6-0 v St Mirren, 2-1 v Rangers were all achieved away from home – and if a revitalised Celtic were to finish champions, Hearts took great credit and satisfaction from edging out Rangers' expensively-assembled squad for second place.

Again, there was a great run in the Scottish Cup where Hearts lost only one goal in wins over Falkirk, Morton and Dunfermline en route to a semi-final against Celtic. A crowd of 65,886 were drawn to Hampden for the game and a freak goal from Whittaker put Hearts in the driving-seat in the second half and within sight of a second final appearance in three years. But calamity was to follow.

With just three minutes left, goalkeeper Smith dropped a corner at the feet of Celtic substitute Mark McGhee and he lashed in the equaliser. Shortly afterwards, Smith was badly at fault again as he dropped a McGhee header and Andy Walker scored the winning goal. It was another occasion when Hearts were dazzled as they approached silverware.

But Hearts, runners-up in two seasons out of three, had obviously turned it around both on and off the park and the disappointments had to be put in the context of where the club was six years previously. Now the club was able to invest in players of the ilk of Dave McPherson from Rangers and was making a profit off the field of play through some imaginative commercial ventures.

Yet there was a huge blow to Hearts fans when prize asset John Robertson, who had been haggling over his future for some months, was allowed to join Newcastle United at the end of the season for a fee of £750,000. The striker was keen to test himself in England but chairman Wallace Mercer took the flak for not settling a new deal with the player and keeping him at Tynecastle. Hearts re-invested the money by purchasing Eamonn Bannon and Iain Ferguson from Dundee United and it was a remoulded Hearts that started the 1988-89 season, which was now back to a ten-team top division and a 36-game format.

There remained a question mark over who would get the goals that Robertson had so frequently provided over the past few seasons and Ferguson gave an early response with a hat-trick in a 5-0 League Cup

John Robertson

FEW of the 512 spectators who witnessed John Robertson's first goal for Hearts – in a pre-season friendly against Blyth Spartans in the North-East of England – would anticipate that he would go on to etch his name on the history of the club.

Hearts have always prided themselves on unearthing great goalscoring talents such as Barney Battles, Willie Bauld, Jimmy Wardhaugh, Willie Wallace and Donald Ford, and Robertson deserves his place up there with the best of them.

Standing just 5ft 6ins, he was diminutive in stature, particularly given the demands of the Scottish game in the 1980s and 1990s but his scoring record in the Scottish Premier League was exceptional.

He was seemingly born to play for Hearts. When he did try his luck in England during a brief spell in Newcastle in 1988-89 (when Hearts reaped a record £750,000 for his services), it was not long before he returned with the Tynecastle club paying the same amount they received for him, also a club record spend.

Robertson went on to score a record 214 League goals for Hearts – a record that will stand the scrutiny of time. Curiously, there was never a Premier League hat-trick amongst them, although Robertson scored hat-tricks in the First Division and in the Scottish Cup. In 720 total appearances for the club, he scored 310 goals in all competitions.

Of course, the supreme irony – and there can be few who follow Edinburgh football who are not aware of it – was that he could have signed for Hearts' arch-rivals, Hibernian.

He had grown up on the east side of the city and was banging in goals for his primary school, Parson's Green, and then for Portobello High School. There was a queue of clubs throughout Britain keen to win his signature after he had been a consistent scorer at Under-15 level for Scotland Schoolboys.

Robertson had trials with Arsenal, Manchester City, Leeds United and Nottingham Forest but there was an obvious attraction to Hibs, his local team. However, the then chairman of the Easter Road club, Tom Hart, tried to exert undue pressure on him to sign when he famously told him during signing talks that if he walked out of his office without signing, then he would never be a Hibs player. The

young Robertson wanted to discuss the matter with his older brother Chris, then playing for Rangers, and the contract remained unsigned. In the event, Robertson signed a Schoolboy form for Hearts shortly afterwards, who were then managed by Bobby Moncur.

It was a period of great upheaval for the club but Moncur was building an impressive youth set-up and, alongside Robertson, Gary Mackay and Dave

Bowman were also recruited. Robertson made his debut for the club when he came on as a substitute for the final 17 minutes of a First Division match against Queen of the South on 17 February 1982. He joined his older brother Chris, who had signed for Hearts from Rangers, but those 17 minutes were as much as they played together in maroon.

Chris left the club at the end of that season and John did not get any more chances to impress until that pre-season tour of the North-East of England when he scored that first goal in a 3-0 win over Blyth Spartans.

Given Hearts' plight, he was thrown into the first-team ahead of schedule but it was evident that Robertson's natural instinct for goals would translate to the highest level of the game in Scotland and beyond. When Hearts returned to the Premier League under Alex MacDonald in 1983, Robertson wasted no time in endearing himself to the Hearts' fans by

scoring twice and laying on the other in a 3-2 win over Hibs at Tynecastle.

In the following years, he was to punish Hibs like no other Hearts player previously – perhaps it was a subconscious response to their former chairman's ill-advised statement – and he scored a record 27 goals against Hibs in Edinburgh derbies, never a season going by when he did not score at least one against them between 1983-84 and 1997-98.

Robertson's ratio of chance-taking was high and he could score with either foot as well as his head and he was a menace to many a defence. He relished the big-game occasion and a fair percentage of his goals came against the Old Firm. Robertson played under seven different managers at Tynecastle and, if at times he was rather unfairly criticised for his work-rate, he was consistently one of the first names on the team-sheet, whoever was in charge.

It was unfortunate that his time at the club coincided with such a long barren spell and, even when Hearts finally won a trophy with the Scottish Cup triumph of 1998, he was an unused substitute. Manager Jim Jefferies fully intended to bring him on in the closing minutes but due to the frantic finish with Rangers pressing for an equaliser, he was loathe to tinker with his team.

Nevertheless, there was finally a winner's medal to show for the long service he had given the club and he left Hearts that summer to join Second Division Livingston where he continued to find the net and helped them win promotion before finally hanging up his boots at the age of 35 to concentrate on coaching. In 2000-01, he helped coach Livingston to promotion to the Premier League and it would be no surprise if he returned to Hearts in some coaching capacity in future.

If the silverware was not forthcoming at Tynecastle, his goals earned him international recognition and he gained 16 Scotland caps and also showed he could find the net for his country with a decent return of goals.

**1980-81-1997-98
Appearances 720
Goals 310**

win over St Johnstone. The former Rangers striker was a class act at times but he was never going to replace Robertson in the eyes of the supporters although he did average a goal every two games in his two-and-a-half seasons at the club.

Bannon also proved a perceptive buy and his experience was vital as Hearts enjoyed their longest run yet in Europe. Domestically, Hearts reached the semi-finals of the League Cup where they lost 3-0 to Rangers at Hampden with Mark Walters scoring twice. Results on the home front were mixed and Hearts were languishing at the foot of the League, but there were nonetheless a few raised eyebrows when Sandy Jardine, who had been appointed co-manager with MacDonald the previous season, was dismissed from his post.

Jardine was a well respected figure in the game and had played over 1,000 top-class matches for Rangers and Hearts and the managerial team seemed to be working well, even given the lack-lustre start to the season. But chairman Mercer had proved that he was not shy at making painful decisions and it would not be his last such intervention as he sought to keep Hearts challenging for honours.

Yet, in spite of the upheaval, the team was progressing in Europe. St Patrick's of Dublin were beaten in the first round of the UEFA Cup on a 4-0 aggregate and, a goalless draw against Austria Vienna at Tynecastle in the first leg of the second round appeared to leave Hearts with too much to do. But Hearts came away with an unlikely 1-0 win in the return in Austria, even if Mike Galloway's winning goal had a huge suspicion of offside attached to it. It was a tactical victory for manager MacDonald who had delegated Jimmy Sandison to man-mark Herbert Prohaska, the Austrian international midfield player, and he did so with great success. Thomas Flogel, who was a youth signing with the Austrians at the time, watched the game from the stands, unaware that he was to join Hearts some years later.

It set up a third-round tie with little-known Yugoslavians Velez Mostar and an inspired first-leg performance saw Hearts virtually book their quarter-final berth with a 3-0 win, with Colquhoun, Galloway and Bannon supplying the goals.

But Mostar proved an uninviting place for the return and Hearts found the most intimidating atmosphere in the Bosnian town. Objects were thrown at the Hearts' dug-out during the game and Hearts players were subjected to a torrent of abuse during a tense tie.

Mike Galloway scores one of Hearts' three goals against Velez Mostar in the 1988-89 UEFA Cup at Tynecastle.

Hearts were a goal down at half-time but midfielder Galloway, who had shown his versatility by playing as a striker for most of the European campaign, scored the valuable away goal to clinch aggregate victory. Hearts lost the return 2-1 after leaking a late goal but went through comfortably on aggregate 4-2. What is more, Galloway had proved a sensation and had notched five goals on the European run and scored in every round.

There was word after the final whistle in Mostar that Wallace Mercer, who had stayed behind in Scotland, had agreed a deal with Newcastle to bring back favourite son John Robertson for a record fee of £750,000. It had proved a great night for Hearts. Robertson was straight back into the starting line-up for the following game against Rangers at Tynecastle where he was given a hero's welcome. Untypically, he did not manage to celebrate with a goal but Hearts still recorded a notable 2-0 victory with the goals coming from Galloway and Ferguson. Indeed, there were only four Robertson goals for the Hearts fans to cheer for the remainder of the season as the striker spent the latter part of the campaign on the bench. However, he did not break his habit of scoring against Hibs and one of his goal gave Hearts a 2-1 derby win on April Fool's Day that season.

But it was in Europe that Hearts were enjoying most consistency. They knew they were in the big-time when they drew top German side Bayern Munich in the quarter-finals as their European interest extended into the March. A crowd of 26,294 packed Tynecastle to see if Hearts could upset the German cracks and they were not disappointed as Ferguson scored a memorable goal when he curled a 25-yard shot over the Bayern wall and into the net following a short free-kick from recent signing Tosh McKinlay. It was enough to separate the teams.

The return game in the Olympic Stadium in Munich was just 17 minutes old when Klaus Augenthaler levelled the tie with one of his hallmark 30-yard shots which crashed into the roof of the net. But Hearts were making chances against a Bayern side that were at times careless. Colquhoun galloped away from their defence in one instance but clipped his shot marginally wide and the former Celtic winger later sent a header against a post. It all came to nothing however and Bayern defender Erland Johnsen scored the decisive second goal towards the end as the German side went through to the last four on a 2-1 aggregate. But it had been a bold European run and no Hearts side had gone, or has gone, further.

Hearts came back to a Scottish Cup quarter-final at Celtic where they were ousted 2-1 and finished the match with nine players when Alan McLaren and

Hearts threaten the Celtic goal during the fifth-round Scottish Cup tie at Parkhead in March 1989.

McKinlay were both sent off in separate incidents. Celtic also had defender Mick McCarthy red-carded. Hearts' season was virtually over and the League rather petered out with no European place and a disappointing final placing of sixth, their lowest for four years.

Hearts had a new striker to lead the line at the start of the 1989-90 with Yugoslavian Husref Musemic bought from Red Star Belgrade and he made himself immediately popular with the supporters when he headed the only goal of a drab August derby game against Hibs. Indeed, Musemic scored in three of the opening five games that season for Hearts but his work-rate left a lot to be desired and there were even rumours that MacDonald had signed the wrong player. Whatever, his spell at the club was to prove brief and he was to make only seven starts for the club before he departed back to his native country a few short months later on a free transfer (Hearts having originally parted with £200,000 for his services).

Scott Crabbe, who was a dyed-in-the-wool "Jambo" and was considerably shorter in stature than Musemic, had been making a name for himself and proved a hit with the fans for his pace, work-rate and eye for goal. He also linked well with Robertson and, with Colquhoun also terrorising defences, Hearts had a mobile, if diminutive, front trio which yielded almost 50 goals between them that season. There were even premature comparisons with the "Terrible Trio" and certainly one performance in the Scottish Cup fourth-round tie against Motherwell when the trio bagged all of the goals in a 4-0 win (Robertson 2, Crabbe and Colquhoun) was perhaps as complete as they put together.

The League season had started with a 3-1 home defeat by Celtic and there was also disappointment in a pulsating League Cup quarter-final with the Parkhead side at the end of the month when, after a 2-2 draw and extra-time, Hearts lost out on penalties with Celtic goalkeeper Pat Bonner proving the heart-breaker. But Hearts made steady progress and were scoring freely. Colquhoun scored a hat-trick in a 6-3 win over Dundee at Tynecastle in November where Robertson and Crabbe also netted.

Hearts' best spell came at the turn of the year. Robertson nabbed both goals in a 2-0 win over Hibs on New Year's Day and Hearts went on to run up five

successive wins, four of which were clean sheets as Henry Smith was proving one of the most reliable goalkeepers in the Premier Division. But a surprise 2-0 defeat at home to Dunfermline in mid-February was a setback, although Hearts put up a brave performance to secure a goalless draw at Ibrox in their next game against eventual champions Rangers.

The cup campaign was looking the most likely route for honours, especially after such an enthralling fourth round win over Motherwell but Hearts' hopes foundered on the turf of Pittodrie in the quarter-finals as they were dumped 4-1 by an Aberdeen side who went on to take the trophy.

It was to be Hearts' last defeat of that season and MacDonald's side finished the League campaign strongly as they were unbeaten in their final ten matches but they were just edged out of second place in the final table on goal difference by Aberdeen with Celtic only managing fifth. Once again, it had been a season that had promised much but silverware was still, frustratingly, from Hearts' reach.

MacDonald, however, had gradually been able to bring in more expensive players and the manager was able to spend another £750,000 in the summer to bring in gifted midfielder Derek Ferguson, matching the club record fee paid to bring back Robertson from Newcastle.

The summer of 1990 had been one which supporters of neither Hearts or Hibs will forget. Wallace Mercer launched an audacious bid to take over Hibs and create one super club in Edinburgh. Though he dressed it up as a merger, the implications for financially-troubled Hibs were that they would be closed down and their ground sold off. Neither set of supporters wanted such a move and it was a gross miscalculation by the Hearts' chairman who had threats on his life from irate Hibernian supporters and he had to have a police guard put on his home in Barnton.

Mercer later backed down and stated that he had won the business argument but not the emotional one. There may have been an element of truth in that as history has shown that there are few occasions when Edinburgh can boast two clubs who can mount a title challenge at the same time. Usually, if Hearts are in the ascendancy, then Hibs have a tendency to wilt and vice-versa. But never has an issue touched a raw nerve with both sets of supporters and even players became embroiled in it all with John Robertson attending a "Hands Off Hibs" rally at Edinburgh's Usher Hall.

Few could believe it when the news broke when it was leaked to a tabloid newspaper and Mercer held a remarkable press conference at the city's Sheraton Hotel for invited media and later expanded on the theme at what can only be described as a "media frenzy" at another city hotel. Had Mercer not backed down under the huge pressure of public opinion, there is no doubt he could have made such a bid happen.

Whatever the underlying intent, it only served to distance Mercer from the fan in the street. Ironically, it was the emotion felt by the fans that had persuaded Mercer to invest his money in football in the first place and he could not ignore it at this juncture. But many believe that he had raised the stakes too much and it had been a misguided step.

Within weeks, Mercer was to prove unpopular with a significant section of Hearts fans again. With clear ambitions, that this could be Hearts' year, Mercer saw first-hand that Rangers were moving further away when the champions came to Tynecastle and won 3-1. In truth, they could have won by a greater margin and the chairman felt it was time for change.

The timing of the decision to dismiss manager MacDonald took everyone by surprise – in the build-up to an Edinburgh derby – and with a UEFA Cup tie with Dniepr Dnepropetrovsk on the near-horizon. MacDonald was certainly not expecting it himself but he made a dignified exit from Tynecastle and could take a lot of satisfaction over what he had achieved, having had the post thrust upon him in the first place. Assistant Walter Borthwick was also sacked and, not only some fans, but also some of the players were critical of the decision to let the management team go.

Sandy Clark, who had returned to the club as coach after a bleak few months as manager of Partick Thistle, took on the role of caretaker-manager. His short tenure was successful – a 3-0 win (Robertson 2, Levein) over Hibs at Easter Road which was Hearts' biggest win over their arch-rivals for 17 years and then Hearts survived the long trip to Dnepr and emerged with a 1-1 draw with Robertson on the scoresheet. It was during the trip that Hearts announced that former Scotland international forward Joe Jordan would take over the managerial reins. Mercer had waited behind to conclude the deal but the news filtered out from Hearts travels.

Gary Mackay

GARY Mackay deserves his place in any Hearts' Hall of Fame. Not that there were any medals to show for 17 years at Tynecastle but his dedication to the club and willingness to give his all for Hearts, on and off the park, could never be called into question.

He has also played more games – 737 – than anyone else and it is a record that is likely to stand the test of time, given that players tend to linger for shorter periods at clubs these days under freedom of contract.

Mackay was blooded at an early age as the club was forced, through a harsh financial situation at the dawn of the 1980s, to give any likely lad a chance. He broke into the first-team around the same time as John Robertson and Dave Bowman and his telepathic link with Robertson at a time when the club was reborn was a major talking point at the time.

Indeed, Mackay made his debut as a raw 16-year-old substitute in a League Cup tie against Ayr United at Somerset Park in September 1980, when Hearts were on the wrong end of a 4-0 result. It was a team that included Jim Jefferies, many years later to be Mackay's manager at Tynecastle.

Mackay had supported Hearts from an early age but had trained, like Robertson, with arch-rivals Hibs who had a good youth set-up at the time and he also trained with Manchester United and Celtic and was regarded as one of the best players in Edinburgh schools' football.

It was Bobby Moncur who signed him for Hearts and, if the former Newcastle United player did not hold the managerial reins for long, he left a great legacy as he also persuaded Robertson and Bowman to put pen to paper.

Mackay was a tireless worker in midfield, who passed the ball precisely and had a fair shot when around the edge of the penalty area. His ability to link with his attacking players and time his runs into the opposing penalty area ensured a regular supply of goals and Robertson, for one, would pay tribute to the number of chances Mackay created with his unselfish play.

When he first came into the Hearts team, Mackay clearly lacked the stature to play at the top level but he worked hard on his fitness under then coaches George McNeill and Bert Logan and was regarded as one of the fittest in the Tynecastle squad during his playing days.

He was fortunate in that in his formative years, he had a player of the experience and knowledge of Alex MacDonald alongside him in midfield. Under MacDonald's management, Mackay was a permanent fixture in the team and he played an important part in Hearts' surge to the brink of a League and Cup double in 1986.

His spectacular strike in the penultimate League game at home to

Clydebank brought Hearts two points and to the edge of the Premier League title but, unfortunately for the club, events at Dens Park and Love Street seven days later dictated otherwise.

But his play was being recognised at a higher level and then Scotland manager Andy Roxburgh, who knew Mackay well from the days when he coached the Scottish youth team, awarded the player his first full cap in a European Championship qualifying game against Bulgaria in Sofia. Scotland were already out of the competition but Mackay came on as a substitute to score a memorable winning goal in the closing minutes. It was enough to give the Republic of Ireland the

qualifying place ahead of Bulgaria and made Mackay an honorary Irishman.

He had been the first Hearts player to win a cap since Donald Ford in 1974 and the first to score a goal for Scotland since Alex Young, 27 years previously.

Mackay went on to win four full caps for his country and, although there were no more goals, he at least has the consolation of knowing that it was a goal that will be long remembered, even if more by Irishmen than Scotsmen.

There were many highlights in Mackay's career and one has to be the four goals he scored in a Scottish Cup third round tie against Inverness Caledonian at Tynecastle in 1985 when Hearts won 6-0.

He played in the 1986 Scottish Cup Final against Aberdeen (which Hearts lost 3-0) and scored in the semi-final of the same competition a year later only for the team to go down to a surprise 2-1 defeat by St Mirren. There were more semi-final defeats to follow before Mackay and Hearts finally made it to the Scottish Cup Final again under Jefferies in 1996.

Mackay played in every round of the competition that season including the Final but there was to be no happy ending as Hearts lost 5-1 to a Brian Laudrup-inspired Rangers. There was a League Cup Final place the following season when Hearts were unfortunate to lose out to Rangers 4-3 and a winners' medal was to prove elusive to Mackay.

The player finally left Tynecastle in March 1997 when he linked up with MacDonald again, who was then manager at Airdrie and Mackay went on to succeed him in the post. However, the financial difficulties at Airdrie meant that Mackay was not given a chance to show what he could do as a manager, although that may well come in the future.

Always a popular figure when he returns to Tynecastle, which he does regularly as a spectator, Mackay is now working at establishing himself as a football agent.

1980-81-1996-97
Appearances 737
Goals 88

The Wait Is Over

JOE JORDAN was thought to be one of the brightest young managers in British football and had done such a marvellous job at Bristol City that many saw him groomed as a future manager of Manchester United, one of his former clubs. Even when he arrived at Tynecastle, he made no secret of the fact that Old Trafford was where his ultimate ambitions lay.

Jordan, who scored the goal that put Scotland through to the 1974 World Cup finals in Munich and ended 16 years in the wilderness, was a hugely popular figure in Scotland. He had only played briefly in Scottish football (for Morton) before a glittering career in England and even on to AC Milan, where he had also been thought of highly. Although there had been better players to don the dark blue of Scotland, few epitomised the lionheart spirit as much as Jordan who scored some precious goals for his country.

As a manager, he was still something of an unknown quantity at the top level. He arrived at Tynecastle intent on bringing his own football philosophy to the club and he was given a budget to spend on players and the remit was simply to end Rangers' growing monopoly of the League title and to finally bring some silverware back to Gorgie for an increasingly impatient support. Given the players who had graced the maroon through the 1970s and 1980s, it was remarkable that not a single major trophy had been collected at some point.

Jordan's first match in charge was a 3-0 defeat at

Joe Jordan arrived at Tynecastle with a reputation as one of the game's brightest young managers.

Celtic Park and it was clear there would be some stutters along the way as Hearts adjusted to their first managerial change for eight-and-a-half years.

But Dnepr were duly ousted from the UEFA Cup with Hearts winning the home leg 3-1 with Robertson scoring twice and Dave McPherson also on the mark and it set up a tasty second-round tie with Italian side Bologna.

Hearts' scorer Wayne Foster battles with Bologna's Biondo in the UEFA Cup game at Tynecastle in October 1990.

With Robertson injured for the first leg tie at Tynecastle, Wayne Foster stepped up to score twice in a 3-1 victory with Iain Ferguson scoring the other goal. But the away goal scored by Bologna was always going to be damaging with no margin for error in the second leg. Jordan was given a rousing welcome by the Italian media on his return as a manager to the country where he made a mark as a player but, on the field, things did not go as planned and Hearts lost 3-0 to go out 4-3 on aggregate.

Hearts returned home to beat Celtic in the League and, while there was another one-sided Edinburgh New Year derby (this time 4-1 in Hearts' favour), there was still plenty of work for Jordan to do as defeats at Ibrox (0-4) in December and Pittodrie (0-5) in February would testify. Hearts finished fifth in the

League and there was a third round Scottish Cup exit at First Division Airdrie. After that 5-0 defeat by Aberdeen, Jordan handed Nicky Walker the goalkeeping gloves for the remainder of the season as Henry Smith, who had missed only one game in the previous 344, was dropped.

By the 1991-92 season, it was evident that Jordan was building his own team and he brought in some experienced players he had known from his time in English football – firstly striker Ian Baird and then Graeme Hogg and Glynn Snodin later in the campaign. Hearts made a whirlwind start by winning their first half-dozen games (four in the League and two in the League Cup) and scoring a dozen goals with Crabbe, Robertson and Baird accounting for 11 of the goals. Smith was back in goal as Walker had suffered a broken cheekbone pre-season.

There was a narrow 1-0 loss to Rangers at home in the League Cup quarter-final with Ally McCoist scoring the only goal. But, in the League, Hearts did not stumble and were unbeaten for the first two months. Jordan's 3-4-3 formation with Gary Mackay and Tosh McKinlay filling the wing-back berths magnificently was proving successful and, if Hearts were not scoring as readily as they had in some previous seasons, little was conceded at the back. In the first 12 games of that season the team only lost eight goals and had six shut-outs.

There was a loss at Celtic Park at the start of October – 3-1 with Robertson on the scoresheet for Hearts – but Jordan had the luxury of a settled team with Derek Ferguson orchestrating things in midfield. Rangers also managed to get the better of Hearts (2-0 at Ibrox) but, up until Christmas, these were Hearts' only two defeats in the League.

After a 1-1 draw with Hibs at the start of November when Robertson inevitably scored the goal, Hearts won nine of their next ten games and yet again it was based on solid defence with only four goals conceded in that spell. What was more, Hearts had avenged the early defeat by Celtic with a 3-1 victory over them in November at Tynecastle with, rather unusually, George Wright and Craig Levein both getting in on the scoring act.

A 5-0 win at St Johnstone in the final game of 1991 when Robertson and Crabbe both bagged a brace brought more festive cheer to Hearts supporters but, given the events of 1965 and 1986, there was no-one talking in terms of titles even though Jordan's side sat proudly at the top of the League.

After a draw with Hibs on New Year's Day when Ian Ferguson, recruited a couple of months earlier from Raith Rovers, scored the Hearts' goal, Jordan's side travelled along the M8 to face Celtic, knowing they had not beaten their opponents in Glasgow for over six years. However, goals from Scott Crabbe and the little-acclaimed yet highly-effective John Millar gave Hearts a 2-1 win.

Having broken the Celtic jinx, there were careless whispers that this was finally to be Hearts' season. After all, the defence with Alan McLaren, Dave McPherson and Levein prominent, had looked solid all season and there had been only two defeats in 28 League games. It was all so encouraging for Hearts and Jordan had built a robust team that, at last, did not have an inferiority complex when up against the Old Firm.

Yet, within a week of the result at Celtic, Hearts were brought crashing back to earth in front of a stunned 16,291 crowd at Tynecastle when Aberdeen visited and left with a 4-0 triumph. Eoin Jess (2) Scott Booth and Paul Mason had shared the goals between them in a classic counter-attacking display in which Aberdeen rather exposed Hearts. The result toppled Hearts from their perch at the top of the League and it was a position they were not to regain.

There followed a surprise 2-1 defeat at Airdrie and, after a drab goalless draw in the Scottish Cup third-round tie at St Mirren, there was a third successive League reversal – most damagingly to Rangers, who went on to win the title. Hearts never really recovered their footing in the title race and, although they did enough to squeeze Celtic out of second place, they finished nine points shy of eventual champions Rangers. There was a feeling that Hearts had simply "run out of gas" as Mackay and McKinlay, who had missed only a handful of games between them, found the punishing wing-back roles more and more demanding as the season wore on. Manager Jordan was later to say that if had been given the funds to go into the transfer market when Hearts had hit their peak at the turn of the year, then the title might not have eluded him.

The Scottish Cup campaign gathered momentum with Robertson hitting a hat-trick in a 3-0 replay win over St Mirren and Dunfermline (2-1) and Falkirk (3-1) also taken care of on the way to a semi-final meeting with Airdrie, now managed by Alex MacDonald. Airdrie included a cluster of former Tynecastle stalwarts including former captain Walter Kidd, Jimmy Sandison and Kenny Black. Given Hearts' record in semi-finals (they had lost their last three in Scottish Cup and League Cup), it always looked a tie fraught with danger for Jordan's side.

Action from the game against Celtic in August 1992. George Wright gets in a tackle on Celtic's Paul McStay.

McPherson had a "goal" disallowed in an untidy 0-0 draw and the replay was another tight affair with Black putting Airdrie ahead in the first-half only for Alan McLaren to score a last-minute equaliser and take the tie to extra-time. Robertson hit woodwork twice in the extra period and it was clear Airdrie were destined to make the Final. It went to a penalty shoot-out which the Lanarkshire side won 4-2 with McPherson and Crabbe missing for Hearts. Ultimately, it was a disappointing season given where Hearts stood at the turn of the year but there was the consolation of a UEFA Cup place.

But Jordan had built a team that had the best defensive record in the League behind Rangers and, given the resources in comparison to the Ibrox side, it was a not inconsiderable achievement. Yet there was apathy from fans at the end of the season with none of the final five League games attracting five-figure attendances.

Alan McLaren of Hearts shadows Tommy Coyne in the same game against Celtic.

Off the field, Hearts had proposed moving to Millerhill on the outskirts of Edinburgh and moving from their Tynecastle base. Projects at Ingliston and on the western outskirts of Edinburgh were also mooted in 1991-92 but Hearts were refused the relevant permission from the authorities to go ahead and a decision was eventually taken to remain at Tynecastle.

Jordan signed the combative midfielder Ally Mauchlen for the start of the 1992-93 season and, with Dave McPherson having gone back to Rangers at the end of the previous season, classy Dutch defender Peter Van de Ven was recruited to fill the void. Although Hearts lost narrowly to Celtic on the opening day of the season, their only other defeat in their first 11 games was in the League Cup quarter-final against the same opposition at Tynecastle when a Gary Mackay goal could not prevent Hearts going down 2-1. Nevertheless, the results were not flowing as smoothly and it took extra-time to get through against Brechin City in the third round of the League Cup.

In Europe, Hearts faced Slavia Prague in the first round of the UEFA Cup and after losing 1-0 in the first leg away from home, Jordan's side raised their game suitably for the return which produced one of those classic European encounters that Tynecastle has a habit of staging. Hearts led 3-2 late in the game but, as it stood, were out of the competition on the away goals rule. Step forward Glynn Snodin to crack an unstoppable 30-yard winner into the top corner of the net and put Hearts through on a 4-3 aggregate.

FC Liege, coached by former Dutch international Arie Haan, were next up and their slick passing play caught the eye at Tynecastle in the first leg which the Belgian side won 1-0. But Haan won himself few friends with some unkind comments about the Edinburgh side and it meant an extra edge to the return in Belgium. This time Hearts looked the better side on the night but FC Liege scored the only goal of the game midway through the second half and it was enough to take the tie beyond Hearts' reach and put Haan's side into the third round on a 2-0 aggregate.

While both home ties in Europe had attracted attendances in excess of 16,000, the average gate at Tynecastle was still disappointing and unless the Old Firm or Hibs were visiting, Hearts struggled to break the 10,000 barrier. Yet, defensively, Hearts were as good as anyone in Scotland but there had been some murmurings of discontent among the Hearts faithful that the team was not as adventurous as in previous years. The popular Scott Crabbe was allowed to leave to join Dundee United in a part-exchange deal with Allan Preston and it was clear at the time that the striker was reluctant to leave Edinburgh.

There was a horrible 6-2 defeat by Aberdeen at Pittodrie at the end of November and this was followed by successive losses at the hands of Falkirk and Airdrie and Hearts appeared to be back to the bad old ways. Yet an Ian Ferguson goal gave Jordan's side a win over Celtic in mid-December and, not long afterwards, Huntly were torn apart 6-0 in the Scottish Cup at Tynecastle with Adrian Boothroyd scoring twice. Boothroyd earned the "distinction" of never starting a game for the club in his season there and this was to be the highlight of his maroon days.

With Rangers running away with the League title again, Hearts were once again left playing for a UEFA Cup place in the League while at the same time keeping another avenue open to Europe in the Scottish Cup. They reached the last four without losing a goal (Dundee and Falkirk were both dismissed 2-0 in the fourth and fifth rounds respectively) and so Hearts made the trip to Celtic Park to face Rangers in the semi-finals. Preston headed Hearts in front to fuel hopes of an upset but Rangers hit back with former Hearts defender McPherson equalising and Ally McCoist, a constant thorn in Hearts' flesh, scoring the winning goal with a typical opportunist effort.

So the Cup was gone for another year and not long afterwards were successive League defeats at the hands of Rangers, Aberdeen and Motherwell and there was growing unrest among the supporters. Matters came to a head with an insipid display at Brockville when Jim Jefferies' side delivered a 6-0 knockout in Hearts' heaviest defeat since they lost so famously to Hibs on New Year's Day of 1973. Jordan was dismissed a couple of days later and it had become clear that he had not seen eye-to-eye with chairman Wallace Mercer. Jordan could not have envisaged it would come to such a sour end especially after he was one of the most sought-after young managers in Britain when Hearts appointed him and he saw the post as a stepping-stone to greater things.

Sandy Clark took up the reins but the season ended with six defeats in the final seven games. Hearts, nevertheless, managed to book fifth place in the table and get into Europe for another year. Clark's previous managerial experience with Partick Thistle had been a chastening one but he approached his new job with enthusiasm and was a popular appointment with the playing staff and he showed himself willing to give youth a fling. In the final three games of the 1992-93 season, he had used Tommy Harrison, Allan Johnston,

Kevin Thomas and Gary Locke in what was a clear statement of intent about how he would approach his new post.

At the start of the 1993-94 campaign against Rangers at Ibrox, Locke was thrust straight into the starting line-up and Johnston was on the bench. There was also a debut for Justin Fashanu, the most surprising of signings by Clark during the close-season. John Colquhoun

Colquhoun scores against Atletico Madrid in 1993-94.

was also brought back from his spell in exile down south as Clark hoped he could recreate the form of a few seasons earlier which had brought the team within reach of the League title.

Clark clearly had his own ideas and the team that started with a narrow 2-1 defeat by Rangers contained only five of the players who featured in the 6-0 defeat by Falkirk at the tail end of the previous season in what was Jordan's last game in charge. There was an inconsistent start to the season with Allan Johnston scoring the only goal of a win against Hibs but there was a disappointing third round exit to Jim Jefferies' Falkirk in the League Cup. Hearts were once again relying on Robertson to get the bulk of their goals but goals were proving hard to come by and Hearts managed only 11 goals in their opening 17 matches in League, League Cup and UEFA Cup. Indeed, in their first ten League games, Hearts failed to score in half of them.

It was clearly going to be a difficult season although Hearts had a noteworthy 2-1 win over Atletico Madrid at home in the first round of the UEFA Cup. Old faithfuls Colquhoun and Robertson kept up Hearts' remarkably good home record in Europe but the Spanish side turned up the heat in the second leg to win 3-0 and go through comfortably on aggregate with two goals in the final 20 minutes of the tie.

Fashanu had proved a colourful character at Hearts but his exploits off the field were creating more headlines than those on it and indeed he only

contributed one goal before being released by the club to pursue his career elsewhere. Clark was as aware as anyone of the need for a striker with a proven scoring record and so he gambled on bringing Maurice Johnston back north of the border after an unsuccessful stint at Everton. Johnston made his debut in a 0-0 draw at Partick Thistle but Hearts' fans did not

John Robertson and John Colquhoun celebrate against Atletico Madrid.

have to wait too long for his first goal – it came in a 1-1 draw with Dundee United at Tynecastle. The former Old Firm striker, who was on a pay-per-play deal, was to go on and play 39 games and score half a dozen goals in his time at the club.

But the goals still did not come as freely as Clark would have liked and Hearts managed to go through the entire campaign without ever scoring more than two goals in any game. They averaged less than a goal a game in the League and, with three teams relegated, Hearts' Premier League future was uncertain right up until the final game of the season. Maurice Johnston scored the only goal of a tight Scottish Cup third-round tie against one of his former clubs Partick Thistle at Firhill to set up a mouth-watering fourth-round tie against Hibs at Easter Road.

It was the first time the teams had met in a cup tie since the quarter-finals of the 1978-79 competition (which Hibs had won 2-1) and Hibs were considered slight favourites going into the tie in spite of the fact that Hearts had built up a long unbeaten run against their rivals. But Robertson scored an early goal to settle Hearts and, although Keith Wright equalised late in the game, Wayne Foster ensured himself a place in Tynecastle folklore with an opportunist winning goal with barely three minutes of the tie left. Foster presented his shirt to a local hostelry and it is still one of the most fondly remembered derby goals by fans of a maroon persuasion.

Hearts drew Rangers at Ibrox in the quarter-final where they went out to goals from John Brown and Mark Hateley and they had to turn their attentions to the League in the closing weeks of the season. The bottom half of the table was tight and Hearts were inevitably thrown into the dog-fight as they only won one of their next ten games after the Cup exit. But there was an important point in a goalless draw with Hibs on the last day of April when the Easter Road side knew they could seriously dent Hearts' survival hopes. There were just two games remaining and Hearts eased their fears with a 2-0 home win over Dundee United with Stephen Frail and Craig Levein getting the goals.

However, going into the final League game against Partick Thistle at Firhill there was still a scenario where Hearts could go down. In a tense game, Alan McLaren scored the goal that ensured Hearts a 1-0 victory and preserved the top-League status. It had been an unconvincing season but dramatic events were to unfold over the summer months and the match at Firhill was to prove Clark's last in charge of Hearts.

Hearts had been the subject of much takeover speculation throughout that 1993-94 season and it all came to a head shortly after the end of the season when Chris Robinson, who had made his name in the catering industry, joined with fellow lifelong supporter and Edinburgh solicitor Leslie Deans to buy Wallace Mercer's 51 per cent controlling interest in the club. It was the biggest sea-change behind the scenes since Mercer himself took over at the helm some 13 years previously. One of the new board's first actions was to remove manager Sandy Clark and his assistant Hugh McCann from their posts and appoint Tommy McLean as the new manager. McLean had impressed with what he had achieved at Motherwell on a limited budget. He had won Motherwell the Scottish Cup in 1991 and had guided them to third place in the previous season's Premier Division – four points ahead of Celtic and just four points behind champions Rangers. Moreover, he had demonstrated that he could get the best out of players and there was a general feeling within the game that he could go on and achieve what his brother Jim had done with Dundee United.

There could hardly have been a more ominous start for McLean with two of his experienced central defenders, Graeme Hogg and Craig Levein, exchanging blows during a pre-season game at Raith Rovers. Both were red-carded and the incident was caught on film and, although Hearts fined both players heavily, the SFA also cracked down later in the season and suspended both of them for nine games.

Hogg did not start another game for the club and, although he came on as a substitute in a 3-0 defeat by Rangers in the September (when Levein was also in the team), he was soon off to pastures new. If the incident hinted that there was disharmony in the team, it was not necessarily the case but results early in the season were again a mixed bag and there was a dreadful 4-2 home defeat by First Division St Johnstone in the third round of the League Cup after Hearts had led 2-0 but then had Frail sent off.

The defeat followed hard on the heels of Hearts

finally surrendering their long unbeaten run against Hibs that had stretched to 22 games. A Gordon Hunter goal at Tynecastle was enough to settle the first derby of the 1994-95 season in Hibs' favour. But, by October, the ship appeared to have steadied with successive wins over Celtic and Aberdeen at Tynecastle. But then Hibs repeated the derby misery with a 2-1 win in the return at Easter Road just to show the tide had indeed turned and a 5-2 defeat by Dundee United at Tannadice in November signalled another setback.

New Hearts manager Tommy McLean had impressed with what he had achieved on a limited budget at Motherwell, but his time at Tynecastle was not a happy one.

By December, Craig Nelson had taken over in goal from Henry Smith and McLean had also recruited the experienced Jim Bett to play in midfield. McLean was changing the playing landscape at Tynecastle considerably and Brian Hamilton, Willie Jamieson, David Hagen, Colin Miller and Colin Cramb were all brought in with varying degrees of success but none was to remain at the club for too long. January was a bright month with wins over Motherwell, Dundee United and Hibs and a draw at Celtic Park but Hearts had to rely on a Robertson penalty on the opening day of the following month to win a replay against Clydebank in the third round of the Scottish Cup.

Robertson and enigmatic striker Kevin Thomas did the needful in the replay to get Hearts through to the fourth round where they drew Rangers at home in a game which attracted live satellite television. It was to prove a memorable night with Hearts ahead 2-0 by half-time through goals from Colin Miller and Dave McPherson only for Rangers to pull level in the second half through Brian Laudrup and Gordon Durie. But Hearts came back again to win it with late goals from Robertson and Thomas to reach the last eight with a 4-2 victory. It was undoubtedly the highlight of McLean's season in charge of the club.

Midfielder John Millar scored both goals in a televised quarter-final with the Cup holders Dundee

United, managed by Ivan Golac, and Hearts were in the semi-finals again with First Division Airdrie, managed by former Tynecastle favourite Alex MacDonald, once more the opposition. Having been put out at the same stage by Airdrie on penalties during Jordan's tenure at Tynecastle, there was surely no way Hearts would slip on the same banana skin twice. But slip they did with Steve Cooper scoring the only goal of the game in the first half and Robertson later sent off to sum up a frustrating afternoon as Hearts once again tripped at the penultimate hurdle. Almost unbearably, this was the fifth successive Scottish Cup semi-final defeat for Hearts and arguably the most frustrating although there had been so many near misses since 1986 it seemed as if Hearts were destined never to grace a major Final again.

The Airdrie loss was sandwiched between four consecutive League defeats but some pride was restored in mid-April when McLean's side travelled to Celtic Park and returned with an unlikely win courtesy of a solitary goal from David Hagen. But defeats by Aberdeen and Hibs meant Hearts could still be left facing a play-off against the First Division runners-up to decide their future status if they did not beat Motherwell in their final League game at Tynecastle. McLean's former club had risen to second in the Premier League under the guidance of Alex McLeish and, although they had nothing to play for, would undoubtedly make it an uncomfortable afternoon.

Over 11,000 fans witnessed the game and their minds were put at rest when Brian Hamilton, not noted for his goalscoring and not wholly accepted after spending much of his career at Easter Road, headed Hearts in front. It was not until the final moments that Robertson struck a penalty to seal the victory but Hearts were safe for another season and the result sparked celebrations on Gorgie. With no silverware to toast, it was becoming too much of a habit now to celebrate retaining top League status. In the end, it was Aberdeen who had to play off with Dunfermline to ensure their survival for another year and avoid the drop.

McLean's time at Tynecastle had not been a happy one in the final few months of the season. A share issue to raise funds for him to spend on players did not raise the substantial amount hoped for and the manager had offered to resign halfway through the season. There was clearly a breakdown in relations between the manager and the boardroom and matters came to a head at the end of the season when Hearts dismissed him for "unreasonable behaviour". For the fourth successive year, Hearts would go into the next season with a new manager and the search was on for a successor to McLean.

There were two candidates in the frame: former Hearts player Jim Jefferies who had built up a decent reputation with Falkirk and looked ready for the step up to a bigger club and Jimmy Nicholl, who had guided Raith Rovers to the League Cup in 1994 and the glamour of a European tie with Bayern Munich in which the Fife side had held their own.

It was no secret that both men were being considered with Jefferies, given his previous Hearts connection, the obvious frontrunner. But the manager was popular with everyone at Brockville and it was no easy task prising him away from Falkirk. After an agreement had been seemingly reached between Hearts and Jefferies, the Falkirk manager went to Brockville to inform chairman George Fulston of his decision. But, after several hours in discussion with Fulston and with the media anxious for news, both men emerged from the Brockville talks to announce that Jefferies would, in fact, be staying.

Jefferies later disclosed that he felt he had made the wrong decision and a persistent Chris Robinson refused to take no for an answer. Twenty-four hours after the Falkirk announcement, it was clear there was to be another dramatic U-turn after what had been an emotional few days for Jefferies, who was unable to be loyal to everyone without being disloyal to himself.

And so it was that Jefferies travelled with Hearts a few days later for a pre-season game at Derby County with caretaker Eamonn Bannon remaining in charge of the team and the new manager watching events from the stand. A 3-0 half-time deficit persuaded the manager that he had to look in to the visitors' dressing-room for some words of encouragement. It finished 3-3, and even then it was clear that Jefferies would be a strong motivational influence on putting Hearts back on an even keel.

Having started out his managerial career rather reluctantly with his local Borders amateur side Lauder not many years previously and having learnt his trade at such unglamorous outposts as Hawick Royal Albert, Gala Fairydean and Berwick, there were those that felt that the step up to Hearts would be too great for the new manager.

But he made a solid enough start and guided the team into the last eight of the League Cup and there was also a self-satisfying 4-1 victory over new-promoted Falkirk. But there was also a 2-0 defeat by Partick Thistle at Firhill for the new manager to digest and then Hearts went out of the League Cup at First Division Dundee on penalties after a 4-4 draw in a game where goalkeeper Henry Smith looked less than convincing. The manager made his first tough decision of his Tynecastle tenure as he axed Smith for the next game at Celtic and the veteran goalkeeper was never to play for the club again.

Craig Nelson came in but also lost four goals against Celtic and the former Partick Thistle goal-keeper lasted only a couple of more games before Gary O'Connor took over between the sticks. He lost nine goals in three games and it was glaringly obvious to Jefferies that an experienced goalkeeper was top of his shopping-list.

Hearts were struggling badly by the time Jefferies returned to Brockville at the end of October for the first time since leaving as manager. He had managed to

Former Hearts player Jim Jefferies had built up a good reputation with Falkirk and was a popular choice as the new manager at Tynecastle.

sign former French international goalkeeper Gilles Rousset in time for the game under the Bosman ruling and it was not the last time that Jefferies and Hearts were to profit from Bosman. Rousset made a solid debut in spite of a 2-0 defeat by Falkirk in which future Hearts' signing David Weir scored one of the goals. That result left Hearts floundering at the foot of the table and hurt Jefferies personally to such an extent that he took the decision that major changes to the playing personnel had to occur.

Jefferies had already dabbled in the transfer market and brought in experienced English defender Neil Pointon and former Celtic midfielder Steve Fulton as well as Alan Lawrence, David Winnie and Paul Smith. But this time, the manager cast his net wider and brought in Pasquale Bruno, a player with vast Serie A experience, and little-known Swedish striker Hans Eskilsson. Both made their debuts the week after the Falkirk defeat and, while Bruno gave the team a much-needed steel, Eskilsson came off the bench to score with a simple tap-in in the 3-0 victory over Partick Thistle.

The new team was taking shape and there was a 2-1 victory over Hibs in mid-November where

Bruno showed his leadership qualities. But, by the time the teams met again on New Year's Day, the tables had been turned and this time Hibs, who had lost 7-0 to Rangers the previous Saturday, came back from a stunning goal from Pointon to win 2-1 and inflict upon Jefferies his first derby defeat as manager. Eskilsson was guilty of missing a golden chance in front of goal, rather bizarrely claiming that the crowd noise had put him off, and it was to be the last game he started for the club and he had departed by the end of the season.

There was no doubt that Jefferies had started to turn things around and there was a remarkable 3-0 win at Ibrox later in January when Allan Johnston scored the sweetest of hat-tricks. Hearts had climbed into a respectable League position and the Scottish Cup was also going well as Hearts had removed Partick Thistle, Kilmarnock and St Johnstone – all away from home – to set up a semi-final meeting with Aberdeen at Hampden. Of course, Hearts still had not managed to shake off their eccentric streak as a 5-2 home defeat by struggling Partick in the League illustrated just a fortnight before the semi-final.

Given Hearts' experiences of semi-final ties, no-one

John Robertson scores for Hearts against Aberdeen in the 1996 Scottish Cup semi-final at Hampden Park.

was taking anything for granted and it looked a familiar tale when, after substitute John Robertson had put Hearts in front late on, Duncan Shearer equalised for Aberdeen with just a couple of minutes left. But this time, fortune smiled on Hearts and, in injury-time, Robertson set up a winning goal for Allan Johnston and Hearts were in the Final for the first time in ten years.

Hearts had signed livewire midfielder Colin Cameron from Raith Rovers and although he helped Hearts to a fourth place finish in the League (just missing out on third to Aberdeen on goal difference), he was ineligible for the Final. It was a proud Gary Locke who – at 21 the youngest Cup Final skipper since Aberdeen's Martin Buchan in 1970 – led out Hearts at Hampden for the Final against Rangers. Winning silverware had been Jefferies' ambition for the club when he took over as he had never managed it as a player with Hearts, but surely winning the Cup in the first season was too much to ask.

Hearts lined up for a Final which was the last at Hampden before major ground reconstruction, thus: Rousset; Locke, Ritchie, McManus, McPherson, Bruno, Johnston, Mackay, Colquhoun, Fulton and Pointon with Lawrence, Robertson and Hogarth the substitutes. Rangers were: Goram; Cleland, Robertson,

McLaren, Gough, Brown, Ferguson, McCall, Durie, Gascoigne and Laudrup with substitutes Petric, Durrant and Andersen.

Celebrations for Hearts against the Dons after a late goal from Allan Johnston put them through to the Final against Rangers.

Hearts had prepared carefully for the Final but their plans were thrown into disarray seven minutes into the game when Locke suffered a freak injury, catching his studs in the turf and damaging ligaments. He was stretchered off and now faced a long period on the sidelines. It forced a rethink but Hearts struggled throughout to cope with the menace of Rangers' gifted Dane Brian Laudrup. He laid on a hat-trick for Gordon Durie and scored two himself, his second being the killer shortly after half-time as the ball squirmed through Rousset's legs. There was a consolation goal from John Colquhoun but, by then, it was much too late.

Hearts – and Rousset – were nevertheless given a rousing reception when they returned to Edinburgh by the Hearts fans, aware of how far their team had come in a few months under Jefferies. There was also the consolation of a place in the European Cup-Winners' Cup with Rangers also winning the League and there was to be a glamour draw with Red Star Belgrade paired with Hearts.

Jefferies was earning a reputation of being a shrewd operator in the transfer market. Not only was he using the Bosman ruling to his advantage with an influx of top-grade foreign players but, in the summer of 1996, he brought in two of the most talented young Scottish players, David Weir from Falkirk and Neil McCann from Dundee as well as the experienced Welsh international Jeremy Goss from Norwich. The outlay for the three players was not much more than £500,000.

Hearts opened the new season with a creditable 0-0 draw with Red Star in Belgrade in the Cup-Winners' Cup where the Edinburgh side gave a decent account of themselves.

But then it took penalty kicks to dispose of Stenhousemuir in the second round of the League Cup before Hearts opened their League campaign with a 3-2 win over Kilmarnock. The second leg of the Cup-Winners' Cup came around quickly and, while Hearts again performed well, the Tynecastle leg finished 1-1 with Dave McPherson scoring the home goal and it meant an early exit from Europe on the away goals rule.

Hearts progressed to the quarter-finals of the League Cup to face Celtic but, three days before the game, Hearts were involved in a remarkable game at Ibrox against champions Rangers. The final scoreline of 3-0 to Rangers only tells part of the story as Hearts finished the game with only seven players with referee Gerry Evans sending off Bruno, Weir, Pointon and Paul Ritchie. Had another player been red carded, then the game would have been abandoned but Hearts managed to play out the final 25 minutes without further mishap.

But suspensions left Jefferies short for the League Cup tie with Celtic. Seventeen-year-old Gary Naysmith was given his first start and Jefferies managed to rush through a short-term loan for English defender

John Robertson celebrates after scoring the only goal of the League Cup fourth-round tie against Celtic in September 1996.

David Weir scores for Hearts against Rangers in the League Cup Final seven-goal thriller at Celtic Park in November 1996.

Andy Thorn from Wimbledon. Stefano Salvatori, an experienced Italian midfield player who had played alongside Baresi, Gullit and Van Basten at AC Milan, also made his home debut after outings at Dunfermline and Ibrox.

The new recruits did not let their manager down and Hearts held firm in defence throughout the 90 minutes and extra-time. Salvatori was sent off for two bookings after an hour but Celtic's Peter Grant was also red carded in extra-time. The only goal of the game came deep into extra-time and it was Robertson who supplied it.

It put Hearts into the semi-finals, and First Division Dundee were duly taken care of in the Easter Road tie with goals from Darren Beckford, Colin Cameron from the penalty spot and French striker Stephane Paille. So Jefferies had guided Hearts into a second domestic Final in as many seasons and, with Rangers the opposition at Celtic Park due to the reconstruction of Hampden, it gave Hearts the opportunity for revenge after the Scottish Cup Final.

The teams were: Hearts: Rousset; Weir, Ritchie, Bruno, Mackay, Cameron, Fulton, Pointon, McCann, Paille and Robertson; Subs: Goss, Beckford, McManus; Rangers: Goram; Gough, Petric, Bjorklund, Moore, Gascoigne, Miler, Albertz, Cleland, Laudrup and McCoist; Subs: Van Vossen, Robertson, Snelders.

Hearts started badly and were two goals down before half an hour had elapsed with Ally McCoist demonstrating his lethal touch around the box to notch both of them. But Hearts contributed to one of the most memorable finals by pulling back to 2-2 through goals from Steve Fulton and John Robertson. But then Gascoigne took a hand in things to steer the Final back Rangers' way. Hearts were aggrieved about his first as they felt Robertson had been a victim of an earlier foul but before the protests had time to die down, Gascoigne had scored a sublime fourth goal. There was a late counter from Weir but Rangers held on to capture the trophy 4-3.

There was a reaction with Hearts going five games without a win following the Final but they bounced back over the festive season and crushed Hibs 4-0 in the

New Year's Day derby in what was Hibs' manager Jim Duffy's first experience of the occasion. There was a certain irony with former Dundee striker Jim Hamilton, one of Duffy's former pupils, scoring two of Hearts' goals.

Hearts went on to finish fourth in the League and beat Rangers 3-1 in the final game of the season but by then Rangers had won the title and the result was academic. In the Scottish Cup, Hearts crushed Cowdenbeath 5-0 in their first game but then went out 1-0 to Dundee United in a fourth round replay at Tannadice.

Action from Hearts' 4-0 win at Easter Road on New Year's Day 1997, as Robertson crashes in a shot.

But Hearts were maturing as a team under Jefferies. Colin Cameron and Neil McCann had proved inspired signings and offered the team the flair and imagination they had perhaps lacked in the more recent past. Paul Ritchie was also looking increasingly accomplished having come through the ranks and, having represented Scotland from Under-15 schoolboy level, was developing into a future senior cap. Dave Weir was also a commanding defensive figure but Jefferies was continuing to trawl Europe for available and affordable talent. So it was that the technically-gifted Thomas Flogel arrived from Austria Vienna and also a French striker Stephane Adam from Metz in time for the start of the new campaign. Could they be the missing pieces in the jigsaw that Jefferies had sought to finally turn Hearts into winners?

Both were included in the squad for the season's opener at Ibrox but Hearts were well beaten 3-1 with substitute Cameron on target. Defeat from Dunfermline before August was through did not suggest it was going to be a vintage year for Jefferies' remoulded team but fortunes soon turned. In the League Cup, Hearts came through tricky away ties at Livingston and Raith Rovers before going out in early September at the quarter-final stage when Allan Moore, signed by Alex MacDonald for Hearts earlier in his career, scored the only goal to give Dunfermline an extra-time win at East End Park.

But, by then, League form had picked up. Five successive wins until a 2-1 defeat by Celtic in mid-October, had led to a new optimism around the club. Just for good measure, Hearts cobbled together another six straight wins after that Celtic setback, including a thrilling 5-3 televised win over Kilmarnock at Tynecastle when Adam, who had already won the fans over with his industry and unselfish front play, contributed a hat-trick. By early December, Hearts were among the front-runners in the League but there were back-to-back defeats by Celtic (0-1) and Rangers (2-5) before Christmas.

But Hearts' results against teams outside the Old Firm were remarkably consistent and the only teams to beat them apart from Celtic or Rangers in the League that season were Dunfermline in that game back in August and a Hibs side desperate for League points in an attempt to beat relegation in the April.

Hearts rather let Hibs off the hook in the New Year's Day derby at Tynecastle when Steve Fulton scored two early goals and a landmark victory looked on the cards but Hibs' manager Jim Duffy won a brief stay of execution as his side fought back for a 2-2 draw. It was Hearts' inability to beat the Old Firm that season that ultimately cost them the League title and Hearts only lost two more games than champions Celtic and one more than Rangers in the final analysis as all three faltered on their approach to the finish.

Indeed, Hearts only won one of their final seven

League games (against Dunfermline on the final day of the campaign) and needless points were dropped in draws with St Johnstone, Motherwell and Kilmarnock in the final weeks. Of course, the Hibs defeat was also painful and, although Hearts scored more goals than eventual champions Celtic, they finished seven points adrift.

Stephane Adam scoring against Falkirk in the Scottish Cup semi-final at Ibrox in April 1998.

Hearts had only managed nine clean sheets in the League all season and had leaked too many goals over the season (46 in 36 matches) to merit the championship. Nevertheless, Fulton had enjoyed an exquisite season in midfield and young Gary Naysmith was playing well beyond his years at left-back.

But Hearts had also been distracted somewhat by a magnificent cup run, albeit with the aid of a kind draw.

No team wins a trophy without a slice of good fortune, even though Hearts rather milked it and never had to meet a Premier League side until the Final. Nevertheless, Hearts were supreme professionals as they disposed of Clydebank (2-0), Albion Rovers (3-0) and Ayr United (4-1) – all at Tynecastle – before facing Falkirk in the semi-final at Ibrox, a team from the First

Adam joins his team-mates in celebration during the Scottish Cup semi-final 3-1 victory.

Colin Cameron scores from the penalty spot against Rangers in the 1998 Scottish Cup Final.

Division but one with a dangerous cup pedigree having beaten Celtic in the previous year's semi-final and having beaten St Johnstone 3-0 in the quarter-finals. Falkirk were particularly stubborn but Hearts finished strongly to win 3-1 with Adam scoring twice and McCann also finding the net to set up another Final against Rangers.

Having already lost two domestic finals to Walter Smith's side, Jefferies was meticulous in his planning for the season's spectacle. He took his squad to Stratford to prepare for the game, where Scotland had prepared for the 1996 European Championship finals. There, Jefferies did as much talking about the game as physical preparation and the one sour note to the build-up was that Gary Locke, so cruelly struck down in the 1996 Final, was ruled out with another injury.

The Final was played at Celtic Park with Hampden still out of commission and veteran striker John Robertson, who had to play for much of the season on the bench, was again missing from the starting team as Hearts lined up: Rousset; McPherson, Naysmith,

Weir, Salvatori, Ritchie, McCann, Fulton, Adam, Cameron and Flogel with Robertson, Hamilton and Murray on the bench.

Rangers were: Goram; Porrini, Stensaas, Gough, Amoruso, Bjorklund, Gattuso, I Ferguson, Durie, McCall and Laudrup; substitutes: McCoist, Durrant and Moore.

There was no Gascoigne by this stage and McCoist only managed a game on the bench but, having already

Neil McCann turns away in jubilation after Hearts score against Rangers in the 1998 Scottish Cup Final.

Gary Naysmith celebrates as Gough looks on.

Hearts could scarcely have been given a better start when Sergio Porrini brought down Fulton in the penalty area before even a minute had elapsed. Cameron kept his cool to beat Andy Goram with the penalty, even though he admitted afterwards that he had changed his mind which way he was going to place his kick during his run-up. It was Jefferies' tactic to allow Rangers possession until they were within sight of goal and then close down the space. In this way, it was hoped his team would conserve their energy and hit Rangers on the break. It was a tactic that worked to perfection as Lorenzo Amoruso failed to cut out a long through ball early in the second half and Adam pounced to put Hearts 2-0 ahead.

But, being Hearts, the huge travelling support was put through emotional turmoil in the final stages. Substitute Ally McCoist pulled a goal back for Rangers and goalkeeper Gilles Rousset was called upon to make several superb saves

lost the League and League Cup to Celtic, Walter Smith faced the possibility of signing off his Ibrox management career without a trophy.

Jim Hamilton (left) and goalscorer Stephane Adam with the Scottish Cup after the victory over Rangers in 1998.

All smiles. Hearts with the 1998 Scottish Cup.

Manager Jim Jefferies and assistant Billy Brown with the Cup.

to ensure the Cup was bound for Gorgie and Hearts won their first silverware for 36 years.

Had it gone to extra-time, few Hearts fans were confident their team could have held out but such was the frantic final few minutes that Robertson, stripped for action and standing on the touchline, could not be brought into the fray for fear of upsetting the fine balance. Still, after such an illustrious career, there was finally a winner's medal for Robertson to cherish.

Fulton, captain for the day, ensured that Locke was able to make his way down from the stands to share in lifting the trophy as Hearts finally removed all of the years of failure with this victory. An estimated 250,000 turned out in glorious sunshine the next day to see the team parade the trophy through the streets of Edinburgh. At long last, the famine was ended and how the supporters celebrated.

Keeping the team together would be the hard part for Jefferies. Football had changed in the previous ten years and it was an occupational hazard for managers that they had to virtually rebuild a team from scratch every couple of years. While Jefferies had undoubtedly prospered under Bosman, inevitably Hearts were also damaged by the ruling. The manager had already seen Allan Johnston go to France on freedom of contract during his tenure,

Celebrations against Lantana at Tynecastle in August 1998. Hearts won this Cup-Winners' Cup game 5-0 for a 6-0 aggregate victory. They then faced Real Mallorca, losing the home leg 1-0 and drawing 1-1 on the Spanish island to go out to the team who would eventually contest the last-ever Final in this competition.

In the final season of the European Cup-Winners' Cup, Hearts were drawn against little-known Estonians FC Lantana in the qualifying round.

The Scots were made to feel most welcome by their hosts in the first leg which was played on a rutted pitch that proved a great leveller. Only 1,300 fans attended the tie – the lowest attendance ever to watch a Hearts' European game – and it was settled by a solitary goal from Lee Makel.

The second goal proved a formality with McCann, Fulton, Hamilton, Flogel and Derek Holmes giving Hearts a 5-0 win for a 6-0 aggregate.

Real Mallorca, a side which was on the move in Spain under Hector Cuper, awaited in the first round and a torrid first leg at Tynecastle ended with Marcelino scoring the only goal for the visitors.

There was controversy at the start of the second leg on the Spanish holiday island as Hearts complained that the goalposts did not measure up and made a formal complaint. The tie was played under protest and finished 1-1 with Jim Hamilton scoring for Hearts and Lopez netting for the Spaniards but the result was allowed to stand as Mallorca went through on aggregate. Mallorca went on to reach the Final of the competition to demonstrate how close Hearts had come to a memorable result.

Hearts did not scale the heights of the previous season and the League produced mixed results. While there was an opening win over Rangers to bask in with Adam and Jim Hamilton getting the goals, there were also damaging

but during the 1998-99 season he was also to lose Neil McCann and David Weir, two of his key players from the Cup-winning year, to Rangers and Everton respectively, the latter for a fraction of his market value.

But players were added. Steven Pressley, a rugged central defender, was brought from Dundee United and striker Gary McSwegan was to follow just a few months later.

early defeats by Kilmarnock and Dundee. Dundee, indeed, were to prove a thorn in the side for Hearts as they won all four League encounters that season.

While Celtic were beaten at Tynecastle in early December, Hearts then suffered a miserable run without a win in 12 League games, including a run of six without scoring. Hearts were suffering from a long-term injury to Colin Cameron who had not played all season and, remarkably, were hovering around the relegation zone come May.

But Cameron's return coincided with a return to form and Hearts survived as they lost only once in the last quarter (to Celtic) and the midfield player crucially scored both of Hearts' goals in a 2-0 win over Dunfermline in early May which was important to the team's chances of beating the drop. In the end, Hearts finished comfortably clear – in sixth place – and just four points off fifth-placed Dundee.

There was also the surprise signing of Darren Jackson, for £300,000 from Celtic in the early spring. The former Hibernian player brought new experience and energy to the team when it needed it most and the move clearly worked as Hearts, who had lost five in a row before his arrival, only lost one of their final nine games of the season with Jackson on the team-sheet.

In the League Cup, Hearts progressed to the semi-finals but then turned in one of their worst displays of the season against St Johnstone at Easter Road and went out 3-0 to goals from Allan Preston, Nick Dasovic and George O'Boyle. Rangers went on to beat St Johnstone 2-1 in the Final. In the Scottish Cup, Hearts tripped over the first hurdle, when they lost 3-1 at Motherwell in the third round.

Colin Cameron

JIM Jefferies used the transfer market shrewdly when he was manager of Hearts and there was no more perceptive buy than Colin Cameron. Bought for just £400,000 in March 1996 from Raith Rovers with John Millar making the journey to Stark's Park in part-exchange, his value has increased significantly since arriving on the Tynecastle doorstep.

Born in Kirkcaldy, he was signed by Raith in 1990 and then farmed out to Sligo Rovers by then manager Jimmy Nicholl in the 1991-92 season for what proved to be invaluable experience.

Cameron helped Raith win promotion to the Premier Division in 1993 and again in 1995 and was also in the team that famously beat Celtic in the 1994 League Cup Final at Ibrox after a penalty shoot-out. For an unfashionable club like Raith, Cameron also had the chance the following season to play in memorable European games against Bayern Munich.

Standing just 5ft 6ins, Cameron has been a livewire in midfield both for club and country and his ability to make darting runs into the opposing penalty area has brought him a rich return in goals. An accomplished finisher for a midfield player and a player who has the engine to motor for 90 minutes, it is no surprise that he has become an integral part of the Scotland international squad.

Quite simply, if Cameron is on song then Hearts are on song and his contribution was acknowledged by Jefferies when he was appointed club captain.

The fact he was Cup-tied meant he missed the 1996 Scottish Cup Final against Rangers but he played in every Hearts' game the following season – a total of 45 – and indeed was the only Premier Division player to play in every League game for his club that season.

Cameron endeared himself to the Hearts' fans early that season when he hit a double in a 3-1 win over Hibs at Easter Road when he even upstaged John Robertson, who predictably hit the other goal.

He was in the Hearts' team that finished runners-up to Rangers in the League Cup Final (and scored in two of the ties on the way to the Final) but he already possessed a winners' medal in the competition from his time at Raith Rovers.

His high level of fitness was obvious but injuries were to hit Cameron hard over the next couple of seasons. There were fears that he would miss the Scottish Cup Final after picking up an injury in the spring of 1998 but he missed only a handful of games and proved his fitness by playing in Hearts' penultimate League game of the season, a 2-2 draw at Pittodrie.

Cameron played a big part in Hearts' push for the double that season and was involved in every tie on the Cup run. He showed ice-cool nerve in the Final against Rangers at Celtic Park when Hearts were awarded a penalty in the first minute.

He swept the ball past Andy Goram to give Hearts the start they were looking for, although he later confessed that he had changed his mind which direction he was going to put it during his run-up, something penalty-takers advise against.

Cameron has proved the most reliable of spot-kick specialists whether it is the first or last minute in a game and he rarely misses. His penalty in the Final set Hearts on the path to their first trophy in 36 years.

He contributed some spectacular goals that season and also showed his worth with his tireless work between the penalty boxes and his willingness to come back and help out his defence.

Unfortunately, injury curtailed Cameron's involvement the following season and it was no coincidence that Hearts struggled to build on their Cup success that season.

As Jefferies struggled to hold on to the squad who had ended the trophy famine, Hearts were not assured of their Premier Division safety until the final few weeks of the season.

The revival in fortune coincided with the return of Cameron. He scored a vital goal in a win at Dundee United and then scored the two goals against Dunfermline in a relegation tussle at Tynecastle that confirmed Hearts would again be playing in the top flight the following season.

Given that he had not played many games, it was a surprise that Craig Brown called him up for his first cap in a friendly game against Germany at the end of that season.

Cameron was appointed club captain at the start of the 1999-2000 campaign and his dedication to the club has been laudable. He has been frequently linked with other clubs, both north and south of the border, but he takes it all in his stride and has always said he is happy at Hearts.

He has the ability to raise his game the more important the match may be and it is anticipated that he still has a few international caps to add to his collection.

1995-96-present
Appearances 185
Goals 56

A Fresh Start

SO there was no European place to anticipate at the start of the 1999-2000 season and indeed a new Hearts team was taking shape. Dave McPherson had left and it was not long into the new season before Paul Ritchie, Stefano Salvatori and Gary Naysmith departed and the team that won the Scottish Cup in 1998 had been scattered to faraway fields. Jim Jefferies could do nothing to prevent players like Ritchie and Naysmith seeking fame and fortune elsewhere, as it was clear Hearts' financial position was worsening in the growing desire to keep apace with the Old Firm.

But there was also the youth policy (which had seldom failed Jefferies before) to fall back on and Scott Severin and Robbie Neilson were two who were pressed into action before too long. Andy Kirk, a young striker from Belfast, had also been signed early in 1999 and would have to wait patiently for his chance as was the case with Gary Wales, bought in the summer of 1999 from Hamilton for £50,000 and a striker of considerable promise.

Hearts started the 1999-2000 season with a thumping 4-1 win at St Johnstone with Gary McSwegan, who had taken time to settle, bagging one of the goals. It was the start of a purple patch for the striker who also nabbed a hat-trick in a 3-0 win over Aberdeen after scoring in the Edinburgh derby and it was all to end in an international call-up by Scotland manager Craig Brown.

In the League, only the Old Firm managed to get the better of Jefferies' side in the opening few months

of the season and it was not until Dundee beat Hearts 1-0 at Dens Park at the end of October that the team lost that record.

After that, Hearts won only one of their next six games and, by early December, Jefferies was impatiently looking towards the transfer market again. Fitzroy Simpson, a Jamaican international midfield player, was brought from Portsmouth for a nominal fee and goalkeeper Antti Niemi (from Rangers), Gordan Petric (from AEK Athens) and Robert Tomaschek (from Slovan Bratislava) were all acquired for a total amount of close on £1.5 million.

Petric made his home debut against Hibs in mid-December and Simpson and Niemi both made their full debuts but it was a calamitous game for Hearts as they tumbled to a 3-0 defeat – their worst to Hibs at Tynecastle since that fateful first day of 1973 – with Dirk Lehmann, Franck Sauzee and Kenny Miller giving Hibs an unexpectedly comfortable victory.

A narrow defeat by Rangers in their next game took Hearts into the winter break with plenty to ponder. But the bonding exercise in Portugal paid off as Hearts returned to beat Dundee and then came back from two goals down to beat Celtic 3-2 in Glasgow with goals from Colin Cameron (2) and Naysmith. The match marked John Barnes's last League game in charge of the home side, coming just days before a Scottish Cup defeat by Inverness Caledonian Thistle on the same turf proved the last straw.

But Hearts were more concerned with their own fortunes and, apart from a disappointing 3-1 defeat by

Steven Pressley's header beats Stuttgart's goalkeeper Hidebrand in the action-packed UEFA Cup tie at Tynecastle early in the 2000-2001 season.

Hibs at Easter Road, results had markedly improved and there was a 1-0 home win over Celtic in early April when McSwegan scored the only goal.

Hearts went into the final League game of the season against Hibs at Tynecastle needing a win to clinch a European place and gave their fans a winning send-off after a troubled season with Spanish winger Juanjo and McSwegan scoring in a 2-1 win.

In the League Cup, Hearts had beaten Queen of the South (3-1) and East Fife (2-0) in the early rounds but then went out meekly at Rugby Park 1-0 to Kilmarnock with Michael Jeffrey scoring the only goal of an untidy encounter. In the Scottish Cup, Hearts recovered from two goals down to beat Stenhousemuir 3-2 in the third round, then beat Clyde 2-0 before going down to Rangers 4-1 in the quarter-finals at Ibrox with a Cameron penalty all they had to show for their efforts.

The positive finish to the previous season raised hopes at the start of the 2000-01 campaign but it was to turn out to be a turbulent campaign. Not that there was much warning of it as Hearts opened the League with three successive draws (against Hibs, St Johnstone and Aberdeen) and there was a comfortable preliminary round UEFA Cup win over Icelandic side Vestmanneyjer. Hearts won 2-0 away with goals from Severin and Jackson and 3-0 at home (Tomaschek, McSwegan and Kris O'Neil).

But it had been clear for some time that there was some friction between Jefferies and the boardroom. Chief Executive Chris Robinson and Leslie Deans, who had jointly bought over Hearts from Wallace Mercer in 1995, had also had a much-publicised fall-out and Deans had left as chairman in September 1999 to be succeeded by Douglas Smith.

There was also a leaked newspaper story which suggested there had been a contingency plan to replace manager Jefferies and this certainly did not help the relationship between Jefferies and Robinson.

But, on the field of play, the team was not doing badly. A narrow 1-0 defeat away to Stuttgart in the UEFA Cup brought an incident-packed second leg at Tynecastle and one of those memorable European nights the stadium has a habit of throwing up every now and then.

A crowd of 14,488 witnessed the occasion as Hearts

produced a storming finish to win 3-2 on the night with goals from Petric, Pressley and a Cameron penalty but it could not prevent them going out of Europe on the away goals rule. The 6ft 7ins Kevin James was thrown into attack in the second half and wreaked havoc in the Stuttgart penalty area and had Petric converted a simple chance right at the death, the outcome would have been different.

Victories over Motherwell (3-0) and Dundee United (4-0) followed and Jefferies had brought on board Gordon Durie from Rangers in a bid to add experience to his attack with Stephane Adam out with long-term injury and young Gary Wales also sidelined for several months. He scored twice in the win over Motherwell and partnered Andy Kirk for the visit to Easter Road in late October as the team looked in good shape to achieve a victory.

It was Kirk who gave Hearts an early lead and even though Hibs came back to lead 2-1 at half-time, it was an evenly-balanced contest. Yet Hearts were swamped in the second half as Hibs went on to win 6-2 with Mixu Paatelainen completing a hat-trick in another derby that Hearts wanted to erase from their minds as quickly as possible.

A 3-0 defeat at St Johnstone followed and then five goals were lost to Celtic in a pulsating League Cup quarter-final at Tynecastle where Hearts performed heroically but went out to three extra-time goals in a 5-2 finish. However, just when it looked as if Hearts had turned the corner with a 3-0 home win over Aberdeen in early November, fans were stunned a few days later when Jefferies and Hearts parted company "by mutual agreement", along with assistant Billy Brown.

"The Board appreciates and values the commitment that Jim Jefferies and Billy Brown have given to the club in their time here," said chairman Douglas Smith at an early evening press announcement. "Their departure provides Hearts with an opportunity to make some fundamental changes in the way our team is managed and that will be reflected in the appointment we make."

Peter Houston took interim control and expressed an interest in doing the job full-time but a 6-1 defeat at Celtic Park harmed his cause. Eric Black, the former Aberdeen striker who had coached at Celtic, was approached but declined the post to concentrate on his football agency business. Many other names were linked with the vacant post – some from south of the border and even abroad – but the future manager was to come from closer to home.

Craig Levein, who had taken on one of the most difficult jobs in football when he agreed to manage Third Division Cowdenbeath, had managed to transform the Fife club with minimal resources and, at the age of 36, was appointed manager of Hearts on 1 December 2000.

He had originally left the club prematurely after being forced to hang up his boots due to injury three years previously and signed a two-and-a-half-year contract in what he admitted had been the realisation of an ambition. With such a young manager, Levein's experience was called into question but he responded by stating as he faced the press for the first time after his appointment: "Some of you here, and probably some people on the terraces as well, might think I lack

Craig Levein (left) was appointed manager of Hearts on 1 December 2000.

Celebrations in the seven-goal romp against Dunfermline in February 2001

the experience for this job, but I believe I have the required skills and standards and a belief in how football should be played that will enable me to make the step up."

Levein could hardly have been given a tougher start, against champions Rangers the following day, but Hearts did well enough in a 1-0 defeat at Tynecastle. It was clear from the outset – and Levein did not hide the fact – that he would be working to a strict budget and players would be leaving the club as he built his own team.

Austin McCann (from Airdrie), Steven Boyack (from Dundee), Kevin McKenna (from Cottbus) and Andy Webster (from Arbroath) were all brought in by the new manager and Darren Jackson, Gordan Petric and Gary Locke all left. Levein did not have the money to go out on a wild spending spree but stressed it would take time to build his own team.

It was a year of renovation for the new manager but one where Hearts did better than expected. There was a narrow 1-0 loss at Celtic Park in the Scottish Cup quarter-final with the inevitable goal from Henrik Larsson after Hearts had reached the last eight by beating Berwick and Dundee, both after replays. In the League, a 7-1 win over Dunfermline at the end of February (Adam 2, Cameron 2, Kirk 2, Tomaschek) showed things were moving in the right direction.

Hearts were pursuing fourth place – and a UEFA Cup berth – right up until the final day of the season with Kilmarnock, who had caused pain to Hearts on the final day of the season before. But there were obvious pitfalls as the team approached the final day as, not only were Kilmarnock in the mix, but Dundee were to provide the final opposition at Tynecastle, the team that had so cruelly deprived Hearts of the League in 1986.

What was more, it was a Dundee team capable of beating both Rangers and Celtic during the season but also one which could lose horribly. But confidence was high – Hearts had booked a European place on the last day of the previous season and Kilmarnock, two points above Hearts in fourth place, were facing champions Celtic who needed a win to achieve the magic 100-point mark for the campaign.

Hearts responded to the challenge in front of 13,554 fans at Tynecastle with Stephane Adam and

Colin Cameron scoring second half goals as Dundee were seen off 2-0 and they knew that even if Celtic could secure a draw at Rugby Park, then a UEFA Cup place would be theirs on goal difference. However, events not under their control once again sealed their fate. Celtic were without prize striker Henrik Larsson because of a hamstring niggle and manager Martin O'Neill chose to rest several of his players ahead of the following weekend's Scottish Cup Final with Hibs.

Kilmarnock, with Ally McCoist playing his final competitive game in Scotland, secured the necessary three points with Alan Mahood scrambling an untidy winner with just a dozen minutes left for a 1-0 victory. Hearts' disappointment on hearing the outcome turned to anger as striker Adam criticised Celtic for fielding a weakened side in a game that was so crucial to the Tynecastle club. Manager Levein was more diplomatic and suggested he may have done the same as the champions in similar circumstances.

There was no hiding his disappointment however, although he must have taken some satisfaction in a top five finish given the turmoil the club had gone through in the previous six months.

Under Levein, Hearts are looking to a bright future. A new football academy to Heriot Watt University on the outskirts of the city will hopefully produce the future talent at the club, in addition to providing state-of-the-art training facilities.

Football has changed a lot over the past century-and-a-quarter since Hearts' formative years. Just as things were in those early days when they were the only east of Scotland team amongst the founder member of the Scottish League, Hearts intend to be play a big part in reshaping the game's future.

Hearts in the League

1890-91

DIVISION 1

	P	W	D	L	F	A	W	D	L	F	A	Pts
Dumbarton	18	7	2	0	35	8	6	1	2	26	13	†29
Rangers	18	7	1	1	31	11	6	2	1	27	14	†29
Celtic	18	7	2	0	26	8	4	1	4	22	13	*21
Cambusling	18	5	2	2	30	20	3	2	4	17	22	20
T. Lanark	18	6	0	3	22	15	2	3	4	16	24	*15
Hearts	18	4	2	3	20	15	2	0	7	11	22	14
Abercorn	18	4	1	4	20	18	1	1	7	16	29	12
St Mirren	18	5	1	3	24	23	0	0	9	15	39	11
Vale of Leven	18	5	0	4	19	18	0	1	8	8	47	11
Cowlairs	18	3	2	4	19	27	0	2	7	5	23	*6

† Dumbarton and Rangers drew 2-2 in a play-off and were
  declared joint Champions.
* Each had four points deducted for infringements.

1891-92

DIVISION 1

	P	W	D	L	F	A	W	D	L	F	A	Pts
Dumbarton	22	11	0	0	55	9	7	1	3	23	18	37
Celtic	22	10	1	0	32	6	6	2	3	30	15	35
Hearts	22	10	1	0	32	11	5	3	3	33	24	34
Leith A	22	8	1	2	34	15	4	0	7	17	25	25
Rangers	22	5	1	5	30	23	6	1	4	29	23	24
T. Lanark	22	4	3	4	27	25	4	2	5	17	22	21
Renton	22	6	1	4	19	18	2	4	5	18	25	21
Clyde	22	5	1	5	38	35	3	3	5	25	26	20
Abercorn	22	3	4	4	25	27	3	1	7	19	32	17
St Mirren	22	3	1	7	23	31	2	4	5	20	29	15
Cambusling	22	1	4	6	11	28	1	2	8	10	25	10
Vale of Leven	22	0	5	6	11	26	0	0	11	13	73	5

1892-93

DIVISION 1

	P	W	D	L	F	A	W	D	L	F	A	Pts
Celtic	18	8	0	1	32	14	6	1	2	22	11	29
Rangers	18	7	2	0	22	13	5	2	2	19	14	28
St Mirren	18	6	1	2	29	14	3	1	5	11	25	20
T. Lanark	18	5	0	4	31	20	4	1	4	22	19	19
Hearts	18	4	2	3	21	15	4	0	5	18	26	18
Leith A	18	5	1	3	22	11	3	0	6	13	20	17
Dumbarton	18	5	1	3	21	12	3	0	6	14	23	17
Renton	18	4	2	3	17	17	1	3	5	14	27	15
Abercorn	18	5	0	4	24	17	0	1	8	11	35	*11
Clyde	18	1	1	7	14	22	1	1	7	11	33	*6

* Abercorn and Clyde relegated to new Division Two.

1893-94

DIVISION 1

	P	W	D	L	F	A	W	D	L	F	A	Pts
Celtic	18	7	1	1	30	12	7	0	2	23	20	29
Hearts	18	4	2	3	21	17	7	2	0	25	15	26
St Bernard's	18	5	1	3	28	19	6	0	3	25	20	23
Rangers	18	6	0	3	29	12	2	4	3	15	18	20
Dumbarton	18	4	3	2	20	18	3	2	4	12	17	19
St Mirren	18	4	1	4	28	20	3	2	4	21	27	17
T. Lanark	18	4	1	4	21	22	3	2	4	17	22	17
Dundee	18	3	2	4	24	23	3	1	5	23	36	15
Leith A	18	3	2	4	24	24	1	0	8	12	22	10
Renton	18	1	1	7	8	21	0	1	8	15	36	4

Dundee and St Bernard's joined Division One

1894-95

DIVISION 1

	P	W	D	L	F	A	W	D	L	F	A	Pts
Hearts	18	7	1	1	27	12	8	0	1	23	6	31
Celtic	18	6	2	1	30	14	5	2	2	20	15	26
Rangers	18	6	1	2	20	9	4	1	4	21	17	22
T. Lanark	18	6	0	3	28	15	4	1	4	23	24	21
St Mirren	18	6	0	3	23	16	3	1	5	11	18	19
St Bernard's	18	4	0	5	18	19	4	1	4	19	21	17
Clyde	18	5	0	4	21	23	3	0	6	17	24	16
Dundee	18	4	2	3	17	11	2	0	7	11	22	14
Leith A	18	3	1	5	19	24	0	0	9	13	40	*7
Dumbarton	18	3	0	6	18	24	0	1	8	9	34	7

* Leith relegated to Division Two

1895-96

DIVISION 1

	P	W	D	L	F	A	W	D	L	F	A	Pts
Celtic	18	8	0	1	39	9	7	0	2	25	16	30
Rangers	18	5	2	2	28	19	6	2	1	29	20	26
Hibernian	18	6	1	2	31	20	5	1	3	27	19	24
Hearts	18	7	0	2	38	11	4	0	5	30	25	22
Dundee	18	4	2	3	21	12	3	0	6	12	30	16
T. Lanark	18	3	1	5	24	26	4	0	5	23	25	15
St Bernard's	18	5	0	4	25	27	2	1	6	11	26	15
St Mirren	18	3	1	5	15	24	2	2	5	16	27	13
Clyde	18	2	1	6	17	24	2	2	5	22	35	11
Dumbarton	18	3	0	6	24	35	1	0	8	12	39	*8

* Dumbarton relegated to Division Two.

1896-97

DIVISION 1

	P	W	D	L	F	A	W	D	L	F	A	Pts
Hearts	18	7	2	0	24	8	6	0	3	23	14	28
Hibernian	18	9	0	0	33	6	3	2	4	17	14	26
Rangers	18	9	0	0	36	10	2	3	4	28	20	25
Celtic	18	6	2	1	20	5	4	2	3	22	13	24
Dundee	18	7	1	1	21	12	3	1	5	17	18	22
St Mirren	18	7	1	1	25	7	2	0	7	13	22	19
St Bernard's	18	4	0	5	20	17	3	0	6	12	23	14
T. Lanark	18	3	1	5	20	24	2	0	7	9	22	11
Clyde	18	3	0	6	18	35	1	0	8	9	30	8
Abercorn	18	1	1	7	12	35	0	0	9	9	53	*3

* Abercorn relegated

1897-98

DIVISION 1

	P	W	D	L	F	A	W	D	L	F	A	Pts
Celtic	18	8	1	0	30	7	7	2	0	26	6	33
Rangers	18	7	1	1	38	6	6	2	1	33	9	29
Hibernian	18	6	1	2	28	12	4	1	4	19	17	22
Hearts	18	5	2	2	30	15	3	2	4	24	18	20
T. Lanark	18	5	0	4	25	15	3	2	4	12	23	18
St Mirren	18	5	1	3	20	13	3	1	5	10	23	18
Dundee	18	4	3	2	20	12	1	0	8	9	24	13
Partick T	18	5	1	3	22	23	1	0	8	12	41	13
St Bernard's	18	4	0	5	24	21	0	1	8	11	46	9
Clyde	18	1	2	6	16	37	0	1	8	5	46	5

1898-99

DIVISION 1

	P	W	D	L	F	A	W	D	L	F	A	Pts
Rangers	18	9	0	0	50	9	9	0	0	29	9	36
Hearts	18	7	1	1	32	13	5	1	3	24	17	26
Celtic	18	7	0	2	28	13	4	2	3	23	20	24
Hibernian	18	5	2	2	23	19	5	1	3	19	24	23
St Mirren	18	5	2	2	24	13	3	2	4	22	19	20
T. Lanark	18	4	2	3	17	17	3	1	5	16	21	17
St Bernard's	18	2	2	5	16	19	2	2	5	14	18	12
Clyde	18	2	3	4	12	15	2	1	6	11	33	12
Partick T	18	1	0	8	8	29	1	2	6	11	29	*6
Dundee	18	1	1	7	15	30	0	1	8	8	35	4

* Partick Thistle relegated

1899-1900

DIVISION 1

	P	W	D	L	F	A	W	D	L	F	A	Pts
Rangers	18	8	1	0	39	14	7	1	1	30	13	32
Celtic	18	6	2	1	25	14	3	5	1	21	13	25
Hibernian	18	5	3	1	22	11	4	3	2	21	13	24
Hearts	18	7	1	1	24	8	3	2	4	17	16	23
Kilmarnock	18	4	3	2	16	16	2	3	4	14	21	18
Dundee	18	3	4	2	20	14	1	3	5	16	25	15
T. Lanark	18	5	2	2	22	16	0	3	6	9	22	15
St Mirren	18	3	4	2	18	13	0	2	7	12	33	12
St Bernard's	18	3	3	3	17	19	1	1	7	12	28	*12
Clyde	18	2	0	7	17	34	0	0	9	7	36	*4

* St Bernard's and Clyde relegated.
Queen's Park joined Division One.

1900-01

DIVISION 1

	P	W	D	L	F	A	W	D	L	F	A	Pts
Rangers	20	10	0	0	37	11	7	1	2	23	14	35
Celtic	20	7	1	2	25	13	6	2	2	24	15	29
Hibernian	20	6	3	1	19	8	3	4	3	10	14	25
Morton	20	6	1	3	24	16	3	2	5	16	24	21
Kilmarnock	20	6	2	2	20	14	1	2	7	15	33	18
T. Lanark	20	5	4	1	14	10	1	2	7	6	19	18
Dundee	20	4	3	3	21	14	2	2	6	15	21	17
Queen's Park	20	4	3	3	18	13	3	0	7	15	24	17
St Mirren	20	5	1	4	23	23	0	5	5	10	20	16
Hearts	20	1	3	6	10	14	4	1	5	12	16	14
Partick T	20	2	1	7	15	23	2	1	7	13	26	*10

* Partick Thistle relegated.

1901-02

DIVISION 1

	P	W	D	L	F	A	W	D	L	F	A	Pts
Rangers	18	6	1	2	18	16	7	1	1	25	13	28
Celtic	18	5	2	2	19	15	6	2	1	19	13	26
Hearts	18	6	2	1	21	8	4	0	5	11	13	22
T. Lanark	18	3	3	3	13	11	4	2	3	17	15	19
St Mirren	18	3	3	3	16	13	5	0	4	13	15	19
Hibernian	18	3	1	5	26	14	3	3	3	10	9	16
Kilmarnock	18	4	2	3	15	10	1	4	4	7	17	16
Queen's Park	18	5	1	3	12	7	0	3	6	9	25	14
Dundee	18	3	3	3	9	9	1	2	6	6	22	13
Morton	18	0	2	7	10	24	1	3	5	10	17	7

1902-03

DIVISION 1

	P	W	D	L	F	A	W	D	L	F	A	Pts
Hibernian	22	8	3	0	23	11	8	2	1	25	7	37
Dundee	22	8	1	2	19	7	5	4	2	12	5	31
Rangers	22	7	3	1	37	17	5	2	4	19	13	29
Hearts	22	6	2	3	23	14	5	4	2	23	13	28
Celtic	22	4	6	1	20	15	4	4	3	16	15	26
St Mirren	22	4	4	3	17	13	3	4	4	22	27	22
T. Lanark	22	6	2	3	25	14	2	3	6	9	13	21
Partick T	22	4	4	3	18	18	2	3	6	16	32	19
Kilmarnock	22	3	3	5	15	20	3	1	7	9	23	16
Queen's Park	22	4	3	4	20	19	1	2	8	13	29	15
Port Glasgow A	22	3	3	5	11	14	0	2	9	15	35	11
Morton	22	2	1	8	13	26	0	4	7	9	29	9

1903-04

DIVISION 1

	P	W	D	L	F	A	W	D	L	F	A	Pts
T. Lanark	26	10	2	1	28	10	10	1	2	33	16	43
Hearts	26	13	0	0	41	9	5	3	5	22	26	39
Celtic	26	11	1	1	44	12	7	1	5	25	16	38
Rangers	26	10	3	0	47	10	6	3	4	33	23	38
Dundee	26	10	1	2	39	12	3	1	9	16	34	28
St Mirren	26	10	1	2	34	13	1	4	8	11	25	27
Partick T	26	7	4	2	28	17	3	3	7	15	23	27
Queen's Park	26	4	7	2	17	19	2	2	9	11	28	21
Port Glasgow A	26	6	3	4	23	17	2	1	10	10	32	20
Hibernian	26	5	3	5	22	19	2	2	9	9	23	19
Morton	26	5	1	7	19	23	2	3	8	12	28	18
Airdrie	26	5	1	7	18	25	2	3	8	14	37	18
Motherwell	26	5	1	7	14	22	1	2	10	12	39	15
Kilmarnock	26	3	3	7	15	27	1	2	10	12	39	13

1904-05

DIVISION 1

	P	W	D	L	F	A	W	D	L	F	A	Pts
Rangers	26	10	1	2	49	17	9	2	2	34	11	41
Celtic	26	8	4	1	31	15	10	1	2	37	16	*41
T. Lanark	26	11	1	1	48	12	3	6	4	12	16	35
Airdrie	26	6	4	3	23	18	5	1	7	15	27	27
Hibernian	26	7	5	1	27	11	2	3	8	12	28	26
Partick T	26	8	0	5	20	20	4	2	7	16	36	26
Dundee	26	8	2	3	26	8	2	3	8	12	24	25
Hearts	26	10	0	3	30	13	1	3	9	13	31	25
Kilmarnock	26	8	2	3	16	17	1	3	9	13	28	23
St Mirren	26	4	4	5	17	15	5	0	8	16	21	22
Port Glasgow A	26	6	3	4	23	20	2	2	9	7	28	21
Queen's Park	26	5	3	5	18	19	1	5	7	10	26	20
Morton	26	6	3	4	16	12	1	1	11	11	38	18
Motherwell	26	4	1	8	13	26	2	1	10	15	27	14

* Celtic won a deciding match against Rangers.

1905-06

DIVISION 1

	P	W	D	L	F	A	W	D	L	F	A	Pts
Celtic	30	13	0	2	36	8	11	1	3	40	11	49
Hearts	30	12	3	0	35	8	6	4	5	29	19	43
Airdrie	30	8	4	3	31	18	7	4	4	22	13	38
Rangers	30	9	2	4	27	23	6	5	4	31	25	37
Partick T	30	9	3	3	25	18	6	3	6	19	22	36
T. Lanark	30	10	0	5	35	15	6	2	7	27	23	34
Dundee	30	8	6	1	26	9	3	6	6	14	24	34
St Mirren	30	10	2	3	29	16	3	3	9	12	21	31
Motherwell	30	7	4	4	33	27	2	4	9	17	37	26
Morton	30	5	5	5	17	20	5	1	9	18	34	26
Hibernian	30	7	1	7	23	22	3	4	8	12	18	25
Aberdeen	30	7	4	4	23	16	1	4	10	13	32	24
Falkirk	30	7	5	3	36	28	2	0	13	16	40	23
Kilmarnock	30	8	3	4	32	22	0	1	14	14	46	20
Port Glasgow A	30	4	3	8	23	33	2	5	8	15	35	20
Queen's Park	30	4	3	8	21	36	1	1	13	20	52	14

1906-07

DIVISION 1

	P	W	D	L	F	A	W	D	L	F	A	Pts
Celtic	34	13	4	0	40	14	10	5	2	40	16	55
Dundee	34	10	5	2	24	10	8	7	2	29	16	48
Rangers	34	9	5	3	35	16	10	2	5	34	17	45
Airdrle	34	12	1	4	36	20	6	5	6	23	24	42
Falkirk	34	12	4	1	45	23	5	3	9	28	35	41
T. Lanark	34	8	5	4	34	26	7	4	6	23	22	39
St Mirren	34	6	8	3	23	19	6	5	6	27	25	37
Clyde	34	9	3	5	27	22	6	3	8	20	30	36
Hearts	34	7	7	3	27	16	4	6	7	19	27	35
Motherwell	34	8	3	6	25	27	4	6	7	20	21	33
Aberdeen	34	7	6	4	24	20	3	4	10	24	35	30
Hibernian	34	7	5	5	22	20	3	5	9	18	29	30
Morton	34	9	4	4	26	15	2	2	13	15	35	28
Partick	34	7	3	7	22	22	2	5	10	18	38	26
Queen's Park	34	7	1	9	27	29	2	5	10	24	37	24
Hamilton	34	5	1	11	27	37	3	4	10	13	27	21
Kilmarnock	34	7	3	7	29	33	1	2	14	11	39	21
Port Glasgow	34	4	6	7	20	27	3	1	13	10	40	21

1907-08

DIVISION 1

	P	W	D	L	F	A	W	D	L	F	A	Pts
Celtic	34	15	2	0	57	11	9	5	3	29	16	55
Falkirk	34	13	2	2	58	17	9	5	3	45	25	51
Rangers	34	10	5	2	35	16	11	3	3	39	24	50
Dundee	34	12	3	2	43	10	8	5	4	28	18	48
Hibernian	34	10	1	6	35	24	7	7	3	20	18	42
Airdrie	34	10	3	4	37	16	8	2	7	21	25	41
St Mirren	34	6	6	5	24	24	7	4	6	26	35	36
Aberdeen	34	9	5	3	25	14	4	4	9	20	30	35
T. Lanark	34	8	3	6	31	29	5	4	8	14	21	33
Motherwell	34	8	2	7	40	25	4	5	8	21	28	31
Hamilton A	34	7	6	4	32	25	3	2	12	23	40	28
Hearts	34	9	1	7	33	24	2	5	10	17	38	28
Morton	34	5	6	6	24	27	4	3	10	19	39	27
Partick T	34	3	7	7	19	30	5	2	10	24	39	25
Kilmarnock	34	5	7	5	22	22	1	6	10	16	39	25
Queen's Park	34	5	5	7	28	29	2	3	12	26	55	22
Clyde	34	4	4	9	21	34	1	4	12	15	41	18
Port Glasgow A	34	3	4	10	21	44	2	3	12	18	54	17

1908-09

DIVISION 1

	P	W	D	L	F	A	W	D	L	F	A	Pts
Celtic	34	11	3	3	36	10	12	2	3	35	14	51
Dundee	34	14	2	1	44	12	8	4	5	26	20	50
Clyde	34	12	2	3	32	16	9	4	4	29	21	48
Rangers	34	10	5	2	48	18	9	2	6	43	20	45
Airdrie	34	8	5	4	38	28	8	4	5	29	18	41
Hibernian	34	12	3	2	28	9	4	4	9	12	23	39
St Mirren	34	11	2	4	35	16	4	4	9	18	29	36
Aberdeen	34	11	2	4	39	22	4	4	9	22	31	36
Falkirk	34	10	4	3	37	18	3	3	11	21	38	33
Kilmarnock	34	11	2	4	32	24	2	5	10	15	37	33
T. Lanark	34	9	4	4	36	19	2	6	9	20	30	32
Hearts	34	8	5	4	26	17	4	3	10	28	32	32
Port Glasgow A	34	6	5	6	20	19	4	3	10	19	33	28
Motherwell	34	8	3	6	31	35	3	3	11	16	38	28
Queen's Park	34	2	6	9	18	31	4	7	6	24	34	25
Hamilton A	34	4	7	6	23	29	2	5	10	19	43	24
Morton	34	5	6	6	24	32	3	1	13	15	58	23
Partick T	34	2	1	14	21	53	0	3	14	17	49	8

1909-10

DIVISION 1

	P	W	D	L	F	A	W	D	L	F	A	Pts
Celtic	34	13	4	0	38	9	11	2	4	25	13	54
Falkirk	34	14	3	0	44	10	8	5	4	27	18	52
Rangers	34	14	2	1	39	9	6	4	7	31	26	46
Aberdeen	34	10	4	3	25	11	6	4	7	19	18	40
Clyde	34	10	4	3	24	11	4	5	8	23	29	37
Dundee	34	12	5	0	37	12	2	3	12	15	32	36
T. Lanark	34	10	2	5	44	19	3	6	8	18	25	34
Hibernian	34	10	4	3	20	12	4	2	11	13	28	34
Airdrie	34	7	5	5	28	26	5	4	8	18	31	33
Motherwell	34	8	5	4	39	25	4	3	10	20	35	32
Kilmarnock	34	10	3	4	35	19	2	5	10	18	40	32
Hearts	34	9	3	5	37	19	3	4	10	22	31	31
St Mirren	34	11	0	6	31	28	2	5	10	17	30	31
Queen's Park	34	8	5	4	37	25	4	1	12	17	49	30
Hamilton A	34	9	4	4	35	34	2	2	13	15	33	28
Partick T	34	6	6	5	24	22	2	4	11	21	37	26
Morton	34	9	1	7	22	18	2	2	13	16	42	25
Port Glasgow A	34	2	3	12	15	36	1	2	14	10	57	*11

* Port Glasgow A relegated.

1910-11

DIVISION 1

	P	W	D	L	F	A	W	D	L	F	A	Pts
Rangers	34	12	2	3	53	18	11	4	2	37	16	52
Aberdeen	34	12	5	0	31	11	7	5	5	22	17	48
Falkirk	34	12	4	1	41	18	5	6	6	24	24	44
Partick T	34	13	4	0	30	12	4	4	9	20	29	42
Celtic	34	11	4	2	31	3	4	7	6	17	15	41
Dundee	34	13	2	2	36	13	5	3	9	18	29	41
Clyde	34	8	6	3	21	8	6	5	6	24	28	39
T. Lanark	34	8	5	4	30	28	8	2	7	29	25	39
Hibernian	34	11	2	4	27	19	4	4	9	17	29	36
Kilmarnock	34	9	3	5	29	22	3	7	7	13	23	34
Airdrie	34	9	4	4	36	24	3	5	9	13	29	33
St Mirren	34	11	2	4	30	17	1	5	11	16	40	31
Morton	34	4	8	5	24	22	5	3	9	25	29	29
Hearts	34	7	6	4	27	18	1	2	14	15	41	24
Raith R	34	6	6	5	26	22	1	4	12	10	33	24
Hamilton A	34	7	3	7	22	24	1	2	14	9	36	21
Motherwell	34	6	3	8	25	27	2	1	14	12	39	20
Queen's Park	34	5	2	10	15	28	0	2	15	13	52	14

1911-12

DIVISION 1

	P	W	D	L	F	A	W	D	L	F	A	Pts
Rangers	34	16	0	1	60	10	8	3	6	26	24	51
Celtic	34	14	3	0	38	11	3	8	6	20	22	45
Clyde	34	10	1	6	25	14	9	3	5	31	18	42
Hearts	34	11	2	4	28	16	5	6	6	26	24	40
Partick T	34	7	8	2	24	14	9	0	8	23	26	40
Morton	34	10	3	4	27	19	4	6	7	17	25	37
Falkirk	34	10	3	4	30	17	5	3	9	16	26	36
Dundee	34	11	4	2	40	18	2	5	10	12	23	35
Aberdeen	34	9	4	4	26	14	5	3	9	18	30	35
Airdrie	34	8	5	4	25	14	4	3	10	15	27	32
T. Lanark	34	10	1	6	26	19	2	6	9	14	38	31
Hamilton A	34	7	5	5	21	16	4	3	10	11	28	30
Hibernian	34	10	3	4	32	15	2	2	13	12	32	29
Motherwell	34	7	2	8	20	21	4	3	10	14	23	27
Raith R	34	6	6	5	25	22	3	3	11	14	37	27
Kilmarnock	34	7	3	7	22	22	4	1	12	16	38	26
Queen's Park	34	6	6	5	18	22	2	3	12	11	31	25
St Mirren	34	5	6	6	19	25	2	4	11	13	34	24

1912-13

DIVISION 1

	P	W	D	L	F	A	W	D	L	F	A	Pts
Rangers	34	13	2	2	46	22	11	3	3	30	19	53
Celtic	34	13	2	2	32	12	9	3	5	21	16	49
Hearts	34	10	4	3	42	18	7	3	7	29	25	41
Airdrie	34	10	4	3	39	22	5	7	5	25	24	41
Falkirk	34	9	4	4	29	14	5	8	4	27	24	40
Motherwell	34	7	5	5	28	19	5	8	4	19	20	37
Aberdeen	34	9	4	4	31	14	5	5	7	16	26	37
Hibernian	34	9	3	5	34	22	7	2	8	29	32	37
Clyde	34	6	8	3	18	12	7	1	9	23	32	35
Hamilton A	34	10	3	4	29	14	2	5	10	15	33	32
Kilmarnock	34	8	4	5	27	22	2	7	8	10	32	31
St Mirren	34	9	4	4	32	26	1	6	10	18	34	30
Morton	34	8	3	6	28	23	3	4	10	22	36	29
Dundee	34	7	7	3	19	14	1	6	10	14	32	29
T. Lanark	34	4	7	6	11	14	4	5	8	20	27	28
Raith R	34	5	7	5	33	28	3	3	11	13	32	26
Partick T	34	9	3	5	33	24	1	1	15	7	31	24
Queen's Park	34	4	3	10	20	32	1	0	16	14	56	13

1913-14

DIVISION 1

	P	W	D	L	F	A	W	D	L	F	A	Pts
Celtic	38	15	3	1	45	6	15	2	2	36	8	65
Rangers	38	14	3	2	40	15	13	2	4	39	16	59
Hearts	38	17	1	1	43	7	6	7	6	27	22	54
Morton	38	16	0	3	45	17	10	2	7	31	34	54
Falkirk	38	14	4	1	44	18	6	5	8	25	33	49
Airdrie	38	10	7	2	46	24	8	5	6	26	19	48
Dundee	38	13	2	4	41	19	6	3	10	23	34	43
T. Lanark	38	10	4	5	30	22	3	6	10	12	29	36
Clyde	38	8	5	6	27	17	3	6	10	17	27	33
Ayr U	38	8	3	8	26	30	5	4	10	30	42	33
Raith R	38	9	4	6	38	22	4	2	13	18	35	32
Kilmarnock	38	8	3	8	34	29	3	6	10	14	39	31
Hibernian	38	6	2	11	27	36	6	4	9	31	39	30
Aberdeen	38	5	8	6	21	18	5	2	12	17	37	30
Partick T	38	9	4	6	25	23	1	5	13	12	28	29
Queen's Park	38	7	6	6	29	33	3	3	13	23	51	29
Hamilton A	38	8	4	7	31	21	3	2	14	18	45	28
Motherwell	38	9	2	8	34	28	2	4	13	12	37	28
Dumbarton	38	7	4	8	24	35	3	3	13	21	52	27
St Mirren	38	6	5	8	22	28	2	1	16	16	45	22

1914-15

DIVISION 1

	P	W	D	L	F	A	W	D	L	F	A	Pts
Celtic	38	18	1	0	56	10	12	4	3	35	15	65
Hearts	38	17	1	1	50	13	10	6	3	33	19	61
Rangers	38	11	1	7	37	23	12	3	4	37	24	50
Morton	38	13	4	2	43	17	5	8	6	31	31	48
Ayr U	38	13	3	3	29	12	7	5	7	26	28	48
Falkirk	38	10	5	4	31	19	6	2	11	17	29	39
Hamilton A	38	9	5	5	37	26	7	1	11	23	29	38
Partick T	38	10	3	6	36	22	5	5	9	20	36	38
St Mirren	38	9	4	6	31	25	5	4	10	25	40	36
Airdrie	38	9	4	6	35	28	5	3	11	19	32	35
Hibernian	38	9	5	5	36	27	3	6	10	23	39	35
Kilmarnock	38	12	2	5	39	24	3	2	14	16	35	34
Dumbarton	38	9	3	7	29	30	4	5	10	22	36	34
Aberdeen	38	7	7	5	21	14	4	4	11	18	38	33
Dundee	38	8	4	7	24	21	4	5	10	19	40	33
T. Lanark	38	7	8	4	32	22	3	4	12	19	35	32
Clyde	38	8	4	7	27	24	4	2	13	17	35	30
Motherwell	38	7	5	7	31	30	3	5	11	18	36	30
Raith R	38	5	8	6	31	27	4	2	13	22	41	28
Queen's Park	38	3	2	14	14	39	1	3	15	13	51	13

1915-16

DIVISION 1

	P	W	D	L	F	A	W	D	L	F	A	Pts
Celtic	38	15	3	1	64	13	17	0	2	52	10	67
Rangers	38	15	2	2	55	17	10	4	5	32	22	56
Morton	37	15	0	3	58	9	7	7	5	28	26	*51
Ayr U	38	12	4	3	39	19	8	4	7	33	26	48
Partick T	38	13	2	4	48	20	6	6	7	17	21	46
Hearts	37	12	1	6	35	23	8	5	5	31	22	*46
Hamilton A	38	13	2	4	49	28	6	1	12	19	48	41
Dundee	38	13	2	4	37	14	5	2	12	19	35	40
Dumbarton	38	9	6	4	33	22	4	5	10	21	42	37
Kilmarnock	38	9	5	5	34	17	3	6	10	12	32	35
Aberdeen	38	8	8	3	31	20	3	4	12	20	44	34
Falkirk	38	8	6	5	21	19	4	3	12	24	42	33
St Mirren	38	11	1	7	37	26	2	3	14	13	41	30
Motherwell	38	5	7	7	34	40	6	1	12	21	42	30
Airdrie	38	8	6	5	25	19	3	2	14	19	55	30
T. Lanark	38	6	5	8	26	23	3	6	10	14	33	29
Clyde	38	7	2	10	30	34	4	5	10	19	37	29
Queen's Park	38	7	5	7	30	34	4	1	14	23	66	28
Hibernian	38	7	2	10	21	28	2	5	12	23	43	25
Raith R	38	8	3	8	21	24	1	2	16	9	41	23

* Morton and Hearts only played each other once.

1916-17

DIVISION 1

	P	W	D	L	F	A	W	D	L	F	A	Pts
Celtic	38	13	5	1	38	8	14	5	0	41	9	64
Morton	38	16	1	2	44	16	8	5	6	28	23	54
Rangers	38	16	1	2	40	9	8	4	7	28	23	53
Airdrie	38	16	1	2	47	17	5	7	7	24	21	50
T. Lanark	38	11	7	1	32	15	8	4	7	21	22	49
Kilmarnock	38	12	2	5	48	22	6	5	8	21	24	43
St Mirren	38	8	7	4	25	15	7	3	9	24	28	40
Motherwell	38	9	4	6	32	28	7	2	10	25	31	38
Partick T	38	9	5	5	28	11	5	2	12	16	32	35
Dumbarton	38	8	6	5	35	31	4	5	10	21	42	35
Hamilton A	38	11	3	5	35	24	2	6	11	18	48	35
Falkirk	38	7	5	7	29	24	5	5	9	29	33	34
Clyde	38	6	7	6	20	23	4	7	8	20	29	34
Hearts	38	9	1	9	25	30	5	3	11	19	29	32
Ayr U	38	6	6	7	21	24	6	1	12	26	35	31
Dundee	38	9	2	8	37	28	4	2	13	21	43	30
Hibernian	38	6	6	7	33	34	4	4	11	24	38	30
Queen's Park	38	7	5	7	34	37	4	2	13	22	44	29
Raith R	38	6	2	11	22	41	2	5	12	20	50	23
Aberdeen	38	6	4	9	24	23	1	3	15	12	45	21

Aberdeen, Dundee & Raith Rovers left League.
Clydebank joined Division One.

1917-18

DIVISION 1

	P	W	D	L	F	A	W	D	L	F	A	Pts
Rangers	34	15	1	1	42	12	10	5	2	24	12	56
Celtic	34	11	4	2	34	13	13	3	1	32	13	55
Kilmarnock	34	12	2	3	45	16	7	3	7	24	25	43
Morton	34	9	6	2	27	17	8	3	6	26	25	43
Motherwell	34	11	3	3	43	21	5	6	6	27	30	41
Partick T	34	10	4	3	36	19	4	8	5	15	18	40
Queen's Park	34	11	4	2	41	15	3	2	12	23	48	34
Dumbarton	34	8	2	7	30	29	5	6	6	18	20	34
Clydebank	34	7	4	6	30	26	7	1	9	25	30	33
Hearts	34	11	1	5	24	15	3	3	11	17	43	32
St Mirren	34	9	6	2	27	12	2	1	14	15	38	29
Hamilton A	34	8	5	4	33	22	3	1	13	19	41	28
T. Lanark	34	6	3	8	29	22	4	4	9	27	40	27
Falkirk	34	8	6	3	29	21	1	3	13	9	37	27
Airdrie	34	8	2	7	26	19	2	4	11	20	39	26
Hibernian	34	7	4	6	27	26	1	5	11	15	31	25
Clyde	34	5	2	10	20	32	4	0	13	17	40	20
Ayr U	34	3	4	10	20	28	2	5	10	12	33	19

1918-19

DIVISION 1

	P	W	D	L	F	A	W	D	L	F	A	Pts
Celtic	34	13	3	1	33	10	13	3	1	38	12	58
Rangers	34	15	2	0	51	7	11	3	3	35	9	57
Morton	34	10	7	0	49	20	8	4	5	27	20	47
Partick T	34	11	1	5	38	21	6	6	5	24	22	41
Motherwell	34	7	5	5	28	19	7	5	5	23	21	38
Ayr U	34	9	1	7	34	22	6	7	4	28	31	38
Hearts	34	8	5	4	31	20	6	4	7	28	32	37
Queen's Park	34	10	1	6	39	29	5	4	8	20	28	35
Kilmarnock	34	6	4	7	30	24	8	3	6	31	35	35
Clydebank	34	7	4	6	31	35	5	4	8	23	30	32
St Mirren	34	6	8	3	26	25	4	4	9	17	30	32
T. Lanark	34	4	4	9	27	34	7	5	5	33	28	31
Airdrie	34	4	7	6	21	27	5	4	8	24	27	29
Hamilton A	34	6	2	9	23	31	5	3	9	26	44	27
Dumbarton	34	4	6	7	16	20	3	2	12	15	38	22
Falkirk	34	3	5	9	28	34	3	3	11	18	39	20
Clyde	34	4	4	9	23	33	3	2	12	22	42	20
Hibernian	34	5	0	12	16	35	0	3	14	14	56	13

1919-20

DIVISION 1

	P	W	D	L	F	A	W	D	L	F	A	Pts
Rangers	42	18	2	1	68	18	13	7	1	38	7	71
Celtic	42	15	6	0	54	14	14	4	3	35	17	68
Motherwell	42	15	6	0	53	22	8	5	8	21	31	57
Dundee	42	16	2	3	48	24	6	4	11	31	41	50
Clydebank	42	12	6	3	47	24	8	2	11	31	30	48
Morton	42	10	6	5	37	15	6	7	8	34	33	45
Airdrie	42	11	6	4	27	11	6	4	11	30	32	44
T. Lanark	42	11	4	6	35	28	5	7	9	21	34	43
Kilmarnock	42	15	0	6	40	31	5	3	13	19	43	43
Ayr U	42	11	7	3	44	19	4	3	14	28	50	40
Dumbarton	42	7	9	5	26	23	6	4	11	31	42	39
Queen's Park	42	11	5	5	41	28	3	5	13	26	45	38
Partick T	42	12	5	4	36	24	1	7	13	15	38	38
St Mirren	42	9	3	9	32	38	6	5	10	31	43	38
Clyde	42	11	4	6	44	31	3	5	13	20	40	37
Hearts	42	8	5	8	31	28	6	4	11	26	44	37
Aberdeen	42	8	7	6	23	19	3	6	12	23	45	35
Hibernian	42	11	3	7	38	27	2	4	15	22	52	33
Raith R	42	10	3	8	33	29	1	7	13	28	54	32
Falkirk	42	10	6	5	36	27	0	5	16	9	47	31
Hamilton A	42	10	5	6	40	34	1	2	18	16	52	29
Albion R	42	7	4	10	27	37	3	4	14	16	40	28

Aberdeen, Albion, Dundee & Raith Rovers joined Division One.

1920-21

DIVISION 1

	P	W	D	L	F	A	W	D	L	F	A	Pts
Rangers	42	19	1	1	50	11	16	5	0	41	13	76
Celtic	42	16	3	2	50	15	14	3	4	36	20	66
Hearts	42	15	2	4	48	16	5	8	8	26	33	50
Dundee	42	13	5	3	35	13	6	6	9	19	35	49
Motherwell	42	11	5	5	46	28	8	5	8	29	23	48
Partick T	42	10	9	2	34	16	7	3	11	19	23	46
Clyde	42	16	3	2	43	17	5	0	16	20	45	45
T. Lanark	42	10	3	8	45	27	9	3	9	29	34	44
Morton	42	10	8	3	44	21	5	6	10	22	37	44
Airdrie	42	9	5	7	46	32	8	4	9	25	32	43
Aberdeen	42	9	7	5	30	18	5	7	9	23	36	42
Kilmarnock	42	13	2	6	43	25	4	6	11	19	43	42
Hibernian	42	9	5	7	31	23	7	4	10	27	34	41
Ayr U	42	10	8	3	40	21	4	4	13	22	48	40
Hamilton A	42	9	8	4	26	16	5	4	12	18	41	40
Raith R	42	14	0	7	38	21	2	5	14	16	37	37
Albion R	42	6	5	10	31	31	5	7	9	26	37	34
Falkirk	42	7	6	8	33	31	4	6	11	21	41	34
Queen's Park	42	6	8	7	24	28	5	3	13	21	52	33
Clydebank	42	6	6	9	33	31	1	8	12	14	41	28
Dumbarton	42	9	1	11	25	27	1	3	17	16	62	24
St Mirren	42	5	2	14	25	39	2	2	17	18	53	18

1921-22

DIVISION 1

	P	W	D	L	F	A	W	D	L	F	A	Pts
Celtic	42	19	2	0	51	4	8	11	2	32	16	67
Rangers	42	15	4	2	45	14	13	6	2	38	12	66
Raith R	42	12	7	2	41	16	7	6	8	25	27	51
Dundee	42	13	8	0	33	8	6	3	12	24	32	49
Falkirk	42	13	6	2	35	11	3	11	7	13	27	49
Partick T	42	12	6	3	32	17	8	2	11	25	36	48
Hibernian	42	11	7	3	31	12	5	7	9	24	32	46
St Mirren	42	11	6	4	43	24	6	6	9	28	37	46
T. Lanark	42	10	7	4	34	22	7	5	9	24	30	46
Clyde	42	12	7	2	36	15	4	5	12	24	36	44
Albion R	42	11	4	6	27	18	6	6	9	28	33	44
Morton	42	14	5	2	39	17	2	5	14	19	40	42
Motherwell	42	15	3	3	49	19	1	4	16	14	39	39
Ayr U	42	11	6	4	30	20	2	6	13	25	43	38
Aberdeen	42	10	5	6	31	17	3	4	14	17	37	35
Airdrie	42	10	4	7	35	23	2	7	12	11	33	35
Kilmarnock	42	12	6	3	44	26	1	3	17	12	57	35
Hamilton A	42	7	8	6	37	29	2	8	11	14	33	34
Hearts	42	9	6	6	34	21	2	4	15	16	39	32
Dumbarton	42	9	4	8	36	39	1	6	14	10	42	*30
Queen's Park	42	5	5	11	22	46	4	5	12	16	36	*28
Clydebank	42	5	6	10	18	37	1	2	18	16	66	*20

* Dumbarton, Queen's Park & Clydebank relegated to Division Two.

1922-23

DIVISION 1

	P	W	D	L	F	A	W	D	L	F	A	Pts
Rangers	38	15	4	0	43	11	8	5	6	24	18	55
Airdrie	38	14	4	1	41	16	6	6	7	17	22	50
Celtic	38	10	5	4	29	21	9	3	7	23	18	46
Falkirk	38	9	10	0	27	7	5	7	7	17	25	45
Aberdeen	38	10	6	3	28	12	5	6	8	18	22	42
St Mirren	38	11	6	2	32	14	4	6	9	22	30	42
Dundee	38	13	2	4	28	11	4	5	10	23	34	41
Hibernian	38	14	2	3	31	13	3	5	11	14	27	41
Raith R	38	9	8	2	18	14	4	5	10	13	29	39
Ayr U	38	11	6	2	31	15	2	6	11	12	29	38
Partick T	38	11	4	4	33	14	3	5	11	18	34	37
Hearts	38	6	10	3	29	20	5	5	9	22	30	37
Motherwell	38	10	6	3	38	24	3	4	12	21	36	36
Morton	38	9	3	7	28	20	3	8	8	16	27	35
Kilmarnock	38	11	1	7	37	26	3	6	10	20	40	35
Clyde	38	10	4	5	24	12	2	5	12	12	32	33
T. Lanark	38	8	5	6	29	22	3	3	13	11	37	30
Hamilton A	38	8	6	5	29	18	3	1	15	14	41	29
Albion R	38	7	3	9	25	22	1	7	11	13	42	26
Alloa	38	3	7	9	16	29	3	4	12	11	23	23

1923-24

DIVISION 1

	P	W	D	L	F	A	W	D	L	F	A	Pts
Rangers	38	14	4	1	38	7	11	5	3	34	15	59
Airdrie	38	13	6	0	48	17	7	4	8	24	29	50
Celtic	38	11	5	3	36	15	6	7	6	20	18	46
Raith R	38	13	3	3	40	12	5	4	10	16	26	43
Dundee	38	12	6	1	48	22	3	7	9	22	35	43
St Mirren	38	10	5	4	37	15	5	7	7	16	30	42
Hibernian	38	12	3	4	41	21	3	8	8	25	31	41
Partick T	38	9	4	6	32	23	6	5	8	26	32	39
Hearts	38	12	4	3	43	17	2	6	11	18	33	38
Motherwell	38	11	4	4	36	26	4	3	12	22	37	37
Morton	38	12	3	4	31	16	4	2	13	17	38	37
Hamilton A	38	11	2	6	37	26	4	4	11	15	31	36
Aberdeen	38	11	5	3	27	14	2	5	12	10	27	36
Ayr U	38	11	7	1	32	16	1	3	15	6	44	34
Falkirk	38	10	4	5	28	15	3	2	14	18	38	32
Kilmarnock	38	9	4	6	28	25	3	4	12	20	40	32
Queen's Park	38	7	7	5	22	21	4	2	13	21	39	31
T. Lanark	38	9	3	7	32	33	2	5	12	22	45	30
Clyde	38	8	6	5	26	21	2	3	14	14	49	29
Clydebank	38	8	3	8	21	25	2	2	15	21	46	25

1924-25

DIVISION 1

	P	W	D	L	F	A	W	D	L	F	A	Pts
Rangers	38	16	3	0	46	10	9	7	3	30	16	60
Airdrie	38	15	4	0	51	10	10	3	6	34	21	57
Hibernian	38	16	1	2	56	16	6	7	6	22	27	52
Celtic	38	13	3	3	51	13	5	5	9	26	31	44
Cowdenbeath	38	13	3	3	52	21	3	7	9	24	44	42
St Mirren	38	12	2	5	36	22	6	2	11	29	41	40
Partick T	38	8	6	5	35	27	6	4	9	25	34	38
Dundee	38	11	4	4	30	14	3	4	12	17	40	36
Raith R	38	11	4	4	34	22	3	4	12	19	39	36
Hearts	38	10	6	3	44	28	2	5	12	20	40	35
St Johnstone	38	8	7	4	38	29	4	4	11	19	43	35
Kilmarnock	38	10	4	5	35	21	2	5	12	18	43	33
Hamilton A	38	10	2	7	29	26	5	1	13	21	37	33
Morton	38	8	7	4	29	23	4	2	13	17	46	33
Aberdeen	38	7	4	8	23	20	4	6	9	23	36	32
Falkirk	38	10	4	5	33	18	2	4	13	11	36	32
Queen's Park	38	9	4	6	30	22	3	4	12	20	49	32
Motherwell	38	9	5	5	42	27	1	5	13	12	36	30
Ayr U	38	7	6	6	28	25	4	2	13	15	40	30
T. Lanark	38	5	5	9	29	32	6	3	10	24	52	30

1925-26

DIVISION 1

	P	W	D	L	F	A	W	D	L	F	A	Pts
Celtic	38	15	4	0	59	15	10	4	5	38	25	58
Airdrie	38	13	3	3	53	22	10	1	8	42	32	50
Hearts	38	14	2	3	52	21	7	6	6	35	35	50
St Mirren	38	12	4	3	37	23	8	3	8	25	29	47
Motherwell	38	15	1	3	41	15	4	7	8	26	31	46
Rangers	38	12	1	6	39	21	7	5	7	40	34	44
Cowdenbeath	38	14	3	2	54	20	4	3	12	33	48	42
Falkirk	38	8	10	1	35	21	6	4	9	26	36	42
Kilmarnock	38	11	4	4	49	30	6	3	10	30	47	41
Dundee	38	9	4	6	29	27	5	5	9	18	32	37
Aberdeen	38	10	4	5	35	23	3	6	10	14	31	36
Hamilton A	38	10	5	4	40	29	3	4	12	28	50	35
Queen's Park	38	10	1	8	43	39	5	3	11	27	42	34
Partick T	38	8	6	5	39	35	2	7	10	25	38	33
Morton	38	9	5	5	35	30	3	2	14	22	54	31
Hibernian	38	8	3	8	48	37	4	3	12	24	40	30
Dundee U	38	7	4	8	31	27	4	2	13	21	47	28
St Johnstone	38	5	8	6	22	31	4	2	13	21	47	28
Raith R	38	9	2	8	30	30	2	2	15	16	51	26
Clydebank	38	7	3	9	37	33	0	5	14	18	59	22

1927-28

DIVISION 1

	P	W	D	L	F	A	W	D	L	F	A	Pts
Rangers	38	17	1	1	67	16	9	7	3	42	20	60
Celtic	38	14	3	2	56	13	9	6	4	37	26	55
Motherwell	38	12	4	3	51	24	11	5	3	41	22	55
Hearts	38	10	5	4	47	20	10	2	7	42	30	47
St Mirren	38	11	6	2	46	26	7	2	10	31	50	44
Partick T	38	10	5	4	48	31	8	2	9	37	36	43
Aberdeen	38	15	1	3	47	15	4	4	11	24	46	43
Kilmarnock	38	10	5	4	41	30	5	5	9	27	48	40
Cowdenbeath	38	8	4	7	32	32	8	3	8	34	36	39
Falkirk	38	12	1	6	55	29	4	4	11	21	40	37
St Johnstone	38	9	4	6	38	27	5	4	10	28	40	36
Hibernian	38	11	6	2	50	24	2	3	14	23	51	35
Airdrie	38	8	3	8	31	31	4	8	7	28	38	35
Dundee	38	12	0	7	46	37	2	7	10	19	43	35
Clyde	38	7	6	6	28	25	3	5	11	18	47	31
Queen's Park	38	10	4	5	52	31	2	2	15	17	49	30
Raith R	38	7	5	7	35	32	4	2	13	25	57	29
Hamilton A	38	9	4	6	46	32	2	2	15	21	54	28
Bo'ness	38	6	8	5	27	27	3	0	16	21	59	26
Dunfermline A	38	4	1	14	22	53	0	3	16	19	73	12

1926-27

DIVISION 1

	P	W	D	L	F	A	W	D	L	F	A	Pts
Rangers	38	15	2	2	41	15	8	8	3	44	26	56
Motherwell	38	13	2	4	46	26	10	3	6	35	26	51
Celtic	38	14	2	3	58	21	7	5	7	43	34	49
Airdrie	38	13	5	1	64	23	5	4	10	33	41	45
Dundee	38	11	3	5	45	21	6	6	7	32	30	43
Falkirk	38	11	7	1	56	23	5	3	11	21	37	42
Cowdenbeath	38	12	3	4	41	18	6	3	10	33	42	42
Aberdeen	38	11	6	2	49	29	2	8	9	24	43	40
Hibernian	38	11	5	3	40	27	5	2	12	22	44	39
St Mirren	38	13	1	5	54	32	3	4	12	24	44	37
Partick T	38	10	3	6	58	39	5	3	11	31	35	36
Queen's Park	38	11	2	6	47	35	4	4	11	27	49	36
Hearts	38	7	7	5	34	25	5	4	10	31	39	35
St Johnstone	38	8	7	4	29	19	5	2	12	26	50	35
Hamilton A	38	7	5	7	34	38	6	4	9	26	47	35
Kilmarnock	38	8	5	6	36	29	4	3	12	18	42	32
Clyde	38	7	7	5	34	26	3	2	14	20	59	29
Dunfermline A	38	7	3	9	29	37	3	5	11	24	48	28
Morton	38	11	0	8	40	38	1	4	14	16	63	28
Dundee U	38	6	5	8	31	34	1	3	15	25	67	22

1928-29

DIVISION 1

	P	W	D	L	F	A	W	D	L	F	A	Pts
Rangers	38	14	5	0	51	8	16	2	1	56	24	67
Celtic	38	13	2	4	38	17	9	5	5	29	27	51
Motherwell	38	12	4	3	49	35	8	6	5	36	31	50
Hearts	38	13	4	2	56	23	6	5	8	35	34	47
Queen's Park	38	13	1	5	69	31	5	6	8	31	38	43
Partick T	38	12	3	4	60	34	5	4	10	31	36	41
Aberdeen	38	14	3	2	55	20	2	5	12	26	48	40
St Mirren	38	9	3	7	46	35	7	5	7	32	40	40
St Johnstone	38	11	4	4	35	22	3	6	10	22	48	38
Kilmarnock	38	9	4	6	45	32	5	4	10	34	42	36
Falkirk	38	11	5	3	41	32	3	3	13	27	54	36
Hamilton A	38	9	6	4	38	31	4	3	12	20	52	35
Cowdenbeath	38	10	5	4	28	18	4	2	13	27	51	33
Hibernian	38	9	5	5	39	25	4	1	14	15	37	32
Airdrie	38	10	4	5	38	24	2	3	14	18	41	31
Ayr U	38	8	3	8	36	33	4	4	11	29	51	31
Clyde	38	9	4	6	32	27	3	2	14	15	44	30
Dundee	38	4	5	10	27	31	5	6	8	32	38	29
T. Lanark	38	8	3	8	46	41	2	3	14	25	61	26
Raith R	38	7	5	7	34	39	2	1	16	18	66	24

1929-30

DIVISION 1

	P	W	D	L	F	A	W	D	L	F	A	Pts
Rangers	38	18	0	1	65	13	10	4	5	29	19	60
Motherwell	38	17	0	2	68	15	8	5	6	36	33	55
Aberdeen	38	14	5	0	50	24	9	2	8	35	37	53
Celtic	38	12	1	6	52	21	10	4	5	36	25	49
St Mirren	38	11	2	6	41	19	7	3	9	32	37	41
Partick T	38	11	4	4	46	27	5	5	9	26	34	41
Falkirk	38	11	5	3	40	21	5	4	10	22	43	41
Kilmarnock	38	12	2	5	47	30	3	7	9	30	43	39
Ayr U	38	10	5	4	46	32	6	1	12	24	60	38
Hearts	38	8	6	5	35	26	6	3	10	34	43	37
Clyde	38	8	4	7	37	32	5	7	7	27	37	37
Airdrie	38	11	3	5	42	26	5	1	13	18	40	36
Hamilton A	38	12	3	4	49	27	2	4	13	27	54	35
Dundee	38	9	3	7	32	26	5	3	11	19	32	34
Queen's Park	38	9	2	8	36	36	6	2	11	31	44	34
Cowdenbeath	38	10	3	6	38	19	3	4	12	26	55	33
Hibernian	38	7	6	6	27	20	2	5	12	18	42	29
Morton	38	7	5	7	46	40	3	2	14	21	55	27
Dundee U	38	5	6	8	33	38	2	2	15	23	71	22
St Johnstone	38	5	5	9	33	37	1	2	16	15	59	

1930-31

DIVISION 1

	P	W	D	L	F	A	W	D	L	F	A	Pts
Rangers	38	16	2	1	55	9	11	4	4	41	20	60
Celtic	38	16	2	1	64	14	8	8	3	37	20	58
Motherwell	38	14	5	0	57	15	10	3	6	45	27	56
Partick T	38	16	2	1	50	16	8	3	8	26	27	53
Hearts	38	12	2	5	58	33	7	4	8	32	30	44
Aberdeen	38	13	3	3	53	20	4	4	11	26	43	41
Cowdenbeath	38	12	3	4	40	21	5	4	10	18	44	41
Dundee	38	13	2	4	40	16	4	3	12	25	47	39
Airdrie	38	11	2	6	38	32	6	3	10	21	34	39
Hamilton A	38	12	4	3	35	15	4	1	14	24	42	37
Kilmarnock	38	11	2	6	33	22	4	3	12	26	38	35
Clyde	38	7	3	9	31	44	8	1	10	29	43	34
Queen's Park	38	9	6	4	45	27	4	1	14	26	45	33
Falkirk	38	10	1	8	43	35	4	3	12	34	52	32
St Mirren	38	8	5	6	28	29	3	3	13	21	43	30
Morton	38	8	3	8	38	33	3	4	12	20	50	29
Leith A	38	5	6	8	30	33	3	5	11	21	52	27
Ayr U	38	8	5	6	37	37	0	6	13	16	55	27
Hibernian	38	8	4	7	32	28	1	3	15	17	53	25
East Fife	38	7	4	8	31	40	1	0	18	14	73	20

1931-32

DIVISION 1

	P	W	D	L	F	A	W	D	L	F	A	Pts
Motherwell	38	18	1	0	72	11	12	5	2	47	20	66
Rangers	38	16	2	1	67	14	12	3	4	51	28	61
Celtic	38	13	2	4	64	24	7	6	6	30	26	48
T. Lanark	38	15	1	3	61	29	6	3	10	31	52	46
St Mirren	38	13	2	4	49	22	7	2	10	28	34	44
Partick T	38	11	3	5	33	26	8	1	10	25	33	42
Aberdeen	38	10	6	3	33	15	6	3	10	24	34	41
Hearts	38	10	5	4	35	18	7	0	12	28	43	39
Kilmarnock	38	13	2	4	50	26	3	5	11	18	44	39
Hamilton A	38	11	3	5	54	29	5	3	11	30	36	38
Dundee	38	9	7	3	38	26	5	3	11	23	46	38
Cowdenbeath	38	11	4	4	38	28	4	4	11	28	50	38
Clyde	38	10	5	4	37	24	3	4	12	21	46	35
Airdrie	38	10	5	4	45	28	3	1	15	29	53	32
Morton	38	10	4	5	54	31	2	3	14	24	56	31
Queen's Park	38	9	2	8	36	38	4	3	12	23	41	31
Ayr U	38	9	1	9	43	32	2	6	11	27	58	29
Falkirk	38	10	3	6	52	31	1	2	16	18	45	27
Dundee U	38	4	5	10	18	49	2	2	15	22	69	19
Leith A	38	6	0	13	23	49	0	4	15	23	88	16

1932-33

DIVISION 1

	P	W	D	L	F	A	W	D	L	F	A	Pts
Rangers	38	14	5	0	67	22	12	5	2	46	21	62
Motherwell	38	15	1	3	66	24	12	4	3	48	29	59
Hearts	38	15	3	1	49	16	6	5	8	35	35	50
Celtic	38	13	3	3	47	18	7	5	7	28	26	48
St Johnstone	38	15	2	2	47	17	2	8	9	23	38	44
Aberdeen	38	13	4	2	63	19	5	2	12	22	39	42
St Mirren	38	12	3	4	48	23	6	3	10	25	37	42
Hamilton A	38	11	5	3	54	31	7	1	11	36	47	42
Queen's Park	38	11	5	3	46	24	6	2	11	32	55	41
Partick T	38	9	3	7	47	28	8	3	8	28	27	40
Falkirk	38	9	5	5	46	25	6	1	12	24	45	36
Clyde	38	12	0	7	42	29	3	5	11	27	46	35
T. Lanark	38	12	3	4	47	27	2	4	13	23	53	35
Kilmarnock	38	8	5	6	45	39	5	4	10	27	47	35
Dundee	38	9	6	4	34	27	3	3	13	26	50	33
Ayr U	38	11	2	6	41	28	2	2	15	21	67	30
Cowdenbeath	38	9	3	7	44	38	1	2	16	21	73	25
Airdrie	38	9	2	8	37	34	1	1	17	18	68	23
Morton	38	4	3	12	29	42	2	6	11	20	55	21
E. Stirling	38	6	3	10	30	44	1	0	18	25	71	17

1933-34

DIVISION 1

	P	W	D	L	F	A	W	D	L	F	A	Pts
Rangers	38	16	3	0	65	18	14	3	2	53	23	66
Motherwell	38	14	2	3	43	20	15	2	2	54	25	62
Celtic	38	12	5	2	47	20	6	6	7	31	33	47
Queen of South	38	11	2	6	44	36	10	1	8	31	42	45
Aberdeen	38	12	4	3	55	12	6	4	9	35	45	44
Hearts	38	11	5	3	52	23	6	5	8	34	36	44
Kilmarnock	38	11	3	5	45	28	6	6	7	28	36	43
Ayr U	38	10	4	5	48	37	6	6	7	39	55	42
St Johnstone	38	11	3	5	43	19	6	3	10	31	34	40
Falkirk	38	12	3	4	49	31	4	3	12	24	37	38
Hamilton A	38	9	5	5	35	30	6	3	10	30	49	38
Dundee	38	10	3	6	39	25	5	3	11	29	39	36
Partick T	38	9	2	8	46	37	5	3	11	27	41	33
Clyde	38	8	5	6	36	29	2	6	11	20	41	31
Queen's Park	38	7	3	9	33	41	6	2	11	32	44	31
Hibernian	38	8	2	9	31	33	4	1	14	20	36	27
St Mirren	38	5	4	10	29	35	4	5	10	17	40	27
Airdrie	38	7	3	9	37	46	3	3	13	22	57	26
T. Lanark	38	6	6	7	38	41	2	3	14	24	62	25
Cowdenbeath	38	4	3	12	33	45	1	2	16	25	73	15

1935-36

DIVISION 1

	P	W	D	L	F	A	W	D	L	F	A	Pts
Celtic	38	17	1	1	71	16	15	1	3	44	17	66
Rangers	38	14	3	2	67	26	13	4	2	43	17	61
Aberdeen	38	15	3	1	52	19	11	6	2	44	31	61
Motherwell	38	12	3	4	46	25	6	9	4	31	33	48
Hearts	38	14	4	1	56	20	6	3	10	32	35	47
Hamilton A	38	11	4	4	56	31	4	3	12	21	43	37
St Johnstone	38	10	4	5	43	27	5	3	11	27	54	37
Kilmarnock	38	10	4	5	46	30	4	3	12	23	34	35
T. Lanark	38	11	4	4	47	29	4	1	14	16	36	35
Partick T	38	12	5	2	47	22	0	5	14	17	50	34
Arbroath	38	6	6	7	22	24	5	5	9	24	45	33
Dundee	38	9	5	5	42	34	2	5	12	25	46	32
Queen's Park	38	8	6	5	36	25	3	4	12	22	50	32
Dunfermline A	38	6	6	7	31	36	6	2	11	36	56	32
Queen of South	38	9	6	4	34	26	2	3	14	20	46	31
Albion R	38	8	2	9	41	33	5	2	12	28	59	30
Hibernian	38	7	3	9	29	31	4	4	11	27	51	29
Clyde	38	10	1	8	35	33	0	7	12	28	51	28
Airdrie	38	8	4	7	44	37	1	5	13	24	54	27
Ayr U	38	8	2	9	30	31	3	1	15	23	67	25

1934-35

DIVISION 1

	P	W	D	L	F	A	W	D	L	F	A	Pts
Rangers	38	14	3	2	50	19	11	2	6	46	27	55
Celtic	38	15	2	2	61	19	9	2	8	31	26	52
Hearts	38	11	5	3	42	19	9	5	5	45	32	50
Hamilton A	38	14	4	1	58	24	5	6	8	29	43	48
St Johnstone	38	13	4	2	45	14	5	6	8	21	32	46
Aberdeen	38	13	3	3	42	17	4	7	8	26	37	44
Motherwell	38	12	4	3	57	27	3	6	10	26	37	40
Dundee	38	10	4	5	35	27	6	4	9	28	36	40
Kilmarnock	38	10	3	6	43	30	6	3	10	33	38	38
Clyde	38	9	6	4	45	29	5	4	10	26	40	38
Hibernian	38	10	7	2	38	20	4	1	14	21	50	36
Queen's Park	38	11	4	4	43	30	2	6	11	18	50	36
Partick T	38	10	5	4	38	25	5	0	14	23	43	35
Airdrie	38	10	3	6	42	31	3	4	12	22	41	33
Dunfermline A	38	8	4	7	35	39	5	1	13	21	57	31
Albion R	38	8	4	7	38	30	2	5	12	24	47	29
Queen of South	38	9	2	8	33	27	2	5	12	19	45	29
Ayr U	38	10	2	7	32	29	2	3	14	29	83	29
St Mirren	38	7	3	9	31	33	4	2	13	18	37	27
Falkirk	38	8	3	8	42	33	1	3	15	16	49	24

1936-37

DIVISION 1

	P	W	D	L	F	A	W	D	L	F	A	Pts
Rangers	38	15	3	1	50	11	11	6	2	38	21	61
Aberdeen	38	15	4	0	53	16	8	4	7	36	28	54
Celtic	38	14	3	2	59	26	8	5	6	30	32	52
Motherwell	38	14	1	4	67	29	8	6	5	29	25	51
Hearts	38	17	0	2	67	22	7	3	9	32	38	51
T. Lanark	38	12	4	3	42	20	8	2	9	37	41	46
Falkirk	38	13	1	5	60	26	6	5	8	38	40	44
Hamilton A	38	12	2	5	54	38	6	3	10	37	58	41
Dundee	38	7	10	2	36	23	5	5	9	22	46	39
Clyde	38	10	4	5	35	28	6	2	11	24	42	38
Kilmarnock	38	10	5	4	36	26	4	4	11	24	44	37
St Johnstone	38	13	1	5	50	25	1	7	11	24	43	36
Partick T	38	8	6	5	43	26	3	6	10	30	42	34
Arbroath	38	9	5	5	33	23	4	0	15	24	61	31
Queen's Park	38	3	7	9	24	36	6	5	8	27	41	30
St Mirren	38	9	2	8	43	35	2	5	12	25	46	29
Hibernian	38	2	11	6	29	34	4	2	13	25	49	25
Queen of South	38	6	4	9	28	35	2	4	13	21	60	24
Dunfermline A	38	3	7	9	34	45	2	4	13	31	53	21
Albion R	38	4	2	13	32	51	1	4	14	21	65	16

1937-38

DIVISION 1

	P	W	D	L	F	A	W	D	L	F	A	Pts
Celtic	38	16	3	0	70	15	11	4	4	44	27	61
Hearts	38	16	2	1	48	16	10	4	5	42	34	58
Rangers	38	11	5	3	44	23	7	8	4	31	26	49
Falkirk	38	9	4	6	43	27	10	5	4	39	25	47
Motherwell	38	12	5	2	49	28	5	5	9	29	41	44
Aberdeen	38	12	3	4	47	18	3	6	10	27	41	39
Partick T	38	12	2	5	45	32	3	7	9	23	38	39
St Johnstone	38	11	4	4	47	29	5	3	11	31	52	39
T. Lanark	38	7	8	4	34	30	4	5	10	34	43	35
Hibernian	38	8	8	3	38	27	3	5	11	19	38	35
Arbroath	38	8	7	4	37	30	3	6	10	21	49	35
Queen's Park	38	6	8	5	33	32	5	4	10	26	42	34
Hamilton A	38	9	3	7	48	30	4	4	11	33	46	33
St Mirren	38	11	2	6	42	25	3	3	13	16	41	33
Clyde	38	6	9	4	41	31	4	4	11	27	47	33
Queen of South	38	6	4	9	26	32	5	7	7	32	39	33
Ayr U	38	6	9	4	42	31	3	6	10	24	54	33
Kilmarnock	38	9	5	5	35	33	3	4	12	30	58	33
Dundee	38	10	3	6	47	27	3	3	13	23	47	32
Morton	38	5	1	13	44	55	1	2	16	20	72	15

1939-40

DIVISION A

	P	W	D	L	F	A	Pts
Rangers	5	4	1	0	14	3	9
Falkirk	5	4	0	1	20	10	8
Aberdeen	5	3	0	2	9	9	6
Celtic	5	3	0	2	7	7	6
Hearts	5	2	2	1	13	9	6
Partick T	5	2	2	1	7	7	6
Motherwell	5	2	1	2	14	12	5
Hamilton A	5	2	1	1	7	11	5
T Lanark	5	2	1	2	9	8	5
Queen of South	5	2	1	2	10	9	5
Albion R	5	2	1	2	12	7	5
St Mirren	5	1	3	1	8	8	5
Kilmarnock	5	2	1	2	10	9	5
Hibernian	5	2	0	3	11	13	4
Alloa	5	2	0	3	8	13	4
Arbroath	5	2	0	3	9	9	4
St Johnstone	5	2	0	3	7	8	4
Ayr U	5	2	0	3	10	17	4
Clyde	5	1	0	4	10	14	2
Cowdenbeath	5	1	0	4	6	14	2

1938-39

DIVISION 1

	P	W	D	L	F	A	W	D	L	F	A	Pts
Rangers	38	16	3	0	62	19	9	6	4	50	36	59
Celtic	38	11	3	5	62	31	9	5	5	37	22	48
Aberdeen	38	16	1	2	64	23	4	5	10	27	38	46
Hearts	38	13	1	5	61	30	7	4	8	37	40	45
Falkirk	38	11	4	4	42	24	8	3	8	31	39	45
Queen of South	38	11	6	2	40	21	6	3	10	29	43	43
Hamilton A	38	13	1	5	39	23	5	4	10	28	48	41
St Johnstone	38	12	2	5	53	32	5	4	10	32	50	40
Clyde	38	10	4	5	46	31	7	1	11	32	39	39
Kilmarnock	38	9	6	4	40	30	6	3	10	33	56	39
Partick T	38	12	2	5	45	30	5	2	12	29	57	38
Motherwell	38	12	1	6	56	42	4	4	11	26	44	37
Hibernian	38	9	5	5	43	23	5	2	12	25	46	35
Ayr U	38	8	6	5	46	33	5	3	11	30	50	35
T. Lanark	38	8	5	6	44	32	4	3	12	36	64	32
Albion R	38	9	1	9	41	44	3	5	11	24	46	30
Arbroath	38	10	3	6	39	31	1	5	13	15	44	30
St Mirren	38	8	5	6	31	30	3	2	14	26	50	29
Queen's Park	38	7	4	8	31	32	4	1	14	26	51	27
Raith R	38	4	2	13	33	44	6	0	13	32	55	22

1945-46

DIVISION A

	P	W	D	L	F	A	W	D	L	F	A	Pts
Rangers	30	12	2	1	45	23	10	2	3	40	18	48
Hibernian	30	11	3	1	42	13	6	3	6	25	24	40
Aberdeen	30	13	1	1	49	10	3	5	7	24	31	38
Celtic	30	7	5	3	30	21	5	6	4	25	23	35
Clyde	30	6	5	4	36	27	5	4	6	28	27	31
Motherwell	30	6	4	5	27	26	5	5	5	27	29	31
Hearts	30	6	5	4	32	23	5	3	7	31	34	30
Queen's Park	30	6	2	7	29	24	5	6	4	31	36	30
T. Lanark	30	9	0	6	36	30	5	2	8	27	38	30
Morton	30	6	7	2	43	26	3	4	8	29	43	29
Falkirk	30	9	2	4	42	30	2	3	10	20	40	27
Partick T	30	8	2	5	34	30	3	2	10	20	35	26
Queen of South	30	7	3	5	40	32	2	3	10	22	50	24
St Mirren	30	5	3	7	29	28	4	2	9	25	42	23
Kilmarnock	30	4	5	6	29	39	3	3	9	27	48	22
Hamilton A	30	2	5	8	26	37	3	1	11	18	51	16

1946-47

DIVISION A

	P	W	D	L	F	A	W	D	L	F	A	Pts
Rangers	30	12	1	2	42	13	9	3	3	34	13	46
Hibernian	30	9	4	2	40	14	10	2	3	29	19	44
Aberdeen	30	11	3	1	32	17	5	4	6	26	24	39
Hearts	30	8	3	4	30	24	8	3	4	22	19	38
Partick T	30	10	0	5	40	20	6	3	6	34	39	35
Morton	30	7	4	4	33	21	5	6	4	25	24	34
Celtic	30	8	2	5	30	27	5	4	6	23	28	32
Motherwell	30	8	3	4	33	23	4	2	9	25	31	29
T. Lanark	30	7	3	5	33	29	4	3	8	23	35	28
Clyde	30	4	5	6	27	33	5	4	6	28	32	27
Falkirk	30	5	4	6	39	33	3	6	6	23	28	26
Queen of South	30	4	4	7	23	33	5	4	6	21	36	26
Queen's Park	30	3	5	7	18	25	5	1	9	29	35	22
St Mirren	30	6	2	7	21	24	3	2	10	26	41	22
Kilmarnock	30	4	4	7	22	30	2	5	8	22	36	21
Hamilton A	30	1	6	8	22	40	1	1	13	16	45	11

1948-49

DIVISION A

	P	W	D	L	F	A	W	D	L	F	A	Pts
Rangers	30	11	3	1	39	18	9	3	3	24	14	46
Dundee	30	13	1	1	41	20	7	4	4	30	28	45
Hibernian	30	9	3	3	37	20	8	2	5	38	32	39
East Fife	30	9	1	5	38	19	7	2	6	26	27	35
Falkirk	30	9	3	3	44	23	3	5	7	26	31	32
Celtic	30	7	3	5	26	17	5	4	6	22	23	31
T. Lanark	30	9	2	4	33	22	4	3	8	23	30	31
Hearts	30	8	2	5	37	22	4	4	7	27	32	30
St Mirren	30	9	3	3	30	16	4	1	10	21	31	30
Queen of South	30	8	3	4	28	19	3	5	7	19	34	30
Partick T	30	4	8	3	25	24	5	1	9	25	39	27
Motherwell	30	7	2	6	29	20	3	3	9	15	29	25
Aberdeen	30	5	4	6	26	26	2	7	6	13	22	25
Clyde	30	5	4	6	27	30	4	2	9	23	37	24
Morton	30	4	6	5	21	22	3	2	10	18	29	22
Albion R	30	3	1	11	18	44	0	1	14	12	61	8

1947-48

DIVISION A

	P	W	D	L	F	A	W	D	L	F	A	Pts
Hibernian	30	13	2	0	52	6	9	2	4	34	21	48
Rangers	30	10	2	3	33	17	11	2	2	31	11	46
Partick T	30	7	3	5	39	24	9	1	5	22	18	36
Dundee	30	10	2	3	43	18	5	1	9	24	33	33
St Mirren	30	9	2	4	31	20	4	3	8	23	38	31
Clyde	30	8	3	4	34	27	4	4	7	18	30	31
Falkirk	30	6	5	4	31	21	4	5	6	24	27	30
Motherwell	30	7	2	6	19	17	6	1	8	26	30	29
Hearts	30	7	3	5	21	18	3	5	7	16	24	28
Aberdeen	30	8	4	3	33	16	2	3	10	12	29	27
T. Lanark	30	8	1	6	33	29	2	5	8	23	44	26
Celtic	30	5	4	6	21	25	5	1	9	20	31	25
Queen of South	30	7	3	5	33	27	3	2	10	16	47	25
Morton	30	3	4	8	18	19	6	2	7	29	24	24
Airdrie	30	7	1	7	26	32	0	6	9	14	46	21
Queen's Park	30	5	2	8	29	32	4	0	11	16	43	20

1949-50

DIVISION A

	P	W	D	L	F	A	W	D	L	F	A	Pts
Rangers	30	11	4	0	32	12	11	2	2	26	14	50
Hibernian	30	13	0	2	50	15	9	5	1	36	19	49
Hearts	30	12	1	2	55	16	8	2	5	31	24	43
East Fife	30	8	3	4	31	18	7	4	4	27	25	37
Celtic	30	11	4	0	37	17	3	3	9	14	33	35
Dundee	30	10	1	4	29	15	2	6	7	20	31	31
Partick T	30	8	1	6	30	20	5	2	8	25	25	29
Aberdeen	30	7	2	6	33	25	4	2	9	15	31	26
Raith R	30	7	3	5	34	29	2	5	8	11	25	26
Motherwell	30	6	3	6	33	25	4	2	9	20	33	25
St Mirren	30	6	4	5	26	15	2	5	8	16	34	25
T. Lanark	30	7	2	6	26	28	4	1	10	18	34	25
Clyde	30	6	3	6	26	19	4	1	10	30	54	24
Falkirk	30	3	7	5	24	29	4	3	8	24	43	24
Queen of South	30	5	5	5	22	25	0	1	14	9	38	16
Stirling A	30	4	2	9	20	32	2	1	12	18	45	15

1950-51

DIVISION A

	P	W	D	L	F	A	W	D	L	F	A	Pts
Hibernian	30	13	1	1	44	9	9	3	3	34	17	48
Rangers	30	10	3	2	36	13	7	1	7	28	24	38
Dundee	30	11	3	1	32	12	4	5	6	15	18	38
Hearts	30	10	3	2	46	17	6	2	7	26	28	37
Aberdeen	30	9	2	4	35	21	6	3	6	26	29	35
Partick T	30	9	4	2	30	15	4	3	8	27	33	33
Celtic	30	6	3	6	29	25	6	2	7	19	21	29
Raith R	30	8	2	5	30	16	5	0	10	22	36	28
Motherwell	30	7	3	5	35	27	4	3	8	23	38	28
East Fife	30	7	4	4	28	24	3	4	8	20	42	28
St Mirren	30	7	3	5	22	20	2	4	9	13	31	25
Morton	30	6	0	9	30	29	4	4	7	17	30	24
T. Lanark	30	7	1	7	22	21	4	1	10	18	30	24
Airdrie	30	7	2	6	39	31	3	2	10	13	36	24
Clyde	30	6	4	5	19	23	2	3	10	18	34	23
Falkirk	30	6	3	6	24	27	1	1	13	11	54	18

1951-52

DIVISION A

	P	W	D	L	F	A	W	D	L	F	A	Pts
Hibernian	30	12	2	1	58	15	8	3	4	34	21	45
Rangers	30	10	4	1	32	13	6	5	4	29	18	41
East Fife	30	11	2	2	44	19	6	1	8	27	30	37
Hearts	30	9	5	1	44	25	5	2	8	25	28	35
Raith R	30	9	2	4	23	14	5	3	7	20	28	33
Partick T	30	7	3	5	28	24	5	4	6	20	27	31
Motherwell	30	8	4	3	33	24	4	3	8	18	33	31
Dundee	30	7	3	5	31	22	4	3	8	22	30	28
Celtic	30	7	5	3	30	22	3	3	9	22	33	28
Queen of South	30	10	3	2	38	18	0	5	10	12	42	28
Aberdeen	30	7	4	4	37	24	3	3	9	28	34	27
T. Lanark	30	7	3	5	28	23	2	5	8	23	39	26
Airdrie	30	7	3	5	31	26	4	1	10	23	43	26
St Mirren	30	9	2	4	28	19	1	3	11	15	39	25
Morton	30	7	1	7	30	23	2	5	8	19	33	24
Stirling A	30	4	4	7	22	40	1	1	13	14	59	15

1952-53

DIVISION A

	P	W	D	L	F	A	W	D	L	F	A	Pts
Rangers	30	12	1	2	49	14	6	6	3	31	25	43
Hibernian	30	10	3	2	45	18	9	2	4	48	33	43
East Fife	30	11	2	2	49	21	5	5	5	23	27	39
Hearts	30	8	3	4	36	18	4	3	8	23	32	30
Clyde	30	8	2	5	43	30	5	2	8	35	48	30
St Mirren	30	6	6	3	29	21	5	2	8	23	37	30
Dundee	30	8	5	2	30	11	1	6	8	14	26	29
Celtic	30	7	3	5	33	26	4	4	7	18	28	29
Partick T	30	6	4	5	32	33	4	5	6	23	30	29
Queen of South	30	8	3	4	31	24	2	5	8	12	37	28
Aberdeen	30	8	4	3	45	26	3	1	11	19	42	27
Raith R	30	5	7	3	25	20	4	1	10	22	33	26
Falkirk	30	7	1	7	29	28	4	3	8	24	35	26
Airdrie	30	6	4	5	33	33	4	2	9	20	42	26
Motherwell	30	7	2	6	34	39	3	3	9	23	41	25
T. Lanark	30	6	2	7	24	24	2	2	11	28	51	20

1953-54

DIVISION A

	P	W	D	L	F	A	W	D	L	F	A	Pts
Celtic	30	14	1	0	40	7	6	2	7	32	22	43
Hearts	30	9	3	3	42	24	7	3	5	28	21	38
Partick T	30	9	0	6	42	22	8	1	6	34	32	35
Rangers	30	9	4	2	35	11	4	4	7	21	24	34
Hibernian	30	9	1	5	38	18	6	3	6	34	33	34
East Fife	30	11	3	1	37	13	2	5	8	18	32	34
Dundee	30	11	3	1	31	12	3	3	9	15	35	34
Clyde	30	8	1	6	36	36	7	3	5	28	31	34
Aberdeen	30	10	2	3	36	14	5	1	9	30	37	33
Queen of South	30	10	2	3	50	28	4	2	9	22	30	32
St Mirren	30	7	3	5	27	22	5	1	9	17	32	28
Raith R	30	7	3	5	37	21	3	3	9	19	39	26
Falkirk	30	5	5	5	31	31	4	2	9	16	30	25
Stirling A	30	8	1	6	27	21	2	3	10	12	41	24
Airdrie	30	4	5	6	29	35	1	0	14	12	57	15
Hamilton A	30	4	1	10	17	35	0	2	13	12	59	11

1954-55

DIVISION A

	P	W	D	L	F	A	W	D	L	F	A	Pts
Aberdeen	30	14	0	1	41	9	10	1	4	32	17	49
Celtic	30	10	4	1	42	16	9	4	2	34	21	46
Rangers	30	13	2	0	40	8	6	1	8	27	25	41
Hearts	30	10	2	3	40	25	6	5	4	34	20	39
Hibernian	30	8	2	5	28	23	7	2	6	36	31	34
St Mirren	30	8	3	4	31	23	4	5	6	24	31	32
Clyde	30	6	7	2	33	20	5	2	8	26	30	31
Dundee	30	9	2	4	32	21	4	2	9	16	27	30
Partick T	30	5	5	5	24	29	6	2	7	25	32	29
Kilmarnock	30	5	3	7	18	24	5	3	7	28	34	26
East Fife	30	6	1	8	32	35	3	5	7	19	27	24
Falkirk	30	6	6	3	28	23	2	2	11	14	31	24
Queen of South	30	7	2	6	22	29	2	4	9	16	27	24
Raith R	30	9	1	5	34	23	1	2	12	15	34	23
Motherwell	30	5	2	8	23	31	4	2	9	19	31	22
Stirling A	30	2	1	12	15	40	0	1	14	14	65	6

1955-56

DIVISION A

	P	W	D	L	F	A	W	D	L	F	A	Pts
Rangers	34	12	4	1	51	13	10	4	3	34	14	52
Aberdeen	34	11	3	3	52	29	7	7	3	35	21	46
Hearts	34	13	2	2	65	17	6	5	6	34	30	45
Hibernian	34	11	4	2	57	24	8	3	6	29	26	45
Celtic	34	9	4	4	31	18	7	5	5	24	21	41
Queen of South	34	12	2	3	46	23	4	3	10	23	50	37
Airdrie	34	8	4	5	41	41	6	4	7	44	55	36
Kilmarnock	34	7	6	4	26	20	5	4	8	26	25	34
Partick T	34	8	4	5	36	22	5	3	9	26	38	33
Motherwell	34	7	6	4	30	21	4	5	8	23	38	33
Raith R	34	6	7	4	30	30	6	2	9	28	45	33
East Fife	34	11	3	3	43	21	2	2	13	18	48	31
Dundee	34	10	2	5	35	24	2	4	11	21	41	30
Falkirk	34	9	2	6	37	28	2	4	11	21	47	28
St Mirren	34	9	2	6	39	23	1	5	11	18	47	27
Dunfermline A	34	6	4	7	26	36	4	2	11	16	46	26
Clyde	34	2	4	11	21	40	6	2	9	29	34	22
Stirling A	34	4	3	10	15	27	0	2	15	8	55	13

1956-57

DIVISION 1

	P	W	D	L	F	A	W	D	L	F	A	Pts
Rangers	34	13	2	2	51	22	13	1	3	45	26	55
Hearts	34	11	3	3	40	23	13	2	2	41	25	53
Kilmarnock	34	9	6	2	35	20	7	4	6	22	19	42
Raith R	34	10	2	5	52	32	6	5	6	32	26	39
Celtic	34	9	6	2	33	14	6	2	9	25	29	38
Aberdeen	34	10	1	6	36	24	8	1	8	43	35	38
Motherwell	34	9	2	6	41	32	7	3	7	31	34	37
Partick T	34	11	3	3	37	18	2	5	10	16	33	34
Hibernian	34	6	8	3	38	20	6	1	10	31	36	33
Dundee	34	10	2	5	38	23	3	4	10	17	38	32
Airdrie	34	8	2	7	45	40	5	2	10	32	49	30
St Mirren	34	8	3	6	37	25	4	3	10	21	47	30
Queen's Park	34	9	2	6	33	19	2	5	10	22	40	29
Falkirk	34	5	2	10	28	35	5	6	6	23	35	28
East Fife	34	7	3	7	33	34	3	3	11	26	48	26
Queen of South	34	8	3	6	36	37	2	2	13	18	59	25
Dunfermline A	34	6	3	8	31	36	3	3	11	23	38	24
Ayr U	34	5	2	10	27	35	2	3	12	21	54	19

1957-58

DIVISION 1

	P	W	D	L	F	A	W	D	L	F	A	Pts
Hearts	34	15	2	0	79	17	14	2	1	53	12	62
Rangers	34	10	2	5	47	26	12	3	2	42	23	49
Celtic	34	7	6	4	42	22	12	2	3	42	25	46
Clyde	34	13	1	3	53	27	5	5	7	31	34	42
Kilmarnock	34	8	6	3	36	24	6	3	8	24	31	37
Partick T	34	11	1	5	37	25	6	2	9	32	46	37
Raith R	34	10	2	5	37	20	4	5	8	29	36	35
Motherwell	34	8	3	6	36	31	4	5	8	32	36	32
Hibernian	34	6	4	7	34	26	7	1	9	25	34	31
Falkirk	34	6	5	6	30	32	5	4	8	34	50	31
Dundee	34	10	1	6	32	22	3	4	10	17	43	31
Aberdeen	34	8	0	9	40	35	6	2	9	28	41	30
St Mirren	34	7	4	6	31	27	4	4	9	28	39	30
T. Lanark	34	6	2	9	32	39	7	2	8	37	49	30
Queen of South	34	6	4	7	33	32	6	1	10	28	40	29
Airdrie	34	8	2	7	47	45	5	0	12	24	47	28
East Fife	34	5	2	10	24	40	5	1	11	21	48	23
Queen's Park	34	1	0	16	18	60	3	1	13	23	54	9

1958-59

DIVISION 1

	P	W	D	L	F	A	W	D	L	F	A	Pts
Rangers	34	13	2	2	41	17	8	6	3	51	34	50
Hearts	34	12	2	3	49	25	9	4	4	43	26	48
Motherwell	34	11	4	2	44	19	7	4	6	39	31	44
Dundee	34	10	5	2	36	25	6	4	7	25	26	41
Airdrie	34	8	3	6	35	32	7	4	6	29	30	37
Celtic	34	11	4	2	48	24	3	4	10	22	29	36
St Mirren	34	8	4	5	38	33	6	3	8	33	41	35
Kilmarnock	34	10	3	4	38	23	3	5	9	20	28	34
Partick T	34	8	4	5	34	27	6	2	9	25	39	34
Hibernian	34	8	3	6	38	31	5	3	9	30	39	32
T. Lanark	34	6	5	6	40	31	5	5	7	34	52	32
Stirling A	34	6	5	6	27	25	5	3	9	27	39	30
Aberdeen	34	7	4	6	42	29	5	1	11	21	37	29
Raith R	34	9	3	5	33	25	1	6	10	27	45	29
Clyde	34	8	2	7	37	34	4	2	11	25	32	28
Dunfermline A	34	7	3	7	41	41	3	5	9	27	46	28
Falkirk	34	6	4	7	32	33	4	3	10	26	46	27
Queen of South	34	4	5	8	24	44	2	1	14	14	57	18

1959-60

DIVISION 1

	P	W	D	L	F	A	W	D	L	F	A	Pts
Hearts	34	14	2	1	56	22	9	6	2	46	29	54
Kilmarnock	34	13	2	2	34	20	11	0	6	33	25	50
Rangers	34	5	6	6	30	22	12	2	3	42	16	42
Dundee	34	11	1	5	41	25	5	9	3	29	24	42
Motherwell	34	9	4	4	42	26	7	4	6	29	35	40
Clyde	34	7	5	5	41	30	8	4	5	36	39	39
Hibernian	34	8	4	5	52	39	6	3	8	54	46	35
Ayr U	34	9	4	4	36	26	5	2	10	29	47	34
Celtic	34	7	5	5	36	24	5	4	8	37	35	33
Partick T	34	10	0	7	26	32	4	4	9	28	46	32
Raith R	34	7	3	7	38	27	7	0	10	26	35	31
T. Lanark	34	7	3	7	45	38	6	1	10	30	45	30
Dunfermline A	34	7	5	5	39	34	3	4	10	33	46	29
St Mirren	34	5	3	9	38	44	6	3	8	40	42	28
Aberdeen	34	8	4	5	35	32	3	2	12	19	40	28
Airdrie	34	5	1	11	31	54	6	5	6	25	26	28
Stirling A	34	4	3	10	28	36	3	5	9	27	36	22
Arbroath	34	4	5	8	29	41	0	2	15	9	65	15

1960-61

DIVISION 1

	P	W	D	L	F	A	W	D	L	F	A	Pts
Rangers	34	14	1	2	52	19	9	4	4	36	27	51
Kilmarnock	34	12	4	1	45	19	9	4	4	32	26	50
T. Lanark	34	11	2	4	55	33	9	0	8	45	47	42
Celtic	34	9	4	4	33	22	6	5	6	31	24	39
Motherwell	34	9	3	5	34	28	6	5	6	36	29	38
Aberdeen	34	9	2	6	38	34	5	6	6	34	38	36
Hearts	34	8	3	6	26	25	5	5	7	25	28	34
Hibernian	34	10	3	4	41	30	5	1	11	25	39	34
Dundee U	34	9	3	5	36	21	4	4	9	24	37	33
Dundee	34	9	3	5	38	23	4	3	10	23	30	32
Partick T	34	8	4	5	36	30	5	2	10	23	39	32
Dunfermline A	34	8	4	5	43	42	4	3	10	22	39	31
Airdrie	34	9	4	4	39	28	1	6	10	22	43	30
St Mirren	34	6	5	6	25	22	5	2	10	28	36	29
St Johnstone	34	7	5	5	30	29	3	4	10	17	34	29
Raith R	34	5	4	8	26	34	5	3	9	20	33	27
Clyde	34	5	7	5	31	29	1	4	12	24	48	23
Ayr U	34	5	6	6	24	26	0	6	11	27	55	22

1961-62

DIVISION 1

	P	W	D	L	F	A	W	D	L	F	A	Pts
Dundee	34	13	2	2	41	23	12	2	3	39	23	54
Rangers	34	12	2	3	43	18	10	5	2	41	13	51
Celtic	34	12	4	1	46	16	7	4	6	35	21	46
Dunfermline A	34	13	1	3	46	15	6	4	7	31	31	43
Kilmarnock	34	10	4	3	41	27	6	6	5	33	31	42
Hearts	34	7	5	5	30	28	9	1	7	24	21	38
Partick T	34	12	0	5	36	21	4	3	10	24	34	35
Hibernian	34	7	5	5	31	30	7	0	10	27	42	33
Motherwell	34	7	3	7	35	34	6	3	8	30	28	32
Dundee U	34	8	3	6	43	30	5	3	9	27	41	32
T. Lanark	34	8	3	6	37	31	5	2	10	22	29	31
Aberdeen	34	6	6	5	33	27	4	3	10	27	46	29
Raith R	34	5	5	7	24	29	5	2	10	27	44	27
Falkirk	34	6	2	9	23	30	5	2	10	22	38	26
Airdrie	34	7	2	8	35	33	2	5	10	22	45	25
St Mirren	34	7	3	7	29	29	3	2	12	23	51	25
St Johnstone	34	4	2	11	14	34	5	5	7	21	27	25
Stirling A	34	5	3	9	22	32	1	3	13	12	44	18

1962-63

DIVISION 1

	P	W	D	L	F	A	W	D	L	F	A	Pts
Rangers	34	13	4	0	53	15	12	3	2	41	13	57
Kilmarnock	34	12	4	1	55	16	8	4	5	37	24	48
Partick T	34	11	1	5	39	26	9	5	3	27	18	46
Celtic	34	10	3	4	33	16	9	3	5	43	28	44
Hearts	34	10	4	3	45	26	7	5	5	40	33	43
Aberdeen	34	10	2	5	38	19	7	5	5	32	28	41
Dundee U	34	10	6	1	41	20	5	5	7	26	32	41
Dunfermline A	34	9	5	3	37	20	4	3	10	13	27	34
Dundee	34	9	6	2	39	20	3	3	11	21	29	33
Motherwell	34	6	7	4	32	23	4	4	9	28	40	31
Airdrie	34	10	0	7	36	33	4	2	11	16	43	30
St Mirren	34	6	4	7	32	36	4	4	9	20	36	28
Falkirk	34	8	1	8	35	35	4	2	11	19	34	27
T. Lanark	34	6	4	7	28	29	3	4	10	28	39	26
Queen of South	34	6	3	8	20	30	4	3	10	16	45	26
Hibernian	34	4	5	8	17	30	4	4	9	30	37	25
Clyde	34	6	1	10	25	38	3	4	10	24	45	23
Raith R	34	0	4	13	16	48	2	1	14	19	70	9

1964-65

DIVISION 1

	P	W	D	L	F	A	W	D	L	F	A	Pts
Kilmarnock	34	12	4	1	38	17	10	2	5	24	16	50
Hearts	34	11	3	3	46	24	11	3	3	44	25	50
Dunfermline A	34	14	2	1	55	14	8	3	6	28	22	49
Hibernian	34	11	2	4	44	26	10	2	5	31	21	46
Rangers	34	9	5	3	42	16	9	3	5	36	19	44
Dundee	34	9	4	4	47	32	6	6	5	39	31	40
Clyde	34	10	3	4	35	22	7	3	7	29	36	40
Celtic	34	9	2	6	33	18	7	3	7	43	39	37
Dundee U	34	10	1	6	38	24	5	5	7	21	27	36
Morton	34	9	4	4	38	21	4	3	10	16	33	33
Partick T	34	5	5	7	28	30	6	5	6	29	28	32
Aberdeen	34	8	5	4	33	27	4	3	10	26	48	32
St Johnstone	34	6	5	6	31	24	3	6	8	26	38	29
Motherwell	34	4	4	9	24	31	6	4	7	21	23	28
St Mirren	34	8	2	7	27	32	1	4	12	11	38	24
Falkirk	34	6	5	6	27	26	1	2	14	16	59	21
Airdrie	34	3	3	11	26	48	2	1	14	22	62	14
T. Lanark	34	2	0	15	11	41	1	1	15	11	58	7

1963-64

DIVISION 1

	P	W	D	L	F	A	W	D	L	F	A	Pts
Rangers	34	13	1	3	43	19	12	4	1	42	12	55
Kilmarnock	34	14	2	1	50	15	8	3	6	27	25	49
Celtic	34	13	3	1	61	16	6	6	5	28	18	47
Hearts	34	8	5	4	39	23	11	4	2	35	17	47
Dunfermline A	34	11	3	3	41	16	7	6	4	23	17	45
Dundee	34	11	3	3	53	27	9	2	6	41	23	45
Partick T	34	11	3	3	30	16	4	2	11	25	38	35
Dundee U	34	10	2	5	43	23	3	6	8	22	26	34
Aberdeen	34	5	5	7	26	26	7	3	7	27	27	32
Hibernian	34	9	4	4	33	22	3	2	12	26	44	30
Motherwell	34	7	5	5	29	24	2	6	9	22	38	29
St Mirren	34	9	4	4	24	23	3	1	13	20	51	29
St Johnstone	34	6	3	8	27	32	5	3	9	27	38	28
Falkirk	34	7	4	6	24	26	4	2	11	30	58	28
Airdrie	34	7	3	7	34	41	4	1	12	18	56	26
T. Lanark	34	5	3	9	27	36	4	4	9	20	38	25
Queen of South	34	3	3	11	23	47	2	3	12	17	45	16
E. Stirling	34	4	2	11	19	36	1	0	16	18	55	12

1965-66

DIVISION 1

	P	W	D	L	F	A	W	D	L	F	A	Pts
Celtic	34	16	1	0	66	12	11	2	4	40	18	57
Rangers	34	15	1	1	49	10	10	4	3	42	19	55
Kilmarnock	34	12	2	3	36	18	8	3	6	37	28	45
Dunfermline A	34	11	2	4	52	29	8	4	5	42	26	44
Dundee U	34	10	3	4	45	27	9	2	6	34	24	43
Hibernian	34	8	6	3	45	22	8	0	9	36	33	38
Hearts	34	7	5	5	28	21	6	7	4	28	27	38
Aberdeen	34	8	3	6	35	26	7	3	7	26	28	36
Dundee	34	9	2	6	35	29	5	4	8	26	32	34
Falkirk	34	10	1	6	32	26	5	0	12	16	46	31
Clyde	34	7	2	8	33	29	6	2	9	29	35	30
Partick T	34	9	5	3	34	25	1	5	11	21	39	30
Motherwell	34	9	0	8	31	26	3	4	10	21	43	28
St Johnstone	34	6	6	5	34	36	3	2	12	24	45	26
Stirling A	34	7	2	8	25	29	2	6	9	15	39	26
St Mirren	34	6	3	8	27	34	3	1	13	17	48	22
Morton	34	4	5	8	18	31	4	0	13	24	53	21
Hamilton A	34	3	1	13	19	56	0	1	16	8	61	8

1966-67

DIVISION 1

	P	W	D	L	F	A	W	D	L	F	A	Pts
Celtic	34	14	2	1	61	17	12	4	1	50	16	58
Rangers	34	13	3	1	54	13	11	4	2	38	18	55
Clyde	34	10	2	5	29	20	10	4	3	35	28	46
Aberdeen	34	11	3	3	44	17	6	5	6	28	21	42
Hibernian	34	10	3	4	43	24	9	1	7	29	25	42
Dundee	34	9	5	3	34	16	7	4	6	40	35	41
Kilmarnock	34	9	5	3	33	18	7	3	7	26	28	40
Dunfermline A	34	9	4	4	46	27	5	6	6	26	25	38
Dundee U	34	7	5	5	36	33	7	4	6	32	29	37
Motherwell	34	7	6	4	37	26	3	5	9	22	34	31
Hearts	34	7	6	4	22	16	4	2	11	17	32	30
Partick T	34	5	8	4	25	21	4	4	9	24	47	30
Airdrie	34	7	1	9	27	27	4	5	8	14	26	28
Falkirk	34	8	1	8	18	24	3	3	11	15	46	26
St Johnstone	34	8	3	6	31	30	2	2	13	22	43	25
Stirling A	34	3	6	8	18	34	2	3	12	13	51	19
St Mirren	34	4	1	12	18	47	0	6	11	7	34	15
Ayr U	34	1	4	12	11	37	0	3	14	9	49	9

1967-68

DIVISION 1

	P	W	D	L	F	A	W	D	L	F	A	Pts
Celtic	34	14	3	0	53	14	16	0	1	53	10	63
Rangers	34	14	2	1	50	13	14	3	0	43	21	61
Hibernian	34	12	2	3	40	17	8	3	6	27	32	45
Dunfermline A	34	9	1	7	38	18	8	4	5	26	23	39
Aberdeen	34	11	1	5	36	17	5	4	8	27	31	37
Morton	34	10	4	3	35	25	5	2	10	22	28	36
Kilmarnock	34	9	4	4	34	23	4	4	9	25	34	34
Clyde	34	9	3	5	39	25	6	1	10	16	30	34
Dundee	34	8	2	7	44	39	5	5	7	18	20	33
Partick T	34	6	5	6	25	28	6	2	9	26	39	31
Dundee U	34	7	7	3	36	30	3	4	10	17	42	31
Hearts	34	9	1	7	24	23	4	3	10	32	38	30
Airdrie	34	7	5	5	26	20	3	4	10	19	38	29
St Johnstone	34	6	2	9	19	26	4	5	8	24	26	27
Falkirk	34	3	6	8	19	25	4	6	7	17	25	26
Raith R	34	5	4	8	32	30	4	3	10	26	56	25
Motherwell	34	4	3	10	20	32	2	4	11	20	34	19
Stirling A	34	4	3	10	18	44	0	1	16	11	61	12

1968-69

DIVISION 1

	P	W	D	L	F	A	W	D	L	F	A	Pts
Celtic	34	12	3	2	50	19	11	5	1	39	13	54
Rangers	34	13	3	1	47	12	8	4	5	34	20	49
Dunfermline A	34	12	4	1	42	20	7	3	7	21	25	45
Kilmarnock	34	10	6	1	30	15	5	8	4	20	17	44
Dundee U	34	12	3	2	40	25	5	6	6	21	24	43
St Johnstone	34	11	2	4	39	22	5	3	9	27	37	37
Airdrie	34	10	5	2	27	16	3	6	8	19	28	37
Hearts	34	7	7	3	26	20	7	1	9	26	34	36
Dundee	34	4	8	5	24	23	6	4	7	23	25	32
Morton	34	8	5	4	34	27	4	3	10	24	41	32
St Mirren	34	7	4	6	24	21	4	6	7	16	33	32
Hibernian	34	9	2	6	38	24	3	5	9	22	35	31
Clyde	34	6	7	4	20	18	3	6	8	15	32	31
Partick T	34	7	3	7	21	24	2	7	8	18	29	28
Aberdeen	34	6	5	6	26	24	3	3	11	24	35	26
Raith R	34	6	2	9	23	29	2	3	12	22	38	21
Falkirk	34	4	6	7	21	27	1	2	14	12	42	18
Arbroath	34	4	3	10	24	34	1	3	13	17	48	16

1969-70

DIVISION 1

	P	W	D	L	F	A	W	D	L	F	A	Pts
Celtic	34	12	2	3	54	18	15	1	1	42	15	57
Rangers	34	13	1	3	38	17	6	6	5	29	23	45
Hibernian	34	12	3	2	40	17	7	3	7	25	23	44
Hearts	34	6	7	4	28	19	7	5	5	22	17	38
Dundee U	34	10	3	4	36	23	6	3	8	26	41	38
Dundee	34	11	2	4	29	15	4	4	9	20	29	36
Kilmarnock	34	10	5	2	37	21	3	5	9	25	36	36
Aberdeen	34	6	6	5	30	19	8	1	8	25	26	35
Morton	34	9	5	3	33	21	4	4	9	19	31	35
Dunfermline A	34	12	2	3	32	17	3	3	11	13	28	35
Motherwell	34	8	4	5	25	18	3	6	8	24	33	32
Airdrie	34	8	3	6	33	26	4	5	8	26	38	32
St Johnstone	34	9	4	4	35	28	2	5	10	15	34	31
Ayr U	34	10	3	4	26	20	2	3	12	11	32	30
St Mirren	34	6	5	6	28	28	2	4	11	11	26	25
Clyde	34	8	4	5	21	18	1	3	13	13	38	25
Raith R	34	4	6	7	15	24	1	5	11	17	43	21
Partick T	34	4	4	9	22	33	1	3	13	19	49	17

1970-71

DIVISION 1

	P	W	D	L	F	A	W	D	L	F	A	Pts
Celtic	34	15	1	1	43	7	10	5	2	46	16	56
Aberdeen	34	11	6	0	38	7	13	0	4	30	11	54
St Johnstone	34	10	3	4	33	20	9	3	5	26	24	44
Rangers	34	10	5	2	33	10	6	4	7	25	24	41
Dundee	34	9	2	6	30	23	5	8	4	23	22	38
Dundee U	34	8	4	5	34	29	6	4	7	19	25	36
Falkirk	34	8	5	4	24	20	5	4	8	22	33	35
Morton	34	9	4	4	25	17	4	4	9	19	27	34
Airdrie	34	8	3	6	33	26	5	5	7	27	39	34
Motherwell	34	7	4	6	30	27	6	4	7	13	20	34
Hearts	34	8	5	4	24	16	5	2	10	17	24	33
Hibernian	34	8	4	5	33	24	2	6	9	14	29	30
Kilmarnock	34	5	6	6	26	31	5	2	10	17	36	28
Ayr U	34	7	5	5	22	15	2	3	12	15	39	26
Clyde	34	5	5	7	19	23	3	5	9	14	36	26
Dunfermline A	34	6	5	6	26	19	0	6	11	18	37	23
St Mirren	34	4	3	10	20	30	3	6	8	18	26	23
Cowdenbeath	34	1	2	14	13	39	6	1	10	20	38	17

1972-73

DIVISION 1

	P	W	D	L	F	A	W	D	L	F	A	Pts
Celtic	34	14	3	0	47	10	12	2	3	46	18	57
Rangers	34	14	2	1	36	10	12	2	3	38	20	56
Hibernian	34	12	2	3	43	17	7	5	5	31	16	45
Aberdeen	34	10	6	1	42	15	6	5	6	19	19	43
Dundee	34	13	4	0	45	10	4	5	8	23	33	43
Ayr U	34	11	4	2	33	21	5	4	8	17	30	40
Dundee U	34	11	3	3	32	24	6	2	9	24	27	39
Motherwell	34	5	6	6	20	23	6	3	8	18	25	31
East Fife	34	8	3	6	26	21	3	5	9	20	33	30
Hearts	34	7	4	6	15	17	5	2	10	24	33	30
St Johnstone	34	8	3	6	35	30	2	6	9	17	37	29
Morton	34	8	4	5	33	21	2	4	11	14	32	28
Partick T	34	4	5	8	17	25	6	3	8	23	28	28
Falkirk	34	6	4	7	24	26	1	8	8	14	30	26
Arbroath	34	8	3	6	31	23	1	5	11	8	40	26
Dumbarton	34	3	9	5	26	30	3	2	12	17	42	23
Kilmarnock	34	6	3	8	23	30	1	5	11	17	41	22
Airdrie	34	2	4	11	16	35	2	4	11	18	40	16

1971-72

DIVISION 1

	P	W	D	L	F	A	W	D	L	F	A	Pts
Celtic	34	15	1	1	48	14	13	3	1	48	14	60
Aberdeen	34	13	3	1	54	13	8	5	4	26	13	50
Rangers	34	11	0	6	41	21	10	2	5	30	17	44
Hibernian	34	11	2	4	34	13	8	4	5	28	21	44
Dundee	34	8	6	3	30	14	6	7	4	29	24	41
Hearts	34	10	5	2	29	17	3	8	6	24	32	39
Partick T	34	9	5	3	35	23	3	5	9	18	31	34
St Johnstone	34	7	5	5	26	21	5	3	9	26	37	32
Dundee U	34	7	5	5	36	37	5	2	10	19	33	31
Motherwell	34	9	3	5	33	26	2	4	11	16	43	29
Kilmarnock	34	7	3	7	27	28	4	3	10	22	36	28
Ayr U	34	5	6	6	20	19	4	4	9	20	39	28
Morton	34	5	7	5	23	20	5	0	12	23	32	27
Falkirk	34	7	4	6	26	23	3	3	11	18	37	27
Airdrie	34	4	6	7	25	37	3	6	8	19	39	26
East Fife	34	2	7	8	19	34	3	8	6	15	27	25
Clyde	34	5	4	8	16	26	2	6	9	17	40	24
Dunfermline A	34	5	5	7	19	24	2	4	11	12	26	23

1973-74

DIVISION 1

	P	W	D	L	F	A	W	D	L	F	A	Pts
Celtic	34	12	4	1	51	12	11	3	3	31	15	53
Hibernian	34	14	2	1	46	18	6	7	4	29	24	49
Rangers	34	9	3	5	32	17	12	3	2	35	17	48
Aberdeen	34	7	9	1	26	9	6	7	4	20	17	42
Dundee	34	7	3	7	32	25	9	4	4	35	23	39
Hearts	34	6	6	5	26	20	8	4	5	28	23	38
Ayr U	34	9	4	4	23	16	6	4	7	21	24	38
Dundee U	34	7	3	7	30	25	8	4	5	25	26	37
Motherwell	34	8	5	4	28	20	6	2	9	17	20	35
Dumbarton	34	7	3	7	23	23	4	4	9	20	35	29
Partick T	34	7	4	6	19	16	2	6	9	14	30	28
St Johnstone	34	3	6	8	20	31	6	4	7	21	29	28
Arbroath	34	5	2	10	24	32	5	5	7	28	37	27
Morton	34	4	5	8	20	27	4	5	8	17	22	26
Clyde	34	5	2	10	13	26	3	7	7	16	39	25
Dunfermline A	34	3	5	9	28	37	5	3	9	15	28	24
East Fife	34	3	2	12	9	30	6	4	7	17	21	24
Falkirk	34	1	11	5	17	21	3	3	11	16	37	22

1974-75

DIVISION 1

	P	W	D	L	F	A	W	D	L	F	A	Pts
Rangers	34	14	1	2	39	15	11	5	1	47	18	56
Hibernian	34	12	2	3	41	16	8	7	2	28	21	49
Celtic	34	11	2	4	47	20	9	3	5	34	21	45
Dundee U	34	10	5	2	41	19	9	2	6	31	24	45
Aberdeen	34	9	6	2	42	20	7	3	7	24	23	41
Dundee	34	11	1	5	32	17	5	5	7	16	25	38
Ayr U	34	9	5	3	29	27	5	3	9	21	34	36
Hearts	34	8	6	3	24	16	3	7	7	23	36	35
St Johnstone	34	8	4	5	27	20	3	8	6	14	24	34
Motherwell	34	8	2	7	30	23	6	3	8	22	34	33
Airdrie	34	7	7	3	26	20	4	2	11	17	35	31
Kilmarnock	34	5	7	5	26	29	3	8	6	26	39	31
Partick T	34	7	5	5	27	31	3	5	9	21	31	30
Dumbarton	34	3	5	9	19	24	4	5	8	25	31	24
Dunfermline A	34	3	6	8	24	32	4	3	10	22	34	23
Clyde	34	4	6	7	25	30	2	4	11	15	33	22
Morton	34	4	5	8	17	28	2	5	10	14	34	22
Arbroath	34	4	5	8	20	27	1	2	14	14	39	17

1975-76

PREMIER DIVISION

	P	W	D	L	F	A	W	D	L	F	A	Pts
Rangers	36	15	2	1	38	12	8	6	4	22	12	54
Celtic	36	10	5	3	35	18	11	1	6	36	24	48
Hibernian	36	13	2	3	37	15	5	5	8	18	28	43
Motherwell	36	11	4	3	29	18	5	4	9	28	31	40
Hearts	36	7	5	6	23	20	6	4	8	16	25	35
Ayr U	36	10	3	5	29	24	4	2	12	17	35	33
Aberdeen	36	8	5	5	27	19	3	5	10	22	31	32
Dundee U	36	9	3	6	27	20	3	5	10	19	28	32
Dundee	36	8	5	5	31	26	3	5	10	18	36	32
St Johnstone	36	3	4	11	19	34	0	1	17	10	45	11

1976-77

PREMIER DIVISION

	P	W	D	L	F	A	W	D	L	F	A	Pts
Celtic	36	13	5	0	44	16	10	4	4	35	23	55
Rangers	36	12	4	2	36	16	6	6	6	26	21	46
Aberdeen	36	11	4	3	30	18	5	7	6	26	24	43
Dundee U	36	8	5	5	26	17	8	4	6	28	28	41
Partick T	36	9	5	4	27	24	2	8	8	13	20	35
Hibernian	36	4	10	4	14	12	4	8	6	20	23	34
Motherwell	36	8	7	3	38	25	2	5	11	19	35	32
Ayr U	36	4	5	9	23	36	7	3	8	21	32	30
Hearts	36	5	6	7	26	28	2	7	9	23	38	27
Kilmarnock	36	4	5	9	21	30	0	4	14	11	41	17

1977-78

DIVISION 1

	P	W	D	L	F	A	W	D	L	F	A	Pts
Morton	39	12	3	5	45	23	13	5	1	40	19	58
Hearts	39	13	4	2	37	18	11	6	3	40	24	58
Dundee	39	14	2	3	52	20	11	5	4	39	24	57
Dumbarton	39	11	8	1	38	20	5	9	5	27	28	49
Stirling A	39	7	6	7	32	27	8	6	5	28	25	42
Kilmarnock	39	8	7	4	29	16	6	5	9	23	30	40
Hamilton A	39	10	5	5	40	27	2	7	10	14	29	36
St Johnstone	39	7	2	10	19	21	8	4	8	33	43	36
Arbroath	39	7	7	6	26	30	4	6	9	16	25	35
Airdrie	39	8	5	7	31	30	4	5	10	19	34	34
Montrose	39	7	5	7	27	25	3	4	13	28	46	29
Queen of South	39	6	7	6	28	31	2	6	12	16	37	29
Alloa	39	4	6	9	28	41	4	2	14	16	43	24
East Fife	39	4	7	9	22	27	0	4	15	17	47	19

1978-79

PREMIER DIVISION

	P	W	D	L	F	A	W	D	L	F	A	Pts
Celtic	36	12	4	2	32	13	9	2	7	29	24	48
Rangers	36	12	5	1	32	10	6	4	8	20	25	45
Dundee U	36	12	4	2	33	16	6	4	8	23	21	44
Aberdeen	36	9	4	5	38	16	4	10	4	21	20	40
Hibernian	36	7	9	2	23	16	5	4	9	21	32	37
St Mirren	36	8	3	7	23	20	7	3	8	22	21	36
Morton	36	9	4	5	34	23	3	8	7	18	30	36
Partick T	36	10	2	6	31	21	3	6	9	11	18	34
Hearts	36	5	5	8	19	25	3	2	13	20	46	23
Motherwell	36	2	5	11	20	38	3	2	13	13	48	17

1979-80

DIVISION 1

	P	W	D	L	F	A	W	D	L	F	A	Pts
Hearts	39	13	6	1	33	18	7	7	5	25	21	53
Airdrie	39	14	2	4	46	21	7	7	5	32	26	51
Ayr U	39	11	5	4	37	22	5	7	7	27	29	44
Dumbarton	39	10	4	5	34	22	9	2	9	25	29	44
Raith R	39	8	7	5	30	22	6	8	5	29	24	43
Motherwell	39	9	7	3	32	17	7	4	9	27	31	43
Hamilton A	39	11	5	3	39	20	4	5	11	21	39	40
Stirling A	39	7	6	7	23	19	6	7	6	17	21	39
Clydebank	39	9	6	5	32	21	5	2	12	26	36	36
Dunfermline A	39	7	7	5	23	24	4	6	10	16	33	35
St Johnstone	39	5	5	9	28	32	7	5	8	29	42	34
Berwick R	39	5	8	7	36	31	3	7	9	21	33	31
Arbroath	39	7	5	7	31	32	2	5	13	19	47	28
Clyde	39	3	6	10	22	34	3	7	10	21	35	25

1980-81

PREMIER DIVISION

	P	W	D	L	F	A	W	D	L	F	A	Pts
Celtic	36	12	3	3	47	18	14	1	3	37	19	56
Aberdeen	36	11	4	3	39	16	8	7	3	22	10	49
Rangers	36	12	3	3	33	10	4	9	5	27	22	44
St Mirren	36	9	6	3	28	20	9	2	7	28	27	44
Dundee U	36	8	5	5	34	24	9	4	5	32	18	43
Partick T	36	6	6	6	17	17	4	4	10	15	31	30
Airdrie	36	6	5	7	19	25	4	4	10	17	30	29
Morton	36	7	2	9	24	28	3	6	9	12	30	28
Kilmarnock	36	3	5	10	14	31	2	4	12	9	34	19
Hearts	36	3	4	11	10	27	3	2	13	17	44	18

1981-82

DIVISION 1

	P	W	D	L	F	A	W	D	L	F	A	Pts
Motherwell	39	12	7	0	41	17	14	2	4	51	19	61
Kilmarnock	39	6	12	2	25	11	11	5	3	35	18	51
Hearts	39	12	2	5	33	19	9	6	5	32	18	50
Clydebank	39	12	3	5	33	27	7	5	7	28	26	46
St Johnstone	39	12	3	4	44	29	5	5	10	25	31	42
Ayr U	39	12	6	1	39	20	3	6	11	17	30	42
Hamilton A	39	10	3	6	20	16	6	5	9	32	33	40
Queen's Park	39	11	5	4	32	17	2	5	12	9	24	36
Falkirk	39	8	8	4	26	19	3	6	10	23	33	36
Dunfermline A	39	3	9	7	24	31	8	5	7	22	25	36
Dumbarton	39	10	1	9	25	30	3	8	8	24	31	35
Raith R	39	5	2	13	13	32	6	5	8	18	27	29
E. Stirling	39	4	6	9	20	35	3	4	13	18	42	24
Queen of South	39	2	5	13	25	50	2	5	12	19	43	18

1982-83

DIVISION 1

	P	W	D	L	F	A	W	D	L	F	A	Pts
St Johnstone	39	17	1	2	34	10	8	4	7	25	27	55
Hearts	39	13	4	3	46	20	9	6	4	33	18	54
Clydebank	39	8	5	6	32	27	12	5	3	40	22	50
Partick T	39	9	6	4	31	23	11	3	6	35	22	49
Airdrie	39	7	3	9	27	27	9	4	7	35	19	39
Alloa	39	8	7	5	31	21	6	4	9	21	31	39
Dumbarton	39	6	7	6	26	32	7	3	10	24	27	36
Falkirk	39	8	2	9	20	22	7	4	9	25	33	36
Raith R	39	8	3	8	32	29	5	5	10	32	34	34
Clyde	39	8	2	10	32	38	6	4	9	23	28	34
Hamilton A	39	7	6	7	27	32	4	6	9	27	34	34
Ayr U	39	9	4	7	29	26	3	4	12	16	35	32
Dunfermline A	39	5	9	6	19	30	2	8	9	20	39	31
Queen's Park	39	3	6	10	24	39	3	5	12	20	41	23

1983-84

PREMIER DIVISION

	P	W	D	L	F	A	W	D	L	F	A	Pts
Aberdeen	36	14	3	1	46	12	11	4	3	32	9	57
Celtic	36	13	5	0	46	15	8	3	7	34	26	50
Dundee U	36	11	3	4	38	14	7	8	3	29	25	47
Rangers	36	7	8	3	26	18	8	4	6	27	23	42
Hearts	36	5	9	4	23	23	5	7	6	15	24	36
St Mirren	36	8	6	4	34	23	1	8	9	21	36	32
Hibernian	36	7	4	7	21	21	5	3	10	24	34	31
Dundee	36	6	1	11	28	42	5	4	9	22	32	27
St Johnstone	36	6	1	11	19	33	4	2	12	17	48	23
Motherwell	36	2	5	11	15	36	2	2	14	16	39	15

1984-85

PREMIER DIVISION

	P	W	D	L	F	A	W	D	L	F	A	Pts
Aberdeen	36	13	4	1	49	13	14	1	3	40	13	59
Celtic	36	12	3	3	43	12	10	5	3	34	18	52
Dundee U	36	13	2	3	47	18	7	5	6	20	15	47
Rangers	36	7	6	5	21	14	6	6	6	26	24	38
St Mirren	36	10	2	6	29	24	7	2	9	22	32	38
Dundee	36	9	3	6	25	19	6	4	8	23	31	37
Hearts	36	6	3	9	21	26	7	2	9	26	38	31
Hibernian	36	5	4	9	23	30	5	3	10	15	31	27
Dumbarton	36	4	4	10	17	29	2	3	13	12	35	19
Morton	36	3	1	14	18	44	2	1	15	11	56	12

1985-86

PREMIER DIVISION

	P	W	D	L	F	A	W	D	L	F	A	Pts
Celtic	36	10	6	2	27	15	10	4	4	40	23	50
Hearts	36	13	5	0	38	10	7	5	6	21	23	50
Dundee U	36	10	6	2	38	15	8	5	5	21	16	47
Aberdeen	36	11	4	3	38	15	5	8	5	24	16	44
Rangers	36	10	4	4	34	18	3	5	10	19	27	35
Dundee	36	11	2	5	32	20	3	5	10	13	31	35
St Mirren	36	9	2	7	26	24	4	3	11	16	39	31
Hibernian	36	6	4	8	27	25	5	2	11	22	38	28
Motherwell	36	7	3	8	23	23	0	3	15	10	43	20
Clydebank	36	4	6	8	18	32	2	2	14	11	45	20

1986-87

PREMIER DIVISION

	P	W	D	L	F	A	W	D	L	F	A	Pts
Rangers	44	18	2	2	45	6	13	5	4	40	17	69
Celtic	44	16	5	1	57	17	11	4	7	33	24	63
Dundee U	44	15	5	2	38	15	9	7	6	28	21	60
Aberdeen	44	13	6	3	32	11	8	10	4	31	18	58
Hearts	44	13	7	2	42	19	8	7	7	22	24	56
Dundee	44	11	6	5	49	31	7	6	9	25	26	48
St Mirren	44	9	5	8	23	20	3	7	12	13	31	36
Motherwell	44	7	5	10	24	28	4	7	11	19	36	34
Hibernian	44	6	8	8	24	30	4	5	13	20	40	33
Falkirk	44	4	9	9	17	28	4	1	17	14	42	26
Clydebank	44	3	7	12	19	40	3	5	14	16	53	24
Hamilton A	44	2	4	16	15	40	4	5	13	24	53	21

1987-88

PREMIER DIVISION

	P	W	D	L	F	A	W	D	L	F	A	Pts
Celtic	44	16	5	1	42	11	15	5	2	37	12	72
Hearts	44	13	8	1	37	17	10	8	4	37	15	62
Rangers	44	14	4	4	49	17	12	4	6	36	17	60
Aberdeen	44	11	7	4	27	11	10	10	2	29	14	59
Dundee U	44	8	7	7	29	24	8	8	6	25	23	47
Hibernian	44	8	8	6	18	17	4	11	7	23	25	43
Dundee	44	9	5	8	31	25	8	2	12	39	39	41
Motherwell	44	10	2	10	25	31	3	8	11	12	25	36
St Mirren	44	5	11	6	22	28	5	4	13	19	36	35
Falkirk	44	8	4	10	26	35	2	7	13	15	40	31
Dunfermline A	44	6	6	10	23	35	2	4	16	18	49	26
Morton	44	3	7	12	19	47	0	3	19	8	53	16

1988-89

PREMIER DIVISION

	P	W	D	L	F	A	W	D	L	F	A	Pts
Rangers	36	15	1	2	39	11	11	3	4	23	15	56
Aberdeen	36	10	7	1	26	10	8	7	3	25	15	50
Celtic	36	13	1	4	35	18	8	3	7	31	26	46
Dundee U	36	6	8	4	20	16	10	4	4	24	10	44
Hibernian	36	8	4	6	20	16	5	5	8	17	20	35
Hearts	36	7	6	5	22	17	2	7	9	13	25	31
St Mirren	36	5	6	7	17	19	6	1	11	22	36	29
Dundee	36	8	4	6	22	21	1	6	11	12	27	28
Motherwell	36	5	7	6	21	21	2	6	10	14	23	27
Hamilton A	36	5	0	13	9	42	1	2	15	10	34	14

1989-90

PREMIER DIVISION

	P	W	D	L	F	A	W	D	L	F	A	Pts
Rangers	36	14	2	2	32	7	6	9	3	16	12	51
Aberdeen	36	12	4	2	33	13	5	6	7	23	20	44
Hearts	36	8	6	4	28	17	8	6	4	26	18	44
Dundee U	36	8	8	2	21	12	3	5	10	15	27	35
Celtic	36	6	6	6	21	20	4	8	6	16	17	34
Motherwell	36	7	6	5	23	21	4	6	8	20	26	34
Hibernian	36	8	5	5	25	23	4	5	9	9	18	34
Dunfermline A	36	5	6	7	17	23	6	2	10	20	27	30
St Mirren	36	6	6	6	14	15	4	4	10	14	33	30
Dundee	36	4	8	6	23	26	1	6	11	18	39	24

1990-91

PREMIER DIVISION

	P	W	D	L	F	A	W	D	L	F	A	Pts
Rangers	36	14	3	1	40	8	10	4	4	22	15	55
Aberdeen	36	12	5	1	30	7	10	4	4	32	20	53
Celtic	36	10	4	4	30	14	7	3	8	22	24	41
Dundee U	36	11	3	4	28	16	6	4	8	13	13	41
Hearts	36	10	3	5	28	22	4	4	10	20	33	35
Motherwell	36	9	5	4	28	18	3	4	11	23	32	33
St Johnstone	36	6	4	8	23	25	5	5	8	18	29	31
Dunfermline	36	5	7	6	23	26	3	4	11	15	35	27
Hibernian	36	6	5	7	17	25	0	8	10	7	26	25
St Mirren	36	4	5	9	14	25	1	4	13	14	34	19

1991-92

PREMIER DIVISION

	P	W	D	L	F	A	W	D	L	F	A	Pts
Rangers	39	14	5	3	50	14	19	1	2	51	17	72
Hearts	39	12	7	3	26	15	15	2	5	34	22	63
Celtic	39	15	3	4	47	20	11	7	4	41	22	62
Dundee U	39	10	7	5	37	25	9	6	7	29	25	51
Hibernian	39	7	8	7	28	25	9	9	4	25	20	49
Aberdeen	39	9	6	7	32	23	8	8	6	23	19	48
Airdrie	39	7	5	10	25	33	6	5	11	25	37	36
St Johnstone	39	5	7	10	21	32	8	3	11	31	41	36
Falkirk	39	7	2	13	29	41	5	9	8	25	32	35
Motherwell	39	5	6	11	25	29	5	8	9	18	32	34
St Mirren	39	2	5	15	18	36	4	7	11	15	37	24
Dunfermline	39	2	7	13	11	35	2	3	17	11	45	18

1992-93

PREMIER DIVISION

	P	W	D	L	F	A	W	D	L	F	A	Pts
Rangers	44	20	2	0	52	11	13	5	4	45	24	73
Aberdeen	44	13	7	2	41	13	14	3	5	46	23	64
Celtic	44	13	5	4	37	18	11	7	4	31	23	60
Dundee U	44	8	7	7	25	27	11	2	9	31	22	47
Hearts	44	12	6	4	26	15	3	8	11	20	36	44
St Johnstone	44	8	10	4	29	27	2	10	10	23	39	40
Hibernian	44	8	8	6	32	28	4	5	13	22	36	37
Partick T	44	5	6	11	26	41	7	6	9	24	30	36
Motherwell	44	7	4	11	27	37	4	9	9	19	25	35
Dundee	44	7	4	11	25	34	4	8	10	23	34	34
Falkirk	44	7	5	10	40	39	4	2	16	20	47	29
Airdrie	44	4	9	9	22	27	2	8	12	13	43	29

1993-94

PREMIER DIVISION

	P	W	D	L	F	A	W	D	L	F	A	Pts
Rangers	44	12	6	4	43	22	10	8	4	31	19	58
Aberdeen	44	11	9	2	33	12	6	12	4	25	24	55
Motherwell	44	11	7	4	31	20	9	7	6	27	23	54
Celtic	44	8	11	3	25	17	7	9	6	26	21	50
Hibernian	44	11	7	4	29	15	5	8	9	24	33	47
Dundee U	44	5	11	6	26	25	6	9	7	21	23	42
Hearts	44	6	9	7	22	24	5	11	6	15	19	42
Kilmarnock	44	6	10	6	18	19	6	6	10	18	26	40
Partick T	44	9	8	5	23	17	3	8	11	23	40	40
St Johnstone	44	7	7	8	24	26	3	13	6	11	21	40
Raith	44	3	12	7	25	35	3	7	12	21	45	31
Dundee	44	6	7	9	26	26	2	6	14	16	31	29

1994-95

PREMIER DIVISION

	P	W	D	L	F	A	W	D	L	F	A	Pts
Rangers	36	11	5	2	31	14	9	4	5	29	21	69
Motherwell	36	8	6	4	29	23	6	6	6	21	27	54
Hibernian	36	9	7	2	37	19	3	10	5	12	18	53
Celtic	36	6	8	4	23	19	5	10	3	16	14	51
Falkirk	36	8	3	7	26	24	4	9	5	22	23	48
Hearts	36	9	4	5	26	14	3	3	12	18	37	43
Kilmarnock	36	8	4	6	22	16	3	6	9	18	32	43
Partick T	36	4	9	5	23	23	6	4	8	17	27	43
Aberdeen	36	7	7	4	24	16	3	4	11	19	30	*41
Dundee U	36	6	6	6	24	20	3	3	12	16	36	36

1995-96

PREMIER DIVISION

	P	W	D	L	F	A	W	D	L	F	A	Pts
Rangers	36	13	3	2	47	16	14	3	1	38	9	87
Celtic	36	12	5	1	40	12	12	6	0	34	13	83
Aberdeen	36	11	1	6	31	17	5	6	7	21	28	55
Hearts	36	10	2	6	33	26	6	5	7	22	27	55
Hibernian	36	7	5	6	25	26	4	5	9	18	31	43
Raith	36	7	5	6	23	21	5	2	11	18	36	43
Kilmarnock	36	8	4	6	25	21	3	4	11	14	33	41
Motherwell	36	6	6	6	15	16	3	6	9	13	23	39
Partick T	36	3	5	10	12	28	5	1	12	17	34	*30
Falkirk	36	4	4	10	17	26	2	2	14	14	34	24

1996-97

PREMIER DIVISION

	P	W	D	L	F	A	W	D	L	F	A	Pts
Rangers	36	13	2	3	44	16	12	3	3	41	17	80
Celtic	36	14	2	2	48	9	9	4	5	30	23	75
Dundee U	36	10	4	4	21	10	7	5	6	25	23	60
Hearts	36	8	6	4	27	20	6	4	8	19	23	52
Dunfermline	36	8	4	6	32	30	4	5	9	20	35	45
Aberdeen	36	6	8	4	25	19	4	6	8	20	35	44
Kilmarnock	36	8	4	6	28	26	3	2	13	13	35	39
Motherwell	35	5	5	8	24	25	4	6	8	20	30	38
Hibernian	36	6	4	8	18	25	3	7	8	20	30	*38
Raith	36	3	5	10	18	39	3	2	13	11	34	25

1997-98

PREMIER DIVISION

	P	W	D	L	F	A	W	D	L	F	A	Pts
Celtic	36	12	4	2	41	9	10	4	4	23	15	74
Rangers	36	13	4	1	46	16	8	5	5	30	22	72
Hearts	36	10	5	3	36	24	9	5	4	34	22	67
Kilmarnock	36	9	4	5	24	21	4	7	7	16	31	50
St Johnstone	36	7	5	6	20	21	6	4	8	18	21	48
Aberdeen	36	6	6	6	20	18	3	6	9	19	35	39
Dundee U	35	5	7	6	23	18	3	6	9	20	33	37
Dunfermline	36	4	9	5	26	30	4	4	10	17	38	37
Motherwell	36	6	4	8	26	28	3	3	12	20	36	34
Hibernian	36	6	4	8	26	24	0	8	10	12	35	30

1998-99

PREMIER DIVISION

	P	W	D	L	F	A	W	D	L	F	A	Pts
Rangers	36	12	5	1	32	11	11	3	4	46	20	77
Celtic	36	14	2	2	49	12	7	6	5	35	23	71
St Johnstone	36	8	7	3	24	18	7	5	6	15	20	57
Kilmarnock	36	8	7	3	24	15	6	7	5	23	14	56
Dundee	36	7	4	7	18	23	6	3	9	18	33	46
Hearts	36	8	2	8	27	26	3	7	8	17	24	42
Motherwell	36	6	5	7	20	31	4	6	8	15	23	41
Aberdeen	36	6	4	8	24	35	4	3	11	19	36	37
Dundee U	36	2	8	8	13	22	6	2	10	24	26	34
Dunfermline	36	4	7	7	18	29	0	9	9	10	30	28

1999-2000

PREMIER DIVISION

	P	W	D	L	F	A	W	D	L	F	A	Pts
Rangers	36	16	1	1	52	12	12	5	1	44	14	90
Celtic	36	12	3	3	58	17	9	3	6	32	21	69
Hearts	36	7	6	5	25	18	8	3	7	22	22	54
Motherwell	36	8	3	7	27	34	6	7	5	22	29	52
St Johnstone	36	5	7	6	16	18	5	5	8	20	26	42
Hibernian	36	7	6	5	30	27	3	5	10	19	34	41
Dundee	36	4	3	11	20	33	8	2	8	25	31	41
Dundee U	36	6	4	8	16	22	5	2	11	18	35	39
Kilmarnock	36	5	5	8	16	22	3	8	7	22	30	37
Aberdeen	36	6	4	8	28	37	3	2	13	16	46	33

2000-2001

PREMIER DIVISION

	P	W	D	L	F	A	W	D	L	F	A	Pts
Celtic	38	17	1	1	49	11	14	3	2	41	18	97
Rangers	38	15	0	4	45	16	11	4	4	31	20	82
Hibernian	38	11	6	2	37	15	7	6	6	20	20	66
Kilmarnock	38	7	4	8	20	25	8	5	6	24	28	54
Hearts	38	11	2	6	36	21	3	8	8	20	29	52
Dundee	38	4	7	8	25	24	9	1	9	26	25	47
Aberdeen	38	6	6	7	24	24	5	6	8	21	28	45
Motherwell	38	5	4	10	22	27	7	3	9	20	29	43
Dunfermline	38	8	6	5	20	17	3	3	13	14	37	42
St Johnstone	38	4	6	9	22	31	5	7	7	18	25	40
Dundee U	38	5	6	8	21	28	4	2	13	17	35	35
St Mirren	38	7	3	9	20	25	1	3	15	12	47	30

League split from 7 April and remaining fixtures played out within the two groups of six.

Subscribers

Brian J Allan
James Allan
Alexander Jeffrey Allan
Callum Anderson
Daniel Anderson
Tom Anderson
Michael Anderson
Dave Anderson
Alison Archibald
Angus Archibald
John Armstrong
Hugh Arundel
Robert Baillie
Graham Baillie
Vivian Bain
Callum Baird
Euan J Ballantyne
Philip Jordan Banks
William Banner
Michael Barrett
Christopher P Beamish
Ian Bennett
Robert Binks
Ross Black
David Black
Graham Blackwood
Kenneth Blake
Andrew Boa
Ronald A Booth
David Borley
Robert Boyd
S. Neil Brailsford
Mark Brand
Ramsay Brand
Martin Bravin
Alan Brown
Alan Brown
Leslie Brown
Robert Brown
Bill Bryce
Mike Buckle
Bob Buckle
Fiona Calder
Richard Callaghan
James Cameron
Dave Campbell
Stan Carroll
Blair Carswell
Kelman D Chambers
Stuart Chapman
George Christine
The Valente Clan
Alasdair Clapperton
Ian Clark
Philip Clark
Maitland Clark
Margaret Clark

Conor Thomas Clark
Scott George Clark
Aidan Forrest Cleland
Jim Cobb
Scott Cockburn
Wm Grant Colligan
Ronald Connolly
Neil Connolly
Peter Connolly
Paul Cook
Steven W Cook
Carol Cooper
Arlene Croall
Ian Cunningham
Gary Curlewis
Rab Currie
Derek Dalgleish
Jamie Darling
Douglas W Davidson
Kelly Dawson
Alan R Dewar
Cameron J Dewar
George Dickson
Scott Dillon
John Dingwall
Bobby Dingwall
Craig Dishington
Joanne Docherty
Ross Donald
Terry Donnelly
Mike Douglas
Sandy Douglas
George Dreaver
Wendy Duffy
Laurie Dunsire
Billy Dyer
Michael A Easton
Matthew Fairfax
Walter Fairnie
John R Falconer
James E Ferguson
Phil Fielding
Stuart Findlay
Atholl G W Finlayson
F M Fisher
Jim Fleming
Morris Flynn
Scott Foley
Pamela Forbes
Calum Forrest
Gordon Forrest
David W Forsyth
Alan J Forsyth
David Foster
George W Fraser
Brian P Fusco
Robert Fyfe

Iain R Galbraith
Murray Gardiner
Aileen Gardiner
Ryan Gardiner
Joe Gardiner
Neil Garwood
Neil Geddes
John Gilchrist
Daniel James Gillan
Thomas L G Gillies
Elaine - Mary Gillings
Stuart Gillings
Michael Gillings
Ian Girdwood
Derek J Golder
Ralph Gordon
Ian Graham
Clark Grant
David D J R Grant
Dorothy Gray
David Green
Mike Greenan
Charles Greenslade
John Greenwood
Ricky Grigg
Douglas Haig
Charlotte Sissi Hall
Kenneth Hamilton
Thomas C Hamilton
Ian Hamilton
Al Hardie
Graham Harkness
Ian Harper
Lynn Hartil
Nicola Hartil
David Harvey
George Hawkins
Peter S Hay
Cameron Hay
G A Headspeath
Tom Heaney
David Heatley
Mr J Henderson
Charles Henderson
Suzanne Hendry
Stuart Henig
Ian Henig
Keith Henig
Ian Henry
Robert Hodge
D Hogg
William Smith Hogg
Tina Hollinsworth
Cameron Hood
Stewart Hood
Lewis Houliston
John Howell

Ronnie Hughes
Andrew Hunter
Robin M Hunter
George Hutchison
Kenneth Imrie
Jack Imrie
Scott Innes
Richard Jacks
Catherine Jansen
Grant Jenkinson
Iain S Jenkison
John Jenner
Paul A R W Jennings
Wallace H S Jennings
Robert M Johnson
Jonathans
Alex W Jones
F. Simon Jones
David V Kaplan
Colin Kay
John Keay
Robert Kelman
John Kerr
David Kerr
D J Kidd
Geoff Kilpatrick
Drew King
Lauryn Nancy King
Alex H Knight
Martin W Laidlaw
Thomas A Laing
Donald Alan Laing
David Laird
Stuart Laird
Jason Law
Ian Lee
Norrie Leithead
Ian K Liddle
George Andrew Liddle
Kevin A Liston
Thomas Lithgow
David Little
Ragnar Lochen
Richard Lockerbie
Jack Lockerbie
Gavin C Lockhart
Michael Lockerbie
David R Lornie
Martyn Lovatt
Elaine Low
Michael Low
Logan Lumsdaine
Mr J M Lumsden
Neil I Macdonald
Stewart D MacFarlane
Mr J W F MacGregor
Karen Mackintosh